the DOGS of SHERBURNE

A Great American Dog Novel

Tom Mody

www.dogsofsherburne.com

Published by Mody Company Creative LLC
56 West Main St., Norwich, NY 13815
www.modycompany.com

Cover portrait by Dale Lewis.
Editorial assistance by Joyce Zummo.

Book design and artwork by Mody Company Creative LLC.

Contributions to this book were made by the following "Masters."
Mark Nigolian, Ellen McDaniel Linhart, James & Marilyn Sherman,
Carter Hillman, Shane Lewis, Kathy Sweet, Scott Braun and Peter Karaman

Library of Congress Cataloging-in-Publication Data

Library of Congress Control Number: 2011925018

Mody, Tom 1966-

ISBN 978-0-9834503-0-6

Learn more about the Dogs of Sherburne and the writing of this novel at
www.dogsofsherburne.com

To Lisa: All my love and all my loving spite.

To Antonia and Julian: This was my life,
my childhood, and nothing has changed.
I'm still in the background somewhere.

To God: Sorry if I've taken this
just a little too far.

To Mark, Ellen, Jimmer, Carter, Shane,
Scott, Peter and the village kids...
- Here's to infamy! -

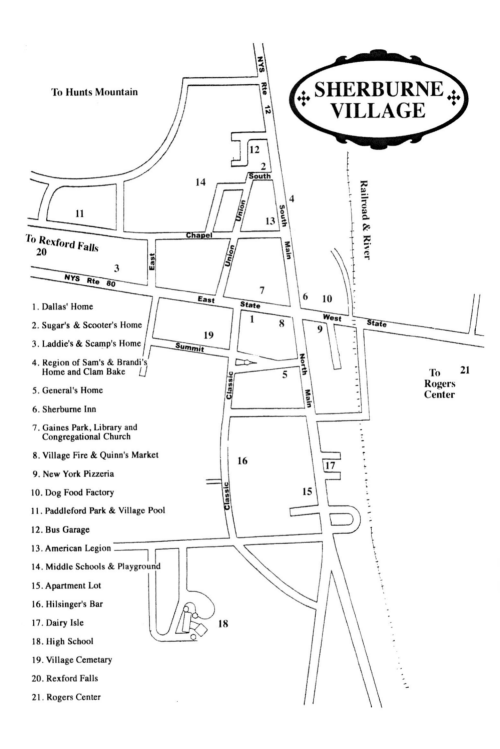

SHERBURNE VILLAGE

To Hunts Mountain

To Rexford Falls

NYS Rte 12
NYS Rte 80
South
Union
Chapel
East
South Main
Railroad & River
East State
West State
North Main
Classic
Summit

12
2
14
4
13
3
20
7
6
10
1
8
9
19
5
16
17
15
18
21

To Rogers Center

1. Dallas' Home
2. Sugar's & Scooter's Home
3. Laddie's & Scamp's Home
4. Region of Sam's & Brandi's Home and Clam Bake
5. General's Home
6. Sherburne Inn
7. Gaines Park, Library and Congregational Church
8. Village Fire & Quinn's Market
9. New York Pizzeria
10. Dog Food Factory
11. Paddleford Park & Village Pool
12. Bus Garage
13. American Legion
14. Middle Schools & Playground
15. Apartment Lot
16. Hilsinger's Bar
17. Dairy Isle
18. High School
19. Village Cemetary
20. Rexford Falls
21. Rogers Center

🐕 Preface

In the following memoir, Master's names
were changed to protect the innocent.

All the dog's names remain unchanged
as they are guilty as sin!

Revelation 1

December 26th 1986

Doggie Heaven does exist!

Revelation 2

Angels take great dictation

I still remember how it felt.

Thwack!

Damn, I hated when they did that. It was one of those times when I really got a good solid jump on it too. That wouldn't have been possible these days. Cars seem to be a lot quieter now that I'm gone. In my day people had a "fix it when you feel like it" attitude about mufflers. A loud muffler from a distance is like getting that car's driving itinerary for the day. The problem is that for a dog who's into this kind of thing, we get way too excited. Any abrupt loud noise, like a siren or a crash, gets echoed throughout the village causing us to respond in over-exaggerated hysteria. Somehow, I let that car kinda' sneak up to the corner of Classic Street before it took a wicked left up East State Street. I happened to be a bit preoccupied roaming the shrubs of the Catholic church. Something smelled awfully familiar to the "mutt-stress" I had tried to hump the night before. I was never very good at tracking, being the spoiled housedog, so I was concentrating real hard on that odor, oblivious to the current opportunity presenting itself.

I was at the far end of the shrubs which ran a ways up East State when that Camaro burned the corner- tires ripping, muffler rumbling. Immediately I was hit with that temporary hysteria and I bolted out well ahead in anticipation of the metal beast. If I had heard the muffler from a distance coming up to the intersection I wouldn't have been so disoriented. But I had bitch on my nose and the sudden burst of the Camaro just went through my dog sensitive ears like thunder. Still, I got a great jump on it, but certainly, I wasn't clear headed. I even had time for a brief pause before I needed to make my move and off I went, hell bent into the street. The ultimate prize hadn't yet built up a full head of steam and I was on it like a cat was dragging from its bumper. My bark was vicious and I was going to let it know I was a bad dog. We were running neck and neck for that first block and in my misguided dog judgment I believed I was prime for the kill. For a moment it appeared I was even getting a step advantage. My head began to clear. I made my move. I actually lunged toward the ultimate prize, a full-metal, rubber-sqealin', piston-pumpin', Detroit-dealin' car.

In all my years it was just a fantasy. Normally I'd just run beside the metal beast with a cautious distance pretending that one day on bark and guile alone I could corral it into submission. Cars were like nothing else to chase in our world. It's the one thing we dogs knew we could never really bring down. Sure, maybe we couldn't bring down a cow but we believed we could. A car though, we knew we didn't have a prayer. Of course, had we known Doggie Heaven existed we might have tried that prayer thing.

It's just that cars seem to encompass the full spectrum of our aspirations- and our nightmares. They can take us to places beyond...? Well, just beyond. We could be with Master at all times- exploring, searching, finding. The sound of a car can break our loneliness as that low hum and crackling stone under the tires tells us that master is pulling into the drive way. Jumping to giddy attention, we rush with wide eyes to greet him- as is our pleasure. It also tells us that finally someone is home to let us out so we can take a leak. And with all the joy we have in it bringing Master home or the oxygen rush of freedom with wind filling our senses as we're lickin' air, heads out the window and loving life down the freeway; it is, in fact, a cold-blooded, animal-treading, road-kill-dinner-serving assassin.

Less dramatic, I guess it could simply be labeled as "spooky." There's nothing natural about them; all metal, plastic & lubricants. A car's aura is very cold and it holds no connection to our instincts. Our instincts can't guide us in our attitudes concerning the car so we simply work off our only other option- response action. And our response action is to chase, catch and pounce.

Now at the time, response action is all that motivated me. In hindsight here in Doggie Heaven, I can tell you that it woulda' been the greatest accomplishment in dog history to "catch" that car. If a dog successfully "caught" a car, a feeling of motivated self-awareness and pride may momentarily overcome him. He would be fearless in all future pursuits. Lack of fear dangerously means that he most likely would soon find his fate under the skidding wheels of a Greyhound bus. That's why dogs really shouldn't feel these things until we're supervised by God.

Anyway, I thought my time had come. I believed I was going to bring down that heartless, cold-blooded, ear-bludgeoning Camaro. I lunged as if a mountain lion had my Master in a death grip and I was going to savagely, fearlessly be the hero. It was destiny, a place in dog lore where all creatures, man and beast, would honor my statute. One fire hydrant in each city would be bronzed in recognition. On this day every year dog wardens would be required to take a national holiday and every dog would have a once-a-year shot to run free and aspire to my greatness.

My lunge was clean and in stride. I had perfect balance as I set on my front paws allowing my hind legs to coil and spring with even distribution of power to each leg. I was airborne. It was slow motion. Poetry in motion. Fate. Destiny. Every dog in America unknowingly gave pause.

Thwack!

Uhhh! Well, bite my bone! The cat-lovin' bastard driver saw me coming, opened his door smack into my oncoming snout swatting me back like a ping pong ball. I hated when they did that. It was a common hazard of car chasing and due to my reputation in the village it happened quite often. In fact, it may have been an actual sport.

"Hey Steve, you bored? Lets go out for a round of Dallas swatting". What other dog gets a sport named after him? Yup, I was a legend.

Damn! There's that word again. The word "was" seems to be finding it's way into my heavenly discovered vocabulary a bit too often as of late. I have no problem with the word "was". I mean, I'm here now and my earthly life has passed so I suspect I'll be using it quite often. The living still use it, "Man, that dog "was" a bastard!" That's fine- I was a bastard in all human definitions. But "was" a legend! No, I AM a legend and am I supposed to quietly sit up here and let the living "was" me out of legendary remembrance? Well, I can't do it! I can't sit up here silently anymore. Not that those in my heavenly surroundings find me silent. But for all the barkin' and humpin' and fightin' I did as flesh, my earthly legend is fading quietly into your new century.

I've been ascended for quite some time now and I realize it shouldn't matter but it does. Time shouldn't matter but it does. I feel powerless to stop it. Powerless to petrify it, fossilize it, canonize it, legitimize it. I can't bury it in a chest, lock it in a safe, sink it in a tar pit or harden it in amber. "It" being time.

I'm not talking about preserving centuries, millennia or eons of self-important human existence. I'm talking about my time. The last great earthly boy/dog era. The era before the over-insured, over-litigated, over-stimulated, sunshine-shunning digital man evolved. I can't store my legend in some silicon mega "bite" hogging chip so I guess the only power I have is the power to rant about "it". And I'll start by making a random example of two dogs in this new century I'm witnessing right now.

They're from opposite sides of the track. They've escaped the shackled confines of the leash, slipped their collars and are bound for forbidden exploration. A sad reminder of how things used to be in my century.

Carefree, they crowd the roadway- cars slow, horns beep. One dog scraps through garbage. The other marvels at a fire hydrant, lost at its purpose. The dog from the north end of town travels south. The dog from the south end of town travels north. Tails in the wind. Paws to the pavement. Noses to the grindstone. Their pace is brisk. In newfound exploration every sensation is fresh and their concentration is too scattered to detect the scent of their oncoming brethren. Seconds from impact their eyes meet. Their bodies freeze, erect and on alert. Two dogs, startled and guarded. Taking in all their canine senses can handle. Adrenaline flows quickly to their brains yet they are cautious to act. They circle slowly- eyes locked, noses reaching.

I'm beginning to feel the rush myself, like I am there again. The right side of my mouth twinges and lifts. My fang exposed to the warm air exiting my snout. The nap of my neck curls, my throat gurgles. It's just like old times. Who will make the first move? Who will stake his claim? Hair will fly. Maybe blood will drip. Bystanders will most definitely gasp. Right?

Don't count on it. All that becomes of their cop-out confrontation is a mutual whiff of ass and off they romp on their merry way. That's not how things were when I left. Sadly, like all dogs these days, they're lame-ass, fat-ass, kiss-ass, sorry-ass excuses of regressed and repressed canine evolution.

What's the use, they're dogs on earth in a new century. The rules have changed. Master has changed. The dogs just don't know any better. They're on Earth living potty break to potty break. I'm here enlightened in a heavenly state. Every day learning the what's and why's of my past life. Revelations are in constant flow about all things my earthly brain couldn't comprehend. It's like living your life all over again in a movie- one you first saw when you were a child.

You ask, what does a dog know of movies? I get a free flowing understanding of your entertainment fix and your political back stabbing and all the human etiquettes such a supposedly advanced species flaunts over us. Yeah, I know all about them here in Doggie Heaven. However, things like movies to me are just a point of reference or useless inane human trivia that helps me make a point from a perspective you possibly couldn't understand. Otherwise, as on earth, I could care less about that stuff- I think.

I do however care about anything past or present that is in the context of dogs. Particularly this dog and the relationships between dog and master, dog and dog- and of course, dog and his place in time. My place in time is getting less clear to those I left behind. A huge part of the problem are two dogs from opposite sides of the track who'd rather politely kiss some ass than seize the moment in a vulgar display of aggression. A vicious dog fight in close proximity to a group of preschoolers on their way to a flower picking contest would be something those kids would remember for the rest of their lives. The more benign and controlled today's dogs are, the more I fade into obscurity.

Earthly dogs have no idea. And not just about Doggie Heaven but about anything. Why we roam and sniff and crap and wait. Why we're whimsical, vicious, vain and needing. Why we sleep with one ear open to the outside world awaiting the creak of the door when Master comes home. All the while locked in the kitchen, with the nose of a dog mind you. Perpetually hungry and debating with blank reason whether to rip open the garbage for a few licks of baby jar pudding scraps. For unimportant creatures like a lion or an alligator there's probably no need for this enlightenment. They'd likely eat Master when the door opened and be on their merry way. Nothing is withheld from them- what is, is what is. But dogs for the most part walk hand-in-hand with Master and are driven with a curiosity that would most definitely kill a cat. I believe that gives us special privilege to receive an explanation of our earthly behavior in the eyes of God.

I have no connection to Master's Heaven but I would guess that it's much like he expected. A state of grace, a fountain of knowledge and peace of mind. Master had preconceived ideas about Heaven and he could explore that and other reasons of his earthly existence while he was alive. He was curious of his existence, realized it and explored it. Dogs were curious too, didn't realize it- explored anyway. I can't imagine why such a single-purposed creature like an alligator would be curious of his existence. Assumably that's why there's no gator heaven. As best that's been revealed even cats don't get this privilege. Although I do believe they serve some function in Doggie Hell. But again, we dogs had no idea of afterlife possibilities. Now that revelations have been streaming at me for some time, there are some things I'm hoping by sheer dogmatic will I can get you to realize.

I had a life and shit happened. I was famous, infamous and notorious. On Earth I didn't know why I had such celebrity but I do now. I didn't know why I chased cars but I do now. In my heavenly revelations I learned why I chased them and putting it into context will tell me how this affected and defined my life and my environment.

Well, that's what I want to do for you now, to make sense of it. What may really interest you is that I'm not just placing activities as they pertained to us dogs. I'm getting a real feel for my times as a whole. I'm perched up here with a view of my old stomping grounds as it exists now and I am understanding the true progression of life and events.

The vibe from my earthly domain is different in this new century. The flow of life seems to have made a turn close to the time of my departure. Master is still there, about the high side of age 6 in dog years. My Master family has tried to replace my legend twice. My immediate successor, Jasmine, was a complete spaz and met her fate getting bumper thumped in front of Master Mother and two horrified little girls.

A few years later they would again try and replace my legend with another. Ciela was her name. I'm not sure if she was a chocolate lab or chocolate slab. The thing weighed a hundred pounds and everyone was goo goo over how well mannered she was. Never ran away. Didn't chase anything. Didn't fight and had these new age dog complexes. You know, got depressed and sullen when her space was violated. I'm not trying to give her a bad rap but it's a different time now. The town has a dog warden and rules about loose dogs. She was so calm and obedient. Walked down the street beside her escort. Came when you called her. Never barked. I understand how this could appeal to a couple of grandparents but let's not lose sight of my 14 years of faithful servitude. And I had personality to boot. I'm the last vestige of a special time. A true changing of an era. The true end of the twentieth century when a boy and his dog had adventures together- and bunches more when Boy Master wasn't around.

A village was was our domain, not a yard or porch or poodle pen in the washroom. What does Ciela know of this? And when the time came to review her life in Doggie Heaven, what comprehension, what context did it all mean. She was beloved... how sentimental. She was beloved because she slept on the bed and gave you the ball and was content to see the world from a back porch and never needed to be leashed. What the hell does she need Doggie Heaven for?

So much had happened, so much was done and deserved an explanation in my earthly life. I suppose it's the right of every dog to know the grand questions but for doggie freakin' sake, do something that will make you want to know why you did it later on. See Spot shit needs no revelation. A whole era of dogs breathed life into a town that today still bellows over a few suds, the stories of their canine companions. Years after my death people still ask Master how I am. Pup, I cannot be replaced.

Master's Heaven I'm sure is full of inner peace and contentment. It's becoming rapidly evident that Doggie Heaven is a bit more territorial when it comes to earthly legacy. Common sense would dictate that this is expected. I live a whole life with no known purpose and little self-evidence. I review that life only to realize now what I meant to a boy and a time. I and my doggie "partners in crime" represent something- a closure of the best of times. As I understand it, the last boy/dog era where real life existed outside in open space. You didn't walk your dog, you chased him. If you were on a bike your dog did the chasing. Your dog was in the top five best friends you hung out with around town. This meant something, it has significance. So if my replacements were getting kudos for good behavior and representing a bit of discipline that maybe I found slightly confining, you could understand that even in my heavenly state I would have some issues with this.

These are new revelations now coming into focus and understanding. This may be a growing period here in Doggie

Heaven as I become fed up with what I'm witnessing down there. Some things are universally inherent to dogs and their territorial nature. As we marked our territory on earth, we also retain the nature to mark our place in time when we're gone.

Think of the great Masters beloved or at least revered for defining their time and place. Caesar, Columbus, Lincoln, even Hitler. When they left Earth to go... wherever, there was a turn in the flow of life. The way we would live from that point was forever changed. I grant you that life's flow took a huge left hook during those guys' time but I have a more subtle change to reveal. A change in life's flow during my tenure which places me and my time as the last boy-dog era. It's a change that rightfully gives me a legendary place above those that follow in my Master's world.

Now I didn't cause this change- cable TV, computers, video games, less parents at home... who knows. From up here you can see the turn and no pansy-ass, mild-mannered, half-dog, half-cow replacement is going to dissipate what I meant to my Master and my time. Just look out the window, that big bay window. The shades of green in the trees are a bit duller. The bark is dingier. Can someone actually verify they witnessed a damn water balloon fight or a gang of kids on bikes? Nobody's kicking cans or playing with cap guns or collecting lightning bugs.

We've gone from reality play to virtual reality play. I don't get it, why do we need virtual reality when we already have reality. Cap guns don't have bullets and virtual reality guns don't have real bullets. Wouldn't you rather pretend shoot your pain in the ass brother than pretend kill some digital cyborg terrorist commando who really has never bothered you at all?

And may I finally say, in the past years since I left did any significant go-lucky, life-affirming, adulthood-grooming, lost-in-the-summer-day event happen in the presence of an unleashed dog? Mark my word and mark my time, I, Dallas, cannot be replaced!

Revelation 3

One feels superior when looking down on birds

Despite my car chasing setbacks, it was one of many typical daily activities for a village dog like myself in the prime of his life when life was prime to be a dog. It was the best of times. It was the last of times. Hmmm, that would have been a great line to open this book. It's so true though. In this new century find me a village with a stoplight and I'll show you a leash law in the village code enforcement books. along with the enforcement officer to back it up.

Country dogs have all the freedom now but there's little glory. You can't make a name for yourself when all you do is see the same people and do the same things every day. That's like being famous only in the eyes of your mother. Farm dogs are the worst. You're just another animal fighting for the feed troth. Sure, you may be allowed in the house but the bottom line is you're still one of the animals in the eyes of Master.

For you farm and country dogs you have very little experience handling cars or mounting the mammas. What's worse, if you don't get shot by some city slicker who can't tell a deer from his duffle bag, your own master will put you out to pasture in the actual pasture.

When Master pulls out his dusty turntable and spins that "Old Shep" 45, I'm tellin' ya, drag your arthritic ass up off the doggie beanbag and look for the next feed tractor-trailer barreling down the dirt road. Just lay there like a lamb for the sacrifice because nothing is worse than watching beloved Master take "Shot Gun Betty" out for your supposed own good. However, that's just one dogs opinion, I'm not really speaking from any practical experience in this matter.

I'd just hate for any of us to get to Doggie Heaven and realize we were shot by Master who then replaced us with some other mutt the next day.

Remember, we are territorial even in this heavenly state. Nope, in my eyes farm and country dogs just ain't livin' life to its dog pesterin' fullest. Your domain must entail at least one red light intersection where clear choices of the day's activities can be made. Do I go North, South, East or West?

When it came to one red light towns, Sherburne, New York in the 1970's was at the very peak of its small town prime. A tree-lined village with an assortment of parks, 30 MPH speed limits, meandering creeks and no ambitious dog wardens trying to climb the political ladder of the three-man police department.

The singular red light sat square in the middle of the village and the streets were lined with beautiful nineteenth-century Victorian houses. Village merchants were in the last great phase of general prosperity and every storefront had an open for business sign. Sherburne was a good hour from the new large malls or super shopping centers. It wouldn't be long before people would shift their spending patterns towards these malls. For the time being, you still bought your sneakers, neckties and watches from village merchants. Sherburne may not stand out as anything special among the hundreds of small towns scattered about America but on a warm spring day with a slight breeze in the air, Sherburne had a distinctive smell, an aroma of a kin that sets it apart from any place like it on earth.

Dog food!

Peel back the wrap on any "Gaines Burger", stick it up to your snouzer and on a good day that was the smell of Sherburne. The Gaines Dog Food Factory was started in Sherburne. The villagers grew up with that smell and with Masters' limited aromatic senses it mostly went unnoticed. Dog food odor was mixed in with the trees and flowers and farm manure and it was simply the smell of home. For us dogs, we woke to the smell of dog food. It filled our senses every conscious minute. We couldn't escape it. It didn't just mix in, it overwhelmed and even with our canine ability to separate smells it could at times dominate our snouts. This may explain why I HATED dog food. It was in me every day, through my nose, in my pours. The last place I wanted it was in my mouth.

The only joy Clarence Gaines contributed to my life was that his family property at the far east end of the village was great for chasing kids on sleds in the winter. For a dog, that's just good clean fun. I doubt his precious Pointers he bred decades earlier enjoyed that luxury.

I suppose he contributed greatly to the economic growth of the village when, in the 1930's, his special compound mix of dog food seemed to jive with his breeds. Some space in the family flour and feed mill was used to make and distribute his dog hash. In a few short years, the mill would be pumping one-hundred-percent dog chow. Within ten years, it was bought by General Foods, thus becoming the world's largest dog food company- all started right here in good ole' Sherburne, New York. Mercifully for me it all ended right here in Doggie Heaven. I haven't smelled dog food since December 26, 1986.

I don't mean to be harsh to Master Gaines. Villagers are rather proud of the fact that the dog food giant started here. But just step back and think about us dog's perspective before you judge me a slanderer. I guess I'm not very tactful in arranging these new thoughts. I didn't realize I was going to know all this stuff as part of my heavenly revelations.

I could go on to tell you that Sherburne was discovered in 1791 by some settlers from Kent, Connecticut that had been shafted by a judge promising them land. Realizing their journey was made for nothing they wandered about and decided to lay down home at Sherburne's current location after meeting some cabin folk. Sadly, when they returned with their families the cabin was burned and the kind folk missing. Rampaging Indians were considered the cause, though I sense a bit of typecasting in that account. A service was held at that spot and an English hymn was sung called "Sherburne," hence they named the settlement. Over the years stuff happened, yadda-yadda, ruff-ruff... then I was born on Thanksgiving Day 1972.

Truth is I was born in Smyrna, New York, just a few miles west of my legendary domain. I was the cutest little black lab you could ever lay eyes on but sometimes I feel it was my very small amount of mutt that gave me that edge. Purebreds just seem so personality challenged. "Stuffy" is Master's term. Think about it, don't purebred British royalty seem absolutely boorish. I said that with a charmingly mocking accent- a heavenly-endowed talent mind you. If you could mix in just a little Irish, American Indian or Aborigine, they would make much better drinking buddies. Again, speaking in Master's tongue.

I spent my first few months suckling and chewing and pissing and crapping until some father had to get his only spoiled son a puppy. My siblings had been shipped off one by one so there wasn't much of a choice when my future Master's parents came calling. Problem was the dog breeder's kids had grown attached to me and a sale was unlikely. Apparently though, fifty bucks is worth disappointing a few screaming and sobbing brats and off I went to be someone's day early birthday pretend half brother. Except he would now be my new Master.

Hours to be seven years old, Master Tom would greet me like he was the loneliest boy on earth. He was so surprised I bet he just about pissed his pants. I'm sure I did. Significant to it all was the white shirt with long blue sleeves Master Tom was wearing at my greeting. It had a big blue star in the middle with silver outline and thus I was forever named Dallas. Within weeks, Master Tom's influential older cousin would insist he become a Pittsburgh Steelers fan due to relatives living in the steel city. And so it was and still is to this day, a die hard, black-and-gold-bleeding, terrible-towel-waving, New York steel head fanatic forever linked to a dog with the name of a sworn enemy. Despite that little embarrassment in explaining my name it never created a problem between us. We were boy and dog in the best town at the best time.

Dubbing a seven-year-old boy Master may seem as silly as giving control of the Nile to little Master Tut but the title Master is not one I have much control over. Master Tom loved me the most. It's a species-transcending emotional bond which places me at his eternal side. I'm starting to get concerned that he has the ability to detach himself from this and let me fade into the past. Fat ass Ceila wasn't really his dog but he sure acted like she was.

Here in Doggie Heaven one might expect me to shed the need for a connection to a Master but it's all part of defining my place in my earthly world. It's not as if I were a slave. It's not as if I obeyed Master Tom, I didn't. When all is said and done it's simply where I belonged. It may seem contradictory to my earthly behavior, and at times my heavenly irreverence, but I am a dog of man, not of the wild.

The fact still remained that Master Tom was a boy and is under the control of his Master Father and Master Mother and so to me they are titled as such. Master Tom would soon have siblings and they loved me and consider me their dog as well but I have no control over giving them title. I can only see them as I am allowed to see them. I would in time come to encounter many free dogs of the village and their owners. If their owners are being referenced in the context of incidents with their dog, I now must give their Master title as well, they just aren't my Master. And finally, in reverence to the title, I must refer to the race in general as Master when appropriate. Again, of all this I have no control.

On the subject of no control, being a puppy is basically the definition of the term. You are either dependent on Master, dependent on your bodily functions or dependent on your instincts. The first two are simply Master's duty as Master. But truthfully, it was Mother Master who had the time and patience to train me to crap on world leaders faces. And it was Mother Master who I was in tune with for the sounds of feeding time. You know, the clanking of certain cupboards. The grinding of the can opener. Even the placement sound of the doggie dish to the floor that only I could differentiate from say, a garbage can or a mop.

Maybe it was this early connection that made me in tune to an instinctive reaction I didn't understand yet surprisingly responded to for such a young pup. Mother Master was pregnant and the explanation of my perception of this goes beyond reason. It must have been obvious because she was aware that I was aware. It had only been a few months since my new family took me in and I had yet to develop the attitude of my glory days. I may not have had the "bite" yet but I was a protector and I stayed by her side often and was certainly capable of the bark.

It's amazing how a little puppy with a big bark can make a cozy apartment feel awfully small to Master. I think it's often evident that the family's first dog generally coincides with an increase in prosperity. One usually follows the other. Get a dog, buy a house or buy a house, get a dog. It's the dream of both our races. Look at me. I went from sharing a box with some other dopey whiney siblings to a five-room apartment and a laundry pole with a twenty paw stride leash. And if you think that was great, what happened next was even sweeter.

I'll never forget that day. The family had been gone most of the morning and there I was chained to that damn laundry pole. I was mad with curiosity. I'd bust ass for ten yards then... snap, back on my butt I'd drop. Maybe the problem was that there wasn't any fence or shrubs or garages to block my view. I could see it all. The entire universe alive with smells I couldn't trail and creatures I couldn't chase.

A bird, a crow actually, landed on the far end of the clothesline and looked down at me with all the knowledge, experience and security of a "wise old bird." It knew I wasn't a player in the grand scheme of things. It knew I was a slave. It knew it was revealing itself to me like a doggie playboy centerfold- or in doggie slang, "she was throwin' me a bone." I was young, a virgin. I knew nothing of the bitter tastes- the joyous contrasts of blood and feathers truly free dogs would savor. I may not have known the taste or how to get me some but I could sure envision that crow with its spindly claws dangling from my jaws.

Tom Mody

The crow waltzed along the line in my direction, casually glancing at me but knowing we were worlds apart. As the saliva began percolating in my glands I strangely could hear the can opener grinding away in my head. With a can of dog food it normally lasts about a few seconds followed by the drop of the dish to the floor. But the seconds went by and it didn't stop, the grinding went on and on as that crow became an obsession to me. "Drop dish, drop, drop", my mind screamed! The dish didn't drop and the grinding went on. What's a dog to do? Well, what any dog does when ravaged with temporary insanity. I barked and barked and barked at that crow. Translated it read like a virtual dirty doggie vocabulary

The crow was amused. Had I known there was a Doggie Heaven I would have simply said "screw you, you're shit in the grand scheme of things". But I just barked and barked. The crow was amused. It walked closer and then stood at the pole right above me. I jumped and clawed and barked like a raving lunatic. I had to have it. The crow was amused. It called out and ruffled its feathers a bit. From the nearby cornfield another half dozen or so came and perched along the line. All safe and secure- beaks snubbed above me and flaunting their freedom. The grinding continued in my head. "How big around is this freakin' can anyway?" My thoughts and fantasies were savage. My mind was drool.

In my head I was crapping crow all over Richard Nixon's face. At the time I didn't know it was Nixon or what a president was. I'm a dog remember. It was just a familiar image every time I lifted a leg or squatted on the kitchen newspaper. I simply associated that image, Nixon, to relieving myself in the properly designated indoor location. And Nixon was eating crow by the crap load in my delusional mind. My barking was fever pitched and I was so distraught with the need to break my leash and show those crows I am a player that I made a few futile lunges to move beyond my ten-yard radius. The leash snapped me back every time. The crows were amused.

There was pain and grinding in my head. My neck sore. My throat burning. My hind legs becoming stiff. What little sanity and normal senses I had left were telling me this isn't right. This isn't how it's supposed to be. My instincts were in complete conflict with my reality. How could these worm eating, tick festering, stick legged squawkers have grander domain than me. I was close to a breakdown.

Immaculately the crows lifted off and scattered. I was stunned at the abruptness of their departure. I turned to see the sight of a familiar "happy trigger." In my ranting I didn't hear the unmistakable sound of the white station wagon with faux wood trim that was my usual delivery of impending happiness. It drove abnormally close to the clothesline pole, which explains why the crows fled. Out jumped Master Tom and he snatched me from my shackles and loaded me into the "happy mobile." It's the happy mobile because I'm always happy when I see it coming or when I'm riding in it. It's the (*insert bad words here*) mobile whenever it leaves without me.

The grinding was gone- my fantasies subsided and off we went. Master Tom whispered in my still ringing ears, "We're going home." It was to a new home and a new start for me. I was determined to become a player in the grand scheme of things in all that I understood to be my universe.

Revelation 4

*Only chase things that are
headed for a finish line*

Location. Location. Location. Master Father was in the real estate business and as he could attest, location is everything when going into business. He had the good fortune of landing one of the best locations in the nearby city of Norwich. A corner office front in the city's heart gave him top exposure and more to my interest, a great view of the action. Yup, Master Father and myself understood that if your going to be a player you need to be in the thick of the action.

Being tied up to some post along the outskirts of town is no place for someone who wants to be king. My humanistic revelations draw me to the great Emperors and Royalty that address their subjects in large masses crowded into the castle courtyard. From high above they emerge from the tower to the balcony and speak of war, speak of peace, or simply stand dignified for their subjects to honor. It also lets their subjects know someone's watching them from above. The tower balcony imposes a sense of greatness directly to those who posses it and utilize it's aura. It's a power base and all that's within view seems to be the domain of the possessor. From high above he is King- he has power.

It was a short side of a mile drive from that damn pole to our new home. Obviously, as a dog I didn't know where we were going or why. I was in the happy mobile and there were no poles and no crows. I was in motion and the grinding and madness were over.

As much as we love the ride... and we really love the ride, the arrival is a whole other sensation. It's a happy, giddy, natural reaction thing a kin to dogs. How excited could say a gofer or a rabbit get arriving to some new place? It just sets off another survival mode for them. They're always looking around for who's going to eat them next. So I guess that means they're looking out for me. They definitely don't want to arrive anywhere new and they could give a cat's ass about the whole car thing. Too bad for them, we dogs love arriving. I truly believe we're the happiest at that moment. Particularly if you're a dog that's been in a car a few times and you can pavlov to the slowing of the motion, the sound of the engine cutting and the overall vibe from your Master that the ride is over. You know it's only moments before you hear the click of the door handle and that arrival euphoria high you've been anticipating the whole trip.

With every high there's a low and that has to be when you are just along for the ride to keep Master company. The motion slows. The engine cuts. Master gives that vibe and then he throws us a bone like a knife through our hearts. Not literally but off they run to the post office or even worse, the grocery store. So we wait and wait while the free world out the window continues merrily on. And you all know the horror stories of leaving the windows rolled up on a summer day. Frankly, I can't even go there... Please, give me a moment

(Pause- "shiver")

Okay. So anyway, being stuck in the car is just like that pole. It confines us from our true nature and our insatiable curiosities when there's no payoff. No arrival high. Master in a sense becomes the crow. Not that we hate him and want to eat him but being left in a car is to our comprehension a slapping down of our being. A new glorious world is just one opposable thumb away and we are teased by the limitations of the paw. Teased by Master freely coming and going at will.

You've got to love a dog's optimism though. Every time that car door opens we are willing to jump in, fully expecting that this time we will accompany Master outside the bubble. Despite all the teasing and whimpering from past trips, the

Tom Mody

quest for that high is too great. The possibility of a trip to the river, the woods, or best of all, the park- oh yeah, there's no better place to take a crap!

It never entered my mind on that mile drive that I could be stuck in the car upon arrival. I was too young and had only been in a car less than a pawful of times. Besides, I was still recovering from my pole-chained madness. Fortunately there would be no disappointment in this trip. The payoff was huge!

The motion slowed. The engine cut. Master got that vibe and "YES," click, the good ole' human thumb clamps that lever and pulls down- in a sense bursting the bubble and out I jump. I'd have to say it was my first real arrival high. After the crow-mocking incident I now had a reference for the joys of freedom and exploration. It's so exhilarating. From tail to tongue your whole body is in peak curiosity. The moment you exit the bubble a whole new world of smells, sounds and sensations bear down on you in an instant. It's one big shot of doggie dope being taken in every pour and every gland. You leap from the bubble and you've arrived. The directions to go from there are infinite. It's delirium as your nose leads in circles and information travels at hyper speed on your brain. It takes seconds for you to get it all in focus and unfortunately for a young pup like myself, those few seconds of freedom, of high, are all you tend to get.

Master out of love, which is why I can forgive him, promptly scooped me up and carried me inside. He knows I was fast enough to elude him in a chase so it certainly was the smart move. Grab me while I'm too buzzed to get my bearings and whisk me to safety.

It wasn't just safety but paradise. Our new home had those three magic words- location, location, location. It was a couple hundred yards from the center of the village and across the street was a beautiful tree lined, squirrel filled park and library. Ironically, Thomas P. Gaines Memorial Park as the round monument tucked in a flowerbed would attest. With all the damn dog food smell all the time I take great joy in the fact I pissed on his monument a couple hundred times over my life. I had yet to be revealed of all that was out there having been cast inside immediately. Little did I know I would soon not only be in the center of the action but I would also have my own version of a tower. My balcony to watch and rule.

Our new house was huge. I tore through the downstairs racing in circles from the kitchen, through the playroom, across the living room and through the dining room back to the kitchen. It was a great skid along the new vinyl floor so I definitely had to give it another run. It was glorious. Even in this new house I felt free and unchained. I ran the circle again and hit that slide... Whack! Face first I went into the refrigerator. My breaking skills needed some developing. Okay, I was tired now of that activity. So I began jumping on the legs of basically anyone who wasn't paying attention to me. Which was everyone since they too were engrossed in the excitement of the moment. They simply swatted me down and I followed them through the new domain.

There was an odd smell of new and old throughout the house. Closets smelled of mothballs. Walls smelled of fresh paint. The floors were lush with carpet upstairs and down. I felt it was my duty to give a sniff-over of every corner of every room to be sure all was acceptable. That's not really why I did it, I'm a dog and that's simply what I do. I've just got to know what's in every corner. I needed to get familiar with all the potential interest points and get comfortable with my surroundings. Problem was, every time I'd get to some curious smell everyone would leave the room and damn if I'll be left behind in a room. There's other rooms to inspect and they can't do it without me.

The upstairs was four bedrooms that seemed to stretch along to the back of the house. When you got to the back it was very isolating. Master Tom would often drag me back there with him when he needed something since he was a bit spooked to go by himself. I never liked it myself and often bolted on him when he wasn't looking. It just seemed so out of the way and I wanted to know what was going on at all times. Back there the world could end and you wouldn't know it. I surely wouldn't have wanted to miss that. It wasn't dirty or dank or anything like that. It was just kinda back there, you know? The floors creaked and the ceiling arched in on you. The downstairs of the house had high ceilings so having to go up in the back you could feel closed in and alone. Particularly for a seven-year-old boy with an active imagination.

After the initial tour everyone settled in to some sort of house activity. Most everything had been moved but there was still some general unpacking and organizing. Master Tom retreated to his room to hang up posters and fill his shelves with stuff. I wandered aimlessly about. The living room was quite large and I was finding the high shag in the carpet a curiosity in its vastness as it spread throughout the room. It was a new sensation to my paws and the fresh smell identified the area.

I continued on with the corner inspection. As I reached the far end of the room I looked up to an extremely bright view. The sun was spraying beams of light in wide doses through what I perceived to be an extremely large portal. It must have been cloudy earlier because I hadn't noticed it but now it was illuminating the room. At the old apartment there wasn't much to see and not a large space to view through so it never occurred to me to make use of windows. But now it appeared as if the outside world was actually coming through that window. The bottom of this window was still much taller than I was so I had a steep look up but I could see sky and trees with great clarity. I like skies and tress because that means there's birds and squirrels and freedom.

Much of my view was still encumbered by the wall being twice my height but there was an abundance of view I never got at the apartment. I was being called, summoned to the light. I didn't quite comprehend what was happening. I just felt like the outside was trying to come in and I wanted it to come in really bad. I could feel the rays warming my nose. As best I could describe, the house was alive in my mind. If only I could see more, get beyond this wall that is standing between my doggie urges to reach, strive and find.

Hours earlier I had been chained and insane. Now the perception of freedom was raining on me in beams of warmth and light. When you don't have the ability to see far into the future it's amazing how fast your fortunes can change. There was no way to predict that my chained madness was temporary or that things can change in an instant. I couldn't predict that since all the apartment furniture had been moved that possibly I would be moving on to new things as well. I was crazy with rage and had no idea it would pass. Over time we do learn to anticipate events from the actions and vibe around us but I was still young. It's taxing to ignorantly ride such a roller coaster everyday.

This probably explains why we constantly act so hyper when things are off from our responsive body clocks. We become accustomed to sounds of the can opener or times when Master comes home. When things aren't as we expect we get confused and agitated. Do you know what it's like when Master opens a can of Alpo? Saliva starts oozing from our glands, our stomachs churn and we react. For a while we often get these sensations at that same time every day even if no food is opened. Even the opening of a can of soup at midnight can set us off. Eventually we learn by the time of day that it's not feeding time so we do have some learned response to keep us from bouncing off walls at every sensation. It's such a hard learn though.

It appeared now that a few hours ago was far in the past. Not forgotten mind you but things were looking up. Actually that was part of my problem. I kept looking up to the life force entering my vision but there was only warmth, no substance. All the substance seemed up, just a few feet above my nose. It was so close, so real.

And as a dog's fortunes can change any instant, mine would again. Had I been paying attention, I may have seen this coming. Master Tom had entered the room to see me staring up to the light. For a brief second I thought I was floating but he was simply picking me up to bring me closer to the light. Then an amazing thing happened. He let me go and I stayed in place. I was fully in the light. The outside world was in complete panoramic view.

It was shades of green, shades of blue. Vast space alive with the daily routine of freedom. Cars in motion. Children playing. Teenagers smoking. Creatures in flight and in trees. Even though I was isolated from it, I knew where it was and it had a sense of attainability. This was the place to be to learn, see and react. To become one of the free like the crow. The park that sat outside this very portal was the very vision I had of freedom and it was real.

The portal was obviously a window, a big bay window. My tower balcony. I wasn't floating in air; I was merely placed on the windowsill. And quite a spacious sill it was. It was a ledge, a platform, a balcony for a king to preside over his domain. I'd guess at length it was a good 6 feet, or 24 paws. The space was great to lie down or stalk back and forth. There was plenty of room for Master to visit me and share in the sights of small town USA.

In my own doggie comprehension I was starting to realize that there wasn't a life force coming down on me and that this wasn't some portal to freedom. It was very much like the experience of being in a car. Life is happening around you and when you get the chance to move outside the bubble the highs are most consuming. But better than a car which moves and leaves a dog a bit disoriented upon exit, this stationary window lets me see and prepare for my exit to freedom. I'm not startled or high with excitement, I'm aware of the environment unfolding before me. I didn't need to be taken into the light, I just wanted to know what the hell goes on out there and bide my time until I could seize the domain.

For those few moments where the realization of the bay window shining down on me was a pseudo heavenly experience, I was sadly the dorkiest dog in creation. I'm not into being this "one with the universe" crap. I'm a dog with a chip on his shoulder. I need to get out there and be a player. I let my excitement of the new environment and discovery of such a window shroud me in human Zen. But once on the sill and with my barring in place I knew this was simply the platform I would need to someday crap crow. Starting at that point I would stay up there and prepare for my entrance to this new domain.

Then Master took me down from the sill and walked away. I was displaced. I gave him a few petulant barks to show my displeasure but he didn't return. I needed to be back on that sill. I was just starting to envision glorious romps through the park and I needed to scout it more thoroughly. Not to mention that there was stuff going on out there and I needed to know what it was.

The ledge was three times my size, a proverbial mountain. My destiny was on that sill and so I determined to climb the mountain- or leap it as the case may be. There was enough room for a running start. I backed up, tucked tail and made the sprint. Up I jumped. Wall I ate. Down I dropped.

My first attempt went flat into the wall. I never "touched rim" in Master speak. I needed to jump sooner as my first attempt was too steep an angle. I could hear the sound of kids on bikes passing by and I was missing it all. I barked, I ran, I leaped. My heave was desperate and I managed to get two paws up to the ledge. My claws grabbed the ledge wood. My bottom paws secured to the wall. Once stable I motored all four paws in a paddling motion but I was losing grip. I reposition my bottom paws but I was sliding off. I dug deep but the sill was freshly painted and my nails hadn't yet dug the grooves of a thousand leaps. Slowly I slid then in an instant I hit ground.

From there I made a few more feeble attempts but my confidence was shot. My energy was spent from trying to grip the ledge on my second attempt. It's not enough that I could hear life happening outside my newly proclaimed balcony. I needed to see it. Again, kids on bikes passed by but this time the bark of man's best friend was heard. It was another dog, I had to see this. I had to know what the doggie hell he was doing free.

On each side of the window there were identical love seats. Freshly purchased with firm cushion. It's not as high as the sill but I thought that maybe I could get a minimal view of the action. I easily leaped up to the cushion level and up I bounced. Startled, I wasn't sure exactly where I was coming down so I reached out my front paws and awkwardly came down on the love seat arm. Using the seat arm to balance I then reactively pushed off with my hind legs, made a second push with my front paws and mildly catapulted up to the sill. Though it wasn't my intent I ended up back in the full light. My destiny led me back to the sweetest place I knew, the sill of the big bay window in my new home. For the time being I would continue to use the seat and arms as a stairway to the sill but soon enough I would grow in size and confidence to ascent to my balcony in one fell swoop. It wouldn't be long.

You'd think this transition would have been a strange time for us all. Master Tom and I were thrust in to a new perception of reality. It was bigger and brighter yet safer and more comfortable. I guess humans would say we entered into the American Dream. Had I known there was a God at the time I would have placed my paw over my heart and said the Pledge of Allegiance. The "American Dream" must be more than a concept though. It has to go beyond ideology because how could a sudden move to a seemingly foreign place make us feel safer and more comfortable.

For me, I've got freedom in my blood baby. I'm all for that "land of the free and home of the brave" stuff. Let's rock, let's roll, let's move it on out. It's that wonderful mix of "call of the wild" and domestication which creates my appreciation for the good life on a shag carpet and a smelly swamp. So, thank you Chris Columbus and George Washington and my all-time favorite American, General MacArthur- who defeated both the Japs and Koreans. The significance here being it was MacArthur who insured that the call of "here boy" would not translate to "soup will be ready in an hour kids."

A boyhood Master Tom does not however hear the "call of the wild." The mocking of a crow is quickly out of sight, out of mind. The freedom of his first seven years were spent entirely with the same small group of neighborhood kids that played on an oversized paved lot behind the apartment. For adventure they could wander into a couple acres of cornfields but that was basically it. Master Father's office was below their apartment and Master's grandparents lived in a house on the same lot. Now that's comfort and safety.

Sure he went to school or to the village swimming pool but that was confined and controlled.

Before the move we lived in a small far corner of the village. In Master Father's day it was called "the quarter" which is where all the immigrant families lived that worked in the mill, which was directly across the street from the apartment. Though decades had passed, Master Tom lived much as his father had but without the prejudice of being an immigrant and of course with indoor plumbing.

Indoor plumbing- how modest of the human race. Why does modesty always create a hassle? Okay, I understand you dress because it's cold and you don't have the fur or body temperament of most mammals but why does that then prevent you from exposing yourself to release an urge you have no control over. I know you want to pretend it's about being clean and sanitary but I think it's about not getting grossed out for sex. You can't handle that the organs function in two capacities even though you know they do. It never affected my species humpin' enjoyment. Who in their right mind would force you to bottle up something you simply can't prevent? You have to eat and your system has to send the waste out of your body. I'd blame Adam and Eve! She eats an apple and now you have to hold it 'til you get to that little room. I guess it's God's punishment- like labor pains.

For a dog, that little room was always quite confusing. We could follow you around the house anyplace but once in a while you'd throw us a bone and slip into this little room while we're left to wait patiently to ponder why we can't go in the little room with all the good smells. After a few hundred times we get the impression that since we never went in with you, we obviously weren't allowed. That's why we usually get "caught" drinking out of the toilet as opposed to simply being "seen" drinking out of the toilet.

So anyway, a little boy in a close-knit environment suddenly is thrust to a grander stage and it's no big whoop, he takes it in stride and it's left no real impression on his psyche. That's the power inherent in the American Dream. It's like a virus and it spreads to a core of a generation and they react as if it's a naturally anticipated growth phenomenon.

The American Dream hit a number of families in that small quarter and off they went to bigger houses and grander stages, all within months of one another. This is the magic of the seed planted by immigrants and it tends to take a generation to blossom but when it does it spreads and scatters prosperity in the most infectious way though all the time making it seem like a natural progression. Animals don't have these kinds of natural progressions based on ideology. One day you are slithering across the ground, you pop out a few offspring and the next thing you know they have mutated feet. There's nothing gradual about the ideology of genetic mutation. So what may seem natural to you as humans as you progress over generations is viewed through my sights as something similarly miraculous as a genetic mutation. That being an idea or a concept which takes on a life and a power of it's own. In time I would develop my own concept, my own chaotic motto which describes my purpose. For humans it's the life force called The American Dream. That is how in the most seemingly safe environment you could casually say, "see ya" and easily move on to the bigger and the better. If the American Dream was just an idea then the adjustment would be troublesome but it's a force of it's own that turns the uncomfortable into the natural. It makes the transition seem safer and more comfortable.

I know it was just a move across town but Master Tom had no geographic comprehension of what Sherburne was. It had existed as a parking lot and a number of short rides to other destinations. Now the heart of the village was pumping its life blood right down the main artery of East State Street, practically up the wazoo of our new domain and Master Tom would waste no time treating the entire village as if it was his little paved lot. I, however, would first need to serve a little more time before I made the village my own.

And so there I was propped up on my balcony for the very first time taking in all I could see and in the back of my head wondering how I was going to get down from this perch. I was studying how far back the perception of the park was. I studied how fast the cars cruised up East State Street. I made note of all the birds and cats and squirrels and people that passed by my view.

Hey, that's not people! That's Master Tom out there in the free world on his merry way. Ruff! Ruff! Ruff! And on I went spewing doggie profanities as Master Tom faded up the street. I whimpered and cried but he just faded like the dot on a tube television.

Despite the safety of the paved lot and close eye of family, the old apartment was situated along the village edge of Route 12, which had a 30 MPH speed limit; though heavy traffic made it unsafe for kids to play near. Traffic generally exceeded the speed limit as it prepared for the 55 MPH change. Often the older neighborhood kids would cross the road but Master Tom was not allowed to cross. Besides a few neighboring yards he didn't do much running off. But now being in the center of town, the village became his new lot and as if it was second nature he just up and walked out the door. Master Tom was the crow as he strode up East State Street and took his first right down Union Street just to explore the safety and comfort of his plush neighborhood. On Union Street he would bump into a core of kids playing and just join in like he'd been there before.

Master Tom was now long gone and that kind of subdued my enthusiasm for being up there so how the hell was I going to get down. Common sense would say, "The same way you got up stupid!" Unfortunately we don't have common sense, we have repetition and getting up here was a one time mistake so maybe I'm stuck here a while. You know, if I just coulda' added one and one together I mighta' figure it out but honestly, math wasn't my best subject as a freakin' dog. I paced left, then right. I stuck a paw out to try and find a spot on the love seat armrest but my balance was unsure. I stuck my nose below the ledge of the windowsill hoping that if I got nearer to the floor the jump would look shorter. Nope, didn't like the view. Pup, I'm stuck up here.

Fortunately, in came Master Dad but he seemed more amused staring at me in the window on his ledge.

T o m   M o d y

"Dallas, what are you doing up there," he yelled!

"I'm stuck for doggie freakin' Sake," I yelled back.

I'm positive that's what I yelled and I'm positive it had to be in clearly understandable universal language. So why was he just looking at me, get me down from here. Then he yells back something which definitely was in clearly understandable English because I didn't know what it was.

So in comes Master Mother. For doggie freakin' sake, he called her in here to look at me. So they're staring at me across the room and I'm whimperin' some crap back. We both think we can understand each other but we can't. They're just yak, yak, yak and I'm just ruff, ruff, ruff. It's all gibberish until I hear yak, yak, Milkbone. I perk up and Master Mother is holding my beloved treat.

I'm airborne baby! See ya ledge, see ya fear, it's Milkbone brand dog biscuit time. So apparently getting down is not an issue any more. I glide to the plush carpet, take a sharp left around the love seat then a quick right past the sofa, across the main living room to snag my treat.

Damn, I love Milkbone brand dog biscuits and I can't explain why. They're just tasty. They're hard enough to get the chewing enjoyment but they have flavor that trickles in your mouth once you crack them. They're not too bacony or chickeny like those little hors d'oeuvres-looking treats. They're not a chore like rawhide which I do enjoy. It's just a perfect combination of flavor, texture and content. And for a good three minutes they do seem to mask that doggie breath which is even a bit harsh on us occasionally.

So I chomped delightfully for a few minutes on my snack. I had a cute little way of holding the milkbone between my two paws and whittling it down to small chunks. The excess that didn't stay in my mouth crumbled to the carpet which was a little bonus treat at the end. Despite how plush the carpet was I usually licked up every crumb. Master needed to give this spot some time to dry of course before they might lie down next to me but the saliva eventually dried so I always could enjoy my treat in the living room comfort.

With all the highs and lows of the day and now digestive processes at work, Master Mother correctly anticipated that I might need some relief. The fact that I was being escorted to the back door by my collar didn't bode well for me getting any free run. Sure enough with all the skill the opposable thumb has to offer she slides the clamp mechanism open on the leash. I can hear the chain dragging across the pavement and in one quick release I'm hooked again. This time to the metal railing on the backdoor stoop. Then comes the customary pat on the head and off she goes doing all-important human stuff. I let out a few "I don't want to be here" barks to no avail but at least the scenery was fresh. Well, it was fresh for the moment- until I did my business.

Once I got that out of the way I expected to get very angry about my confinement but that didn't happen. Angry barking never solved anything. I had seen my destiny up on my balcony and as best as I could comprehend time, I knew my time would come. As angry as I got at the crow, so my circumstances changed just as fast. I went from hysteria to euphoria in a matter of hours and so I could move from confinement to freedom just as fast. If I was to be free I needed to be prepared when my opportunities did arise.

That first year in our new domain could best be described as uneventful. Unless you factor in the baby girl born in December. I had a strange doggie karma about Master Mother being pregnant but it really didn't bind me much after her birth. If it's possible to enjoy instinct I can say I enjoyed the instinctive realizations that I'm a protector to my Master but I somehow understood that once she was born my job was done. For the most part, Baby and myself kinda' ignored each other. The house was big enough for the both of us. Besides, when it came to Master Tom he knew his priorities- baby sister or loyal dog? No contest pup. With all the attention given to Baby, we stared to click.

That first summer I didn't know where he'd go as he was exploring the village- making friends and such. Living my ideal life for the most part. Once school started and the routine kicked in I could every day watch him walking home from school on my balcony. We'd often wrestle and play once he came home. At night I would sleep under his bed. It was a large and cozy space since it could house a second rollaway. Normally it was pushed aside so I could crash under there.

I was growing as well. Making the leap up and down from the balcony with ease. Comprehending the short brisk barks necessary to relay my need to eat or to go outside. And oh, how I studied. From my balcony I would spend time every day scanning that park for the routines of all that habituated there. From the animals to the people and even the maintenance machinery. Quite often I would be escorted out there by leash and I'd get to see first hand the details of the flowerbeds and the pacing distance from the "Y" tree to the stone fence. I could smell the dogs I'd seen there earlier in the day and I could hear the wind jump from one tree to the next. The density of the leaves giving each tree it's own distinct voice.

By winter I started to be a regular village fixture as "that dog in the window." My throne was displaced for a few weeks as the Christmas tree was set up in front of the window. I began to get disgruntle not knowing what this exterior monstrosity was doin' in the interior of my domain. I have to admit the lights were kinda' soothing at night and there really is a feel I could pick up as to the anticipation of the season. Baby hadn't been born yet so I didn't mind spending evenings at the side of Master Mother. However, once Christmas was over and Baby was born a few days after, that tree needed to get the hell outta' my space. My wish was granted shortly there-after and it became an inconvenience I learned to accept year after year. Occasionally I found a way to jump up around it but then I couldn't tell what was goin' on in our own house because the tree was in the way.

Over the course of the following year something was becoming very apparent. Dogs were on a daily basis running by my window with no Master in tow. As spring turned to summer and maybe the heat or whatever was getting me agitated, I found myself more and more compelled to let that dog know, "hey, I see you" in a loud manner. More than once I got the old paper swat on the ass from Master Father but damn it, that's my life out there and I don't know what else to do but bark.

Sitting patiently on my balcony wasn't cuttin' it any more. I needed to let it be known I'm ready for more. Yes, I was a happy dog and I regularly got outside and escorted around but note- I said dog, not puppy. I was all grown up and would be all of two years that fall. That old crow was probably carcass and bones by then and I matured enough to forget about that old bird and do this for myself. I knew the territory. I'd been walked around the neighborhood a few hundred times. I've got this super sense of smell so I could find my way back home. What's out there that could hurt me? I'm the predator. I'm the carnivore. I could stand on my own two feet (for three seconds). I needed a plan to bust outta' this place and show Master I was ready.

Sometime around the beginning of September there seemed to be what I would consider excessive yellin' and excessive cryin' coming from the kitchen. The details aren't important but as can happen, subject "A", the eight year old displeased subject "B" the work stressed adult. Subject "B" then displaced his anger from subject "A" to subject "C," the storm door, by use of boot. Master Father's swift kick was the strike of luck I needed and would eventually exploit. Aside from a foot-size dent in the tin storm door, the handle mechanism became stripped and loose. This I noticed as subject "B" ran out of the house sobbing without having to use any opposable thumbs. A simple push on the door would open it with say, a palm or possibly a long snoozer.

I nudged up to door and pressed on it but Master Father continued with the boot theme and thumped me back. I quickly ran to the balcony and took an extra-excited leap, which sent me face first into the window almost knockin' me back off the sill. My excited purpose was to take a good look around the park as I felt I would soon have uninhibited run of the place.

But how would I get there? The weather in the autumn was turning colder so the main door is commonly shut, preventing me access to the storm door. I needed a diversion. What would cause Master Mother to get half way out the door then run back in leaving a free path to the storm door?

Baby!

Maybe when she takes the garbage out I could stroll up on Baby in her walker and slime her up with a tongue bath across the face. Thus she starts cryin', Master Mother rushes in to check on her and I slip by without a thought. Now that's a great plan except for one problem, I'm a dog. I don't have those cognitive reasoning skills. I do have instinct, intuition and gut feelings, which sometimes resemble motivated deviant behavior. Baby is a defenseless slab of skin waiting to be licked and well, you can't stop my inherent need to cleanse. So why waste my time with forethought and hours of trouble shooting every permutation when the natural course of my canine behavior will suffice.

And that's exactly what happened after a few days. My super sensitive ears could hear the metallic vibrations of the storm door opening. I leaped from my balcony where I was watching the village kids playing in the park. Any door rattling, creaking or vibrating serves an automatic notice to my brain that an investigation of sorts is in order. As I'm heading towards the coatroom to inspect who might be entering or exiting I see Baby lying face up in the kitchen on a floor mat. I figure I could use a little salt on my tongue so I give her a quick face full of perfectly germ free dog tongue. I know it was germ free because I had just finished cleanin' my crotch and who in their right mind would wash their privates with something full of germs. I then head to the coatroom as Baby makes it known she's unhappy with our chance encounter. Master Mother quickly returns to her upset child leaving a loose dented storm door between me and my freedom.

Did I say there was something between me and my freedom? No way puppy, I'm gone! A quick little nose nudge to test the door's return pressure... It's loose, it's light and I'm FREE! I'm FREE! I'm FREE!

Squirrel!

Damn the steps. I leap off the back porch in airborne fashion. I'll be flossin' squirrel outta' my teeth all night, I thought. Spittin' up bushy tail hairballs and unleashing the most enjoyable flatulence of my young life. All I've got to do is continue my momentum another ten yards and the spoils flashing in my mind would be mine. I had never chased a squirrel before but I studied them from my balcony day after day. They're so tiny and consumed with playfulness that a quick strike ambush should easily overwhelm the dazed prey.

I was so freakin' excited that the ten yards was a blur. I reached the spot. I jumped. I pounced. My motion halted. My eyes focused, I felt this lump between my paws and it was dead, lifeless, unmoving. My paws crushed the puny thing as my weight indented it in the turf. I Dallas, newly anointed king of the land, trounced the life out of... a defenseless pine cone.

That squirrel saw me comin' before my paws left the porch. By the time I hit the spot it was probably enjoying a cold beer and chips at the local Tree & Grill. Needless to say I was confused and befuddled. So, first lesson of the free world... squirrels are fast. Lesson learned. Time to move on.

The back yard off the back stoop is kinda' poodle sized. Since God doesn't seem to consider Doggie Heaven an "all knowing" place, my lawn size guesstimate in yards would be fifteen long by eight wide. As you jump off the stoop you would land on pavement which extends into the yard for a basketball court. Beyond that the lawn area is only ten yards long. There's a large two-car garage to the left. A short (someday) leapable iron fence with dull spiked tips to the right. The very back is bordered with tall dingy brush. I took two quick inspection laps around the perimeter, momentarily stopping to perform the necessary one leg lift, and then approached the big decisive moment. Do I take the left side or the right side? You can exit the property on either side of the house straight to Gaines Park. Dodging the occasional metal beasts of course which run up and down East State Street.

Tom Mody

Facing the house I could take the left route which is a secluded thin strip of lawn bordering the house. I could also go right which is directly down the driveway passing the kitchen window and in potential view of Master Mother. The grand question is, was I really considering these options? The answer is no. I was a dog on the loose for the first time pissin' and sniffin' my brains out. I had no deductive reason to go either way. I'm just trying to paint you a picture for future reference.

It's not like I hadn't been outside before. I get chained to the basketball post most everyday and I get walked with a leash. I was familiar with walking down the driveway-Master in tow. So, I chose to go right and went freewheelin' down the driveway. Paws smackin', tail waggin', tongue draggin'. I saw park and trees and kids. Even Master Tom himself. It was freely obtainable and I was seconds from jumpin' in this ocean of my dreams.

What happened next may have been the most important earthly revelation that I would carry with me for the rest of my life. I'm not sure if it was the hours of mental notes I made chilled out on my balcony or if my ears just had a sensitivity to rubber rollin' on pavement but my stride towards the park stopped cold as I reached the roadside. I paused patiently yet eagerly. I did a left to right rotation of my head using not just my eyes but also my ears to detect potential danger. The danger came; the danger past and I marched forward.

They say humans only use fifteen percent of their brain and I would imagine those that use only one or two percent more have definite intellectual advantages. I don't know if I used more brain or if I had a special aptitude to recognize from my balcony that the road is a dangerous place but I understood that early on. I crossed the road when to the best of my senses I felt safe. When I reached the other side that moment of recognition came over me that I definitively learned and comprehended my actions. It was that positive comprehension which stayed with me the rest of my life and allowed me to roam and rule at will. The temporary enthusiasms of chasin' tail or game or rubber did sometimes trump my good sense to check the road for streaking metal beasts but the occasion was rare.

So there I stood, at the edge of my dreams. I could close or open my eyes and the reality would be the same. No leash weighted my neck. No escort held me taught. The entire park was before me and any movement in any forward direction would be in unrestricted stride and in perfect balance. I burst right towards the stone fence that bordered the park dividing it from the library. Using the stone fence as my guide I ran straight and true. I ignored the squirrels and the birds. The new smells would have to wait in idle before I'd notice them. I had no purpose- I just wanted to suck sweet wind through my nose. The dank leaves sprayed off my feet like tire smoke from burnin' rubber.

I had never run so far and so free in one continuous burst. The wind had a voice I never recognized before. It pitched high then fluttered as my ears rippled along waves of air I was creating with every gallop. Over the years I would learn that freedom has many voices but when you can get the wind to speak to you in high tones you never have to look over your shoulder and that is the ultimate feeling of being free.

The wind itself also has many voices and I would soon learn another. That would be the sound of the laughing breeze zipping past your ear as you hit the wall. No I don't mean literally, I had run the length of the wall that ended midway up the perimeter of the park. I meant figuratively as in either hose me off or dig my grave because I am dog-beat tired and my tongue is hangin' like a fifth leg. There's no freedom in a panting, half-comatose state waiting for the dog warden to haul you off to the kennel. Fortunately this is Sherburne circa 1970's and I'll have plenty of opportunity to get in "freedom" shape without worrying about dog wardens catching a tired dog.

I must say that young pups recover quickly and the minimal recovery time allowed me to take in the sights and smells I ignored in my initial burst. The fact is, I was halfway into the park and there's no way to trap me with this abundance of uncluttered real estate in my surroundings. I could chase or sniff around with relative security and I did for a short time. But I must say it got a bit lonely. Why should I be lonely when only a short distance away Master Tom and friends were roughin' it with a ball game I had seen them play often. I like rough play. I like kids. And, I like balls. This was the perfect solution for my loneliness. From what I could tell they were chasing whichever kid had the ball. Dog, that had to be the best game ever invented.

I wanted to run right over there and jump in the fun but there seemed to be a pause in the action. The kids were just standing around talking in groups. I recognized the kids in each group doing all the talking. In the far group was Captain. Him and his little brother, Cappy, were over to the house often. They were Kinda-Master's to two poodles, Tago & Pierre. They actually were their sister's dogs and it would be a rare instance I would even see them outside the house.

In Master Tom's group Big Lew was doing all the talking. Him and his little brother Lew (let's just call him Lew- I'm not specifying "little" every damn time his name comes up) were Masters to yet another poodle, Tuffy. Like Tago & Pierre, Tuffy never left the house except when he was riding in the back of his Master Mother's Mercedes with his gal pal poodle, Mitsy.

In fact, since I've been here in Doggie Heaven I have yet to see a poodle about the grounds. Granted this is a pretty big park we reside in but still, where are all the poodles? My guess is that humans screwed up the genus of the species and poodles really aren't canine at all. I always suspected they were more like a large hairy rodent. Yeah, I know that's stretching it but they have a rat like vicious streak in them. I always thought human science never properly grouped and divided species. Sure, mammals and reptiles and birds are large subheadings but just because a few bones and brain cells are the same we canines get stuck with poodles in our class.

If it's a mammal and it's got four legs and a tail can't we group it by a generalized personality? Maybe a large, horny rat did the nasty with an overly curly haired gopher and- voila, I bring you the poodle. I mean seriously, no man was there to see the dawn of the poodle. You get the rat and the gopher mating; throw in a bolt of lightning or some toxic meteorite dust to contaminate the act and who's to say how the DNA might mutate. How smart can science be when it's obvious that poodles are a species unto themselves? I guess if my theory doesn't hold water the only other explanation is that here in Doggie Heaven, like on earth, the poodles are huddled up in the back of some rear window in Doggie Heaven's parking lot. I never saw one loose down there, why would they be up here.

Another interesting study would be why poodle Masters seem to be the bossy ones but there they were ordering the kids around. Even after they broke from their little groups and spread out, Captain and Big Lew were barking orders. Master Tom walked up to the spongy egg shaped ball, or in human speak, the nerf. He apparently was told to give it up because he shuffled it from the ground to Big Lew upon command. Then the fun rough play started again. All the kids seemed to be bumping into each other and Big Lew was running in all directions trying to avoid everyone.

Big Lew wasn't actually big at all. But he was the oldest, very tough and wicked fast. The kids kept missing him or were unable to wrestle him down. Finally Big Lew avoided everyone he intended to avoid and started running away with the ball. I couldn't take it anymore; I had to get in on the fun. Chasing a kid with a ball had to be even more fun than it looked. I burst on over to the scene.

Some of the kids stopped chasing and seemed to be resigned to cheering for Big Lew to keep on running. I blew past them in full stride, much to the shock of Master Tom who now realized I was loose and running wild. Most of those in the Captain's group seemed to be more enthused with the game and they were chasing Big Lew, though unsuccessfully. With dog's speed I made their pathetic two legged bumbling chasing skills look slow motion at best. Quite frankly, they ate my dust.

Big Lew was heading comfortably for the mid section of two hats that were laid out on opposite sides of the field. He was cocky to my eyes. I had noticed that every time someone got to this point with the ball they stopped running and slammed the nerf to the ground. Big Lew was getting close to that spot. Master Tom kept screaming, "Dallas, come back" but in fourteen years I never listened to the kid. I got to the point where I could have jumped on Big Lew in stride but I wanted the gold, puppy. I wanted the ball.

I passed Big Lew and cut sharply in front of him. A little too sharp actually and Big Lew came tumbling over me. With his duff now in the dirt he wasn't happy. I snapped at the ball in his grasp. He raised his hand to smack me but in true athletic perseverance, Captain and his group came and jumped on top of Big Lew. I kinda' just danced and yelped around the whole group who seemed to have me a little hyper with their rough play. Master Tom seemed to finally be getting in the spirit too as he rushed towards the pile. Though, I was his destination and he made the first of his thousands of feeble attempts over the years to corral me in public. I, however, was a free dog. I could no longer be corralled and escorted to the confines of a leash. I could be tricked of course, quite easily mind you, but that would come later.

Captain got up and told Master Tom to leave me alone. He said I was a hero for tackling Big Lew and preventing him from getting a touchdown. I understand now that means I caught him before he reached the hats. Master Tom seemed rather upset that I was out loose and he ran home to get Master Mother and let her know of my escape. She came out with Baby, dry-faced and in tow. With the help of the kids I was finally caught and escorted to the house. No punishment came, as they were more scared than mad. I think my point was made though. I had the kind of experience from which there is no turning back. Like Master's revolutionary kin, once you taste real freedom and understand its rewards in your life, you will accept no other way.

But unlike the Brits of centuries past, Master seemed to embrace my needs and understand my yearnings. Or maybe he just got sick of having to get his lazy butt out of his chair to let me in off the leash or walk me around the block as the season turned cold. Over the next two months someone would escort me freely to the park or let me roam the back yard as they watched from inside. I'd also take trips to the school ball fields and run unencumbered as Master Father and Mother hit golf balls into empty spaces. They must have been impressed with my aptitude and instincts; and of course it started to get wicked cold because by December I needed no overseer. I might have gotten a quick check as I left the door runnin' but they often put their thoughts to Baby or other things and left me alone. I too was not oblivious to the cold and I quickly learned that a few sharp yelps at the door would soon bring a warm body to let me in from the elements.

This was a lesson my predecessor Jasmine would never fathom. One gruesome February night Master Mother put her on her leash to let her do her business and never bothered to give her a second though. Poor, poor little Jasmine was practically frozen stiff to Master Mother's frantic dismay early the next morning. Fortunately a warm blanket and lots of hugs and tears made everything all right. The kicker here is that if you put that stupid dog out in the morning she barks like a rooster until half the neighborhood is cursing her being. But when she's crystallized her bloodlines at 3:00 A.M. in a dead February winter, she doesn't utter a peep. There's no way they could love that dog more than me.

It had been a year and half since the crow madness incident. It had been a year and a half of growing, learning, studying and comprehending. I had put in my two months of free roaming training. It was the mid 1970's when human acceptance of loose dogs was at its final apex. I was about to show Sherburne what this beast could do when given free reign. I was soon to find out I was not alone.

Revelation 5

A cockpit is a lonely place for a dog fight

I was lying in the middle of the living room carpet lickin' my balls. It was the Christmas season of 1974 and the house was a bustle with activity. The family was setting up an artificial tree and...

What? What's the problem?

Oh! I get it. You are a little uncomfortable with my genital cleaning terminology. Up here in Doggie Heaven I get these little gasps in my right ear every time I trample on some human etiquette or I use verbiage that slaps at the grand frigid humility of humans. Fake as you are about it, comprehending Master's comfort levels with certain subjects is part of my ongoing revelations.

It's hard to verbalize in a manner that is foreign to my personality. I am privy up here to the slang and verbiage that a "proper" and "respectful" storyteller might use to ease over a vulgar topic with his cleverly dancing tongue. I can be respectful at times. Earlier in this memoir I think I used the term "mounting the mamma's" or something to that effect instead of a more vulgar approach. It's a mildly clever line and I didn't have to try and dance around my personality.

Dogs don't dance. We are blatant and obvious and void of all humility. Had I been the type of creature that would slip away to a far corner with obstructed views to cleanse myself, then I may have used verbiage like "wash my privates" or something as discrete. The fact is that I was a dog in the middle of the living room, exposed to the family-young and old, man, woman and child. I took my head and stuck it in my crotch and began to lick vigorously under every crevasse and over every exposed part. I enjoyed it. It was pleasurful. When I had extracted every last enjoyable sensation and was satisfied that my effort was thorough, I stopped... and began lickin' my ass.

There, take that! It's the unadulterated truth. It's also very necessary. It's how we stay clean. The alternative is that you stick us in the shower every night and you have the permanent smell of wet dog labeled to your house. My point is that my original line of this chapter was brief, to the point and worded exactly as my personality as a dog and as Dallas would describe. Had you not been so uncomfortable I wouldn't have continued on describing the activity in all its tongue slobbering detail. I'll even spare you my theories concerning human male jealousy of the act since it's so obvious.

So may we begin again as I intended?

I was lying in the middle of the living room carpet lickin' my balls. It was the Christmas season of 1974 and the house was a bustle with activity. The family was setting up an artificial tree and the overall mood was very festive.

Master Tom had been developing a pattern of getting sick every year when the celebratory pine was in place so this was the first year of decorating an artificial tree. The little irony is that Master Father for many years was in the Christmas tree growing and harvesting business and to now raise a son with allergies to pine is a note of mild humor.

Though I'd only experienced a few Christmases, the positive human vibe this time of year was something that transcended to us canine brethren. I enjoy family and the feeling of everyone being together. Despite the species differences we're all part of the same collective as a family. Master Father comes home from a hard day at the office and reads the paper. Master Tom comes home from school and enjoys an evening of Monday Night Football. I come home from a long day of chasing little girls and terrorizing other small mammals and enjoy... "cleaning my privates" on the soft shag carpet. It's all good- we're all together in the warmth and comfort of home after a long day. And Christmas is a strong concentrated feeling of that family togetherness. I like it.

I also liked the artificial tree. It was much narrower than the natural one from the previous year, which made access to my balcony a little less perilous. When I was younger and weaker I had more than one miscue with my leaps up. On my descent down I also was prone to knocking over and breaking a few ornaments which had been past down through the generations. I could create plenty of other reasons for my Masters to be upset with me so I didn't need little crap like that compounding into something big all because of some fat ass tree.

The tree was fresh out of the box and as it was nearing completion everyone seemed to have an odd look about them. It smelled funny. In fact, I had noticed a peculiarity as well- I couldn't smell the dog food factory. Could we all smell the same thing? That's hardly possible.

Once the tree was completely set up Master Mother went upstairs to get the decorations. Everyone downstairs though was still perplexed at the odd smell of the tree and comments were abound at its smoky aroma. Master Father decided to open the front doors to let some fresh air in. That of course gathered my attention and I raced to the door- clean genitals and all.

Oddly, the smell got worse with the doors open. There was an unusually bright glow emanating from the village center as well; considering it was evening. Seems there was a perfectly logical explanation for all this. The village was on fire!

Sherburne's ablaze, has anyone seen a distant cousin of Mrs. O'Leary's cow... you know, Mrs. O'Leary's cow?

Yes?

No?

Burned Chicago down in the previous century?

Anyway, imagine a duffus cow burns down a whole city. What an animal.

It's pathetic the abundance of useless trivia that streams into my heavenly consciousness. Why do I need to know what a cow does in this century or any other century? It's a freakin' cow! Did the city of Chicago apprehend and convict this cow. Because if obliviance was ever an excuse for a crime then the cow was home free. Duh! "Stupid cow. Stupid cow. I'm a stupid cow." And the judge sets her free. If a cow can torch a city then why isn't there a cow warden? If we dogs piss on the wrong side of a fire hydrant our ass gets booted to the pen. A little justice please! I hope her owners eventually enjoyed her a little extra well done.

Anyway, no cows were suspiciously spotted on that fateful December night. The whole town wasn't actually on fire. Just a quarter of the business district- our quarter. In Sherburne's layout there is one red light in the center of town. If you exit the front door of our house and take a right you would be heading west down East State Street to the center of the village, which wasn't far. Mere seconds in fact. There are only two other residents between us and the row of businesses, most of which were burning.

Despite the fire department being situated in the village and a long stones throw to the fire, the blaze grew quickly and was well out of control before help arrived. Across the street from the burning buildings is a smaller walking park area owned by the Congregational Church on the corner. This corner of the village's main intersection happens to represent most postcard pictures of Sherburne as the large brick Church has a tall picturesque clock steeple. This corner intersection is also represented by the large Civil War Monument standing a couple stories tall with a life size granite soldier at it's top. The park section has some walkways and trees and a smaller Pioneer monument. A nice setting to relax in the brisk December evening and bask by the warm fire with family and friends.

Did I say bask? I meant gasp by the warm fire. The park was quickly filling with villagers; all with contorted faces from the heat and jaws open wide in shock. Sherburne's fire department is volunteer so those on duty diligently got the trucks on their thirty-second ride to the scene. Sirens from all directions quickly began grating on my ears as the off duty volunteers sped to the emergency. It was one hundred percent dog lovin' chaos.

Back at home, once it was realized that the tree was fine and the village wasn't, everyone bolted out the door to watch the toasting of the town. Myself included trotted along with Master Tom to the scene. Master Tom tried to guide me with a loose hold on my collar but he was certainly distracted by the severity of the fire and I quickly scampered into the crowd.

It was quite a spectacle. Windows were exploding Debris was falling. The brave humans were dodging around it all with ladders and hoses. Even from across the street the heat was searing. A particularly large explosion sent one little boy into tears as his watch was on repair at the jewelers.

Turner's Jewelers was one of a few businesses to be leveled that evening along with Pudney's Clothiers and Alice's Restaurant. There were also apartments on the second floor. These businesses were located in the middle of the block of buildings. Firewalls saved the businesses on either side from any major damage.

From a young dog's perspective there was a lot of stimulus happening all at once. The fire wasn't the only focal point of my evening. The constant piercing sirens kept my adrenaline at its peak. The tension and dare I say it, excitement from the park full of villagers is sensed by us and can create a frenzied state in our brains. Just being loose was still a new rush every time I was out and now to be among this whole scene, this spectacle of a roller coaster. It was as I stated, dog lovin' chaos.

I weaved a less than agile route between legs of the mass of people. Often bumping children and even the elderly. I barked from enthusiasm and howled in response to the sirens. I jumped on an able body or two and took a dump near the church brush. No one noticed me at all. I approached the curb with an attempt to potentially cross the road but even in my doggie ignorance as to the situation, the large fire trucks, pulsing water and blinding heat intimidated me. I quickly turned back and began to clumsily mill about the crowd. I could see Master Tom in a synchronized zombie stare with all the other humans. I considered going over to him but in a decisive moment I opted to turn and head further into the crowd at an aggressive pace. That's when this sharp whack on my head occurred.

Damn, did someone kick me? There's too many legs in too much confusion to account for them all. Before I could get my barring there was an angry snarl at my ear then a sharp pierce on my neck. I quickly flicked my head back and damn, I smacked my head again. Now there's more snarlin' but this time from a backed off distance. In response I snarl myself and looked to my left. Hey, it's another mutt in this whole mess. And fetch me a bone, a familiar one as well. And he tried to bite me!

There was many a day when I'd be sitting on my balcony before I realized the dream of being out there. I'd be studying the park terrain and right before my eyes I'd see a brown blur peripherally below my stare. Quickly I'd bounce to my feet and press my nose against the glass to try and extend my vision range but the blur would be gone. One day however with the side screen windows open I could hear some squealing from a young boy. It caught my attention. As he came across my view he was having trouble navigating his bike around the brown blur that was antagonizing his tires. He stopped to take a few swats at the blur and then the blur stopped. The blur was clearly a dog in the free world. A freakin' dog out there just doin' it, being a player. Seizing an opportunity to chase and pounce on whatever crosses his path. I had yet to make my debut but damn I had a hero, a role model. I'm not equipped to fly like the crow so I can much more relate to this stud of the free world.

Now, months later, there he is in the "fur" trying to bite me. Sugar, the brown blur, had been running the same ragged routes through out the mass of people. Experiencing my same adrenaline rush and been off his radar enough to butt heads with me in a moment of fateful coincidence. Having experienced this type of surprise confrontation before, he knew the proper reaction- growl, snip and tuck. Establish a quick non-committal strike. More of an offensive defensive posture.

Had we been in an isolated environment this might have turned ugly right away. But amidst all that surrounded us we both seemed to feel a bit secure among the large crowd and were in no real need to get protective of ourselves or our space- just yet. I was actually feeling a bit star struck. Okay, that's not really a doggie term but I realized this was the dog I'd seen free and whom I pictured in emulation. I was in a real moment of duality here. The fact is that this was a dog in my face. I've never been in this situation before. He's made an aggressive move on me but with the fire and crowd and everything it's hard to focus on that point. I'd give him a sniff-over but there's so much smoke and other sensory overload that I see no point. Under the circumstances I kinda' wanted to just stare at him. I could sense a difference in us right off like the two dogs from opposite sides of the track in my opening remarks.

If ever there was a Mutt, Sugar was it. Not just in breeding but his whole short life to that point was a mish-mash. He was light brown with big whiskers. Dingy at times and like strays, friendly to a point. Though he was only a little older than me he was so far advanced in the ways of being stray, yet you couldn't technically call him a stray. He was more of a foster puppy bouncing around. Up here in the world of all things revealed I still don't know where he originally came from. I think it's because his final and most prominent Master didn't know and thus it becomes unrevealed or inconsequential.

I do know that like me, his first known location was Smyrna, New York. I don't know if he was born there. He must not have liked to be crowded because when his first Master's girl friend moved in he bolted for the big city-Sherburne. He knew it well often running away there even in his earliest days only for his then Master to get a call from some local to come pick him up. Eventually he learned that if you can avoid the kindness of strangers looking out for your best interests you could call your own shots, lonely as it might be. Eventually he settled for simply hanging out at the Sherburne Inn.

The Inn was located at the center intersection of the village, kitty corner to the currently burning carcasses of downtown businesses. There was a large patio where he could hang and it was similar to my balcony. He could oversee the village and learn to react to his surroundings.

Somehow he always found food. Probably because he could look mangly and needy without being unapproachable. His hours away from the Inn were constantly honing his skills in mischief and bedlam. These were perfectly acceptable dog attributes in the pre cable TV era of humanity. He learned the short cuts through the residential yards. He learned the open spaces he could run at full stride. He learned the village brush to hide and the creeks to wade. He may have been the village mutt but the village is not a Master. Despite his loner tendencies he was of sound mind and capable of the "doggie need".

On Earth we do not understand that there is a Doggie Heaven or why we need a Master. God gives us a path we can choose if we aren't fortunate enough to be born and bought into the perfect situation like myself. During humanity's Old Testament you all had a kinda' fatalistic heathen approach to life and death. Rituals and rules that involved sacrificing animals as a potential path to the afterlife or to please God. Despite your savage ways towards animals, God chose you as His preferred earthly creation and fulfilled this (with some human debate) in the New Testament. At some point, as you began domesticating us dogs, He decided to please you and make sure afterlife possibilities would exist for "man's best friend" (since it wasn't common to slaughter us at an altar). The key word here being domesticated. The lost souls of all the wild dogs and savage canine predecessors weren't risen from dust on that day. To simply understand, they didn't have souls to be risen as they were Masterless.

Only through Master can we be filled with a soul and get to Doggie Heaven. It woulda' been nice of God to give us a few more brain cells to know this. Maybe a Moses of the dogs or something. Maybe there coulda' been a doggie shrine where we get summoned to once a year. It smells like Doggie Heaven there and we carry this perfect smell with us all our days instinctively knowing we want to end up at this place. I'm thinkin' kinda' a manure and fresh fish combo odor. That'll wag your tail. For all I know this exists. I just couldn't notice it through the blanket of dog food hazing the village 24/7.

Without a Moses we had to respond to the "doggie need." It's a pull towards domestication when that potential situation arises. For offspring of a domesticated dog it's an easy path as pups are usually advertised to potential owners. A stray dog of good mental health must bare a more difficult path. If a dog is stray without any pull towards a Master than he suffers an imbalance- he's mental. There are some variable soul allowances for mental imbalance, abandonment and other cruelties of life. These circumstances, however, do not guarantee a soul will be endowed to that beast. There's only One who can make that call.

Sugar wasn't mental. A bit irrational, but not mental. The path for a soul was open and he just needed to stumble his way down it. On a hot summer day there's a couple perfect spots bordering the village to take a nice cool soak. Heading west the village is bordered by the Chenango River and off the roadside and under the bridge is a nice shaded locale with some water depth. It's also ideal for skipping rocks, another pre internet activity of humanity. For those of you too young to remember when humans weren't permanently tethered together with coax cable, fiber optics and blue teeth, skipping rocks was a slightly purer activity than spending three hours trying to hack your dad's password to some sorority spy cam web site.

So, shaded under the bridge of Route 80 crossing the Chenango River, two boys were skipping rocks in a Huck Fin kinda' way. They would halt this seemingly dorky activity to pay notice of the bushes rustling. Lions and tigers and bears oh my! No, not in upstate New York. It was just some brown mutt looking to take a dip. Sugar cautiously approached the boys. One in particular made an effort to bend down in a friendly manner and extend his hand.

It's hard to say what makes a loner like Sugar connect with a potential Master. I think it was the wholesome scenario. Boy and dog on a hot summer day, playing by the river and just hangin' out. Sugar had been runnin' and jumpin' and humpin' on his own for a while and it was a long time since he was in a situation to bond. He had gone down there to swim but instead he gave the boy a sniff-over on the hand and then sat there as the boys continued on with their skipping. He must have been in deep contemplation because when boys skip rocks, dogs naturally go chasing into the water with utter futility expecting the rocks to be there floating. If cats could talk I'm sure they would have a series of "dumb dog" jokes. One of which would focus on us chasing rocks into the water.

The boys petted him on occasion as he sat there like the perfect little angel- which he was not. Eventually the boys had exhausted their nearby supply of round flat stones and headed up the bank. Once up the bank you could follow the railroad tracks as a short route to getting anyplace on the south side of town instead of heading to the village center. One of the boys lived at the far south end of the village so he headed down the tracks towards home. Even on the sunniest of days there's usually only one shadow per person. It however seemed on this day the boy had two shadows, an upright thin one and a lagging shaggy one.

The mutt had all of a sudden taken on an uncharacteristic sheepish persona as he followed the boy like an unwanted tag-a-long little brother. The boy yelled at him to go home and Sugar backed off a little more. About a half mile down the tracks the boy turned left and made a dash through a yard to try and distance himself from his shaggy shadow. It seemed to work and the boy headed to his home located on the appropriately named South Street. After a refreshing glass of Kool-aid the boy exited his home again only to realize he had become a Master for the second time.

Congratulations Master Mark, It's a mutt.

Sugar was smitten. It's something that happens to dogs on occasion when they connect with humans. We don't get smitten with female dogs because it's just not good genetics. Why complicate a system of breeding that's worked for animals by socializing it. Look at what you humans do. You've made coffee, alcohol and cigarettes prerequisites for the mating ritual. Coffee, Alcohol and cigarettes... Yuk! Coffee as the enticer, alcohol as the elixir and cigarettes as the after deed relaxant. You've got all that crap involved in the process and then you still have to account for social etiquette. I'll tell ya, if you can manage all that and still enjoy it then I totally understand how your species was able to put a man on the moon- and then get him back!

When you can take sex out of the equation then you have grounds for a bonded relationship. Isn't that how it works, the longer you stay together, the less sex you have? This is why the bond in our relationship between our species lasts well into the afterlife- no sex. And I'm not even going to conceive that it actually occurs. Despite the fact it's as immoral and disgusting an act that's ever been conceived, I must be honest and say with no offense intended, your asses are too smooth. Who wants too look at or feel a bare skin ass when they're humpin'.

Now I have no problems with simulated interspecies sex. It's a flat out necessity when nature controls your glands and you've been stuck in the house all day. You could not domesticate a dog that by some miraculous means was prevented from acting out. True, it can be quite the ugly scene when our urge comes at holiday diner time and little Suzie is wearing her new dress but simply accept it as a bygone way of the wild and be glad you've "attempted to" evolved above it.

It's hard to say what connected Sugar to Master Mark. It could be that opposites attract. Sugar, though young, was much older and scruffier looking. Master Mark was a cute blonde boyish looking child. By boyish I mean much younger looking than his age, which happened to be the same as Master Tom's. He was already a new Master to a beagle named Scooter (dossier to come). There wasn't the desire for another dog in the family but then again, Sugar wasn't looking to move in. As I said, he was just smitten. He felt comfortable around Master Mark from the moment his hand was extended at the river. When he hung out at the Sherburne Inn patio he never knew if he was going to get a hand or a boot for his troubles. As he followed Master Mark along the tracks he sensed a freedom in his back road hike that was relatable on a simple level. Master Mark enjoyed a nice summers day romp through the not so beaten path and Sugar, though a ways behind, had some much-needed companionship while enjoying the same.

As days went by, Master Mark would find the scruffy mug he originally called "Brown Sugar" waiting for him every morning. He wondered how this dog was surviving with no home or steady food supply. They shared many a day together in the summer of '74 and as the winter season approached Master Mark was becoming concerned that his occasional companion would suffer. Most villagers by now had assumed that Sugar was their family's dog and it may be reasonable to officially take him in. When Master Mark brought this up to his parents he was surprised to learn that they considered him the neighbor's dog.

What Master Mark didn't know was that his neighbors, after seeing Sugar around so much, had taken it upon themselves to feed and even house him. They called him either Snickers or Whiskers never settling on a name, which shows how loosely he was considered part of the family. Once he left their house he was out of sight and out of mind. So here's where the Master designation gets a bit screwy. These Neighbors already had a dachshund named Gomer. Master Mark had his beagle Scooter. Both could have some claim to Sugar but neither considered the dog theirs. Does Sugar get to Doggie Heaven?

Yes, he does.

Scooter had it made being Master Mark's first dog and he also serves a place in Sherburne dog lore. To the village though it was Sugar who was more notably Master Mark's dog and by maintaining that connection of boy and dog throughout the rest of his life, Sugar has ascended. He just better stay on his side of Pearly Gates Park.

Staying on his side of the park was not something he would adhere to on earth so I shouldn't expect it up here. The middle and elementary schools were seconds away from South Street and Sugar simply needed to walk through the back yard of Master Mark's to have full run of the freshly manicured fields. So why then was he harassing me clear across town in my parks? I can't blame him now. We lived

Tom Mody

for these moments. It seems that when there was already enough commotion, chaos and stress in a given environment, you could count on us to take it one step further. One step over the edge. Children, the elderly, defenseless animals, objects of human importance- all trampled in our dog-eat-dog world.

Sherburne currently looked like a scene from a Godzilla movie but the real monsters for the most part are obscured in a crowd of weary and shaken legs. I was still just kinda' watching Sugar with no intent to pursue the matter. After his initial petulant strike he digressed to a defensive posture. I didn't know what to do. I didn't want to take my eye off him. Despite the heat from the blaze the air was brisk and I could see the mist rising from his snout. It was exiting at an increased pace which would suggest his adrenaline level was rising. This observation was of no use upon my first confrontation but it was noted. There was something in the subtle lowering of his head and the penetrating stare that was making my comfort level change. The crowd around me didn't seem to have the same soothing presence it did minutes earlier. I found myself wanting to slowly turn and find another spot to settle. I had no intention of engaging the situation nor did I have any experience foreseeing my future reactions.

I tried to nudge backwards but that just increased the intensity of Sugar's stare. It froze me. His stare became so encompassing that the environment around me became blurred. I felt nothing. The heat of the fire. The brushes of legs upon my sides. The pockets of cold air whisked in by the December breeze. This was very disconcerting. To have to keep all of my attention on Sugar's glare was becoming stressful. All in my peripheral view may have become mush but my ears were well attuned to the continued drama around me. Human voices in harmonic gasp. The continuous water jets pulsing rhythms. The sharp crackling of oxygen being sucked out of the wood facades. The sirens in a cyclical wave making the flaps of my ears quiver. When you loose a portion of your senses the others become magnified and my ears were becoming large magnetic dishes with the various frequencies piercing my drums. Being stuck in a stare down with seemingly no comfortable route of escape was twisting the fibers of my sanity.

I didn't realize I was on the edge, the edge of thousands of years of animal instinct and response action. A place where reactions of a miniscule proportion can conjure up savage undomesticated violence. I thought I wanted to divorce myself from the situation but I was held captive by my inability to differentiate my senses. The blur in my peripheral vision and my confusion elevating in my ears made Sugar the only object of any real focus. That singular focus was all that was keeping me from plunging into pure animal. My focus was now so tight that potentially any indiscreet sensory perception could snap the thin thread binding me in the present.

Then Sugar gave me some lip. I don't mean he started trash talkin' like he was wearing knee low baggy shorts and hundred dollar Nikes. These were decades away from being linked to urban rap gone mad on cable sports channels. I mean he raised his upper lip to expose the curved bone of the most dangerous animal attribute.

The fire, a few hundred paws behind me, was emanating at its infernal peak. It was brilliant enough to make a sharp sparkling gleam off Sugar's now exposed left fang. A shimmer that snapped the treads and corroded the edge of my evolution. The flames reflected off his fang like a spark jumping into gasoline. My focus broke and I exploded. Something internal, something of a past life or vestigial instinct sent the command to my brain that an exposed fang means strike first. And so I struck!

Vicious gurgling yelps flowed in piercing waves from my lunges just nano seconds ahead of my attacking jaw. Sugar was momentarily stunned but hoisted his hind legs to an upright position to try and gain the upper advantage. My lunge was too quick and I secured myself upon him with my front paws combating him back to four legs where he belonged. If I only had a damn thumb. Once on top I had no way to grip the fur and flesh beneath my puny claws. Sugar shrugged me off and we proceeded to clash snout first in harmless head smacking. We were both too young and too agile to really allow the other to gain any type of advantage. Being dogs we had no way to secure ourselves to one another other than by jaw and that would be a lucky strike that was probably beyond our ultimate intentions.

This was not about survival or territory. One might think it was about ignorance, foolishness, jealousy and pride. A true model of the twentieth century human war machine. No matter how far back we may have seemed to slip in our domestic evolution, Sugar and I had no intention of killing each other. We didn't like each other at this point- I don't know why. For myself it was a matter of him getting in my face and then setting off a trigger I didn't know existed. For him it was about a more evolutionized motive. He didn't need to digress into survival mode. There was no danger present to him. It was twentieth century earth in a domesticated environment. His motive was a lesson I would learn well. It was about self-promotion.

We were free dogs in a golden age. We had reached the peak of our evolution. This was the ultimate point of our species existence.

You don't believe me? You think maybe dogs of the wild west had it better? You think dogs of the revolution had it better. You think dogs roaming with the Indians or posing with Pharaohs had it better?

Think again. In the 1970's in the village of Sherburne, dogs reached the absolute pinnacle of their being. Pup, we lived in houses, had health care, specialized food and cool toys. We could run free without fear of leash laws, bears or bobcats. We had the lowest rate of rabies in our history. Humans didn't commonly carry guns anymore and it wasn't kosher to eat us. We're just riding the coat tails of the American Dream. It's no longer about survival and protection and packs and hierarchy. We reached the point where we didn't have to cower in corners and roam cold in the night. Having shed all this we could now become beings of a purer purpose, a greater consciousness.

Sugar's reaction towards me though seemingly violent was in truth an act of a dog at a higher level of existence. In an environment charged to it's max with human drama, Sugar stepped to the plate and marked another notch of notoriety for free dogs of his generation. Our little brew-ha was a genius play of ego. A credo of "I can therefore I will." I can open the cupboard therefore I will rummage the trash. I can run faster than you therefore I will steal your shoe. I can make you appalled therefore I will start a fight while your village burns.

I'll state it again, "dog lovin' chaos." No three words were ever so perfect together. It was our motto. As Sugar and I carried on with his instigated theater, the humans gasped. Mothers hoisted their children. The elderly clung to the nearest stable body. In melodramatic panic a few overly uptight ladies even tried to get the attention of the firemen to help control the situation. Finally some brave stud with a big boot swung his foot between the two of us. A few others then landed in some secondary swipes and we parted. One lady was so upset she cried- cried at the fact that we would even dare to engage in a confrontation during the epithet of the business district. Another spectator vehemently wanted to know where the owners were and cursed them for letting these savages loose.

Master Tom and family were too far away from the fight to notice the chaos we were causing and Master Mark had yet to arrive at the social engagement. Once apart, Sugar and I ran off to settle down a bit. My heart was pounding and I was still mad at who was once a creature of envy for me. I found a spot back near the library that separates Gaines Park from the Congregational Church Park and the crowd of villagers. When this all started I had been weaving through large groups of people like a ghost. Despite the crowd it was no fun going unnoticed. Similar in a way to running free in the park yet not involved in the football game close at hand. The revelation was that even though I achieved my dream of freedom it was hollow. My instincts pushed me to become free but my evolution as a species now required more. It wasn't enough to be free. Now everyone I encountered had to know just how free I was.

The problem being that I was a dog. I only had a certain level of comprehension of how to accomplish this. By nature I know how to run and jump and play and fight. These were the only intellectual tools I had at my disposal to make my freedom accountable. Chasing a stick and following Master was not going to always fulfill this new consciousness. Unfortunately, the easiest way was to create bedlam and chaos. To stick my nose in where it didn't belong. I didn't want to misbehave; I just knew no other way to express myself in a noticeable manner.

The cause of the village fire was believed to have been a grill left on at Alice's Restaurant. Arlo Guthrie fans around the world can now bow your heads in a moment of silence. Over the 175 years of the village there have been numerous fires that destroyed churches or businesses- the Sherburne Inn in particular. But it had been many decades since a fire of this magnitude gutted anything. I was lovin' it.

The air was crisp with a soot smell. No, it wasn't tops on my list of odor stimuli. Soot doesn't have a pungency that wets your whistle. More to my liking is what the smell lacks... dog food! Soot can bury the best of smells and I was getting a nice "breather" away from that damn dog food factory. Us village dogs were the only ones taking anything positive away from the fire because the village was a bit of a mess. The winter is muddy and slushy and dingy enough even without the eyesore of the burned buildings. Oh, I guess there were other positives. No one was injured- fireman or pedestrians. In the eyes of little boys there was something neat about walking by the wreckage and inspecting around the caution tape. As noted earlier, some businesses were spared flame damage by the firewalls bordering them. Two businesses of icon stature were among the spared.

For the sake of historians, the Sherburne News went unscathed through the ordeal. In fact, they probably made out just fine. Nothing like having the biggest story in the past ten years right under your nose. I'm sure they easily made an extra twenty or thirty dollars in sales the following week with the "big fire" headlines. Located on the very end of the

East State business row, the family owned Sherburne News even to this day is a symbol of the small town purity to which the villagers fervently cling. It was one of only a handful of printers that still used archaic type setting of each individual letter to make its articles. Early Twentieth century steel gears turned the mammoth press as sheets of smoky cream paper slid off the line to the floor littered with metal file clippings.

Once printed the type was slightly crooked and pictures often lacked any reasonable clarity. Each little surrounding town had a section of article in the paper. You could read about the Smith's having cake and coffee at the Jones' in the Columbus section or someone from Poolville may have just harvested the ripest turnips of the season. Yearly subscriptions cost about the same as a couple hamburgers. It was a notoriously famous paper in dorm rooms around the country as parents had subscriptions mailed to their lonely co-ed children. Often to be the source of amusement for their big city frat mates who were use to more sorted tabloid gossip and the occasional murder headline.

On the opposite end of the burned business row near the corner intersection is another generationally infamous family owned business, which survived destruction. Quinn's Market in the eyes of a eight year old was like finding gold. Upon his move to East State Street, one of Master Tom's first ventures was downtown to Quinn's where upon initial view of the candy selections he just about became the youngest victim of an overly excited coronary artery.

It was a general grocery store with foods and a butcher and dairy section. It had its moments of notoriety in other ways. Often expiration dates on candy and canned goods could be measured in years. Though it's now out of business I would still venture a guess that if you looked hard enough in some corner or back in some store room you could still find a box of "Kaboom" cereal which garnished their shelves years after the cereal went extinct. It was also the only store that would sell eggs on Halloween to citizens under eighteen years of age.

For myself, Quinn's was generally the first stop on my normal days routine. Old man Quinn would often leave crates of plumbs or peaches in wood baskets out front for customer to pick through. As I headed out the door and down the street it was those very fruit filled baskets that were the target of my first urination break of the day. If I hadn't ventured downtown in the morning, by midday I was bound to be at the village center as the noontime fire whistle had me scampering to the intersection and howling like the daily crier.

Over the years the villagers came to expect my daily noontime singing exhibition and I often would be joined by any nearby mutts. I would suspect the first time I was really noticed though was a wet spring day in mid March 1975. Sugar had enlightened me to my internal need of self-promotion. I was doing my best at that point to pick up on the general pest tendencies which suited my personality. A lot of barking at seemingly nothing and occasional chasing was the best I could come up with so far. It was Master Tom who actually spiced up my self-promotion to a new level.

One Saturday it had been raining all morning. The spring rains had yet to wash away the excess mud left around with winter snow melting away. He had been racing sticks down the gullies with rushing water from the heavy rains but soon found that tiresome so he ventured inside for some pretend super hero play. Before the days of wise-ass cartoon losers (grunt! grunt!) there were "The Super Friends" of the Justice League. Life-saving, teeth-sparkling humanoids with super powers and dull stagnant cartoon backgrounds. With a simple blue cape and an iron-on "S" on your shirt it was easy to transform yourself to a Superman-Batman hybrid- no phone booth necessary. Master Tom had a better idea. Why not transform your dog- he could become more heroic than Underdog.

Underdog? That's the best twentieth century minds could come up with for a super hero dog cartoon. Gimme' a break, it's a cartoon. There are no rules, no limits to the powers and greatness a super hero dog could achieve. Aside from flying (which is way cool!), what was his other great power... beer guzzling. Have you seen the beer gut on this mutt? I mean he must have had hellacious super strength just to get his fat ass flying off the ground unless he was propelled by flatulence from all the beer. Dogs and beer are a sure fire recipe for super power intestinal gas. I understand the play on the name Underdog but the only image that pops into my head is his lifeless carcass under a car. I want to call him "Underthat."

Why do we care about bringing ugly puke green villains to justice? That's not our gig. A super hero dog should be able to catch anything- anything! Bullets. Buses. Trains. Jets. Rockets. Meteors. UFO's. In fact we should be running over cars instead of the opposite. A super hero dog should be able to procreate in more than one position. A super hero dog should be able to piss on a dog warden and melt him in acid urine. A super hero dog should be able to smell shit carried by winds of the jet stream and identify not only the geographic location of the load but from what animal it originated. Forget that, he should be able to smell shit from alien planets. I'll tell ya what, just give me a damn super hero dog that can open an industrial meat locker with gadget opposable thumbs and I will endorse that cartoon.

I had never worn any type of clothing until Master Tom slipped my head and front legs through his Superman T-shirt. It didn't really bother me but I could take it or leave it. If you can handle two years with a collar constantly around your neck, a thin cotton garment is barely noticeable. The blue cape though was a bit much.

I pranced around the house amusing Master Tom. Whenever he got me running the cape would float a few inches off my back simulating flight. It was something to do on a Saturday Morning, I guess. Inevitably I had to take a leak so I motioned to the front door and gave my usual quick yelps that I needed a break. He must have been feeling as if he'd outgrown the outfit because he just opened the door and let me out- cape and all.

Can you hear the trumpets sounding my presence? It's Super Dog! Saving children from danger, rescuing small animals from their savage predators and spreading good will between species. Yeah, that's me all right. I looked more like Dumb-Ass Dog. Chemically unbalanced, viciously unstable and obviously blind as a bat because I looked ridiculous. Particularly when that first car came rumbling down from the Route 80 hill. I started chase with my tail wagging out my cape. Down the street I went barking and making a scene. Hoping to catch and pounce the steel beast. I got close but sure as shit the passenger opened her door at me and took a swipe, just missing my less than super hero strong head. Once the two girls driving got a look at me they just started laughing at this absurdity as they zipped through the green light at the village center. Obviously I'm not faster than a speeding bullet or a Chevy Nova.

If I had any humility I would have tucked tail under my cape and tried to summon my Super Dog invisibility shield as I fled for home. Unfortunately the church clock struck twelve and the fire departments noontime whistle went screaming through the air. If you think about it comparatively, I do have super human hearing and that whistle just rips through my eardrums directly to my brain. Having been stranded by the car at the village intersection I was left with no choice but to respond to the fire whistle by howlin' my mid day song. I was directly under the damn red light holding up traffic in all directions wearing a Super Man shirt and cape in a mild downpour just wailing back at that whistle. Patrons from Quinn's, the Sherburne Inn and the corner post office all braved the rain to see self-promotion P.T. Barnum could appreciate. Eventually the whistle subsided, car horns started voicing their irritability and I relented heading to the street corner near the Inn.

You know you're a fool when another dog can give you the look of "moron." Hobie was a dog that had taken Sugar's place by gracing the steps of the Sherburne Inn. He was just another brown mutt and that's all I can really describe about him. I had noticed him shortly after the Sugar fiasco and I crossed his path a few times over the months without incident. There was something different about Hobie. In his presence you didn't feel any of those repressed aggressive dog tendencies. You just accepted him as a part of kin. He had a way of communication I didn't understand. He instilled a sixth sense in all us village dogs. When you saw this walking scruffy brown mutt you just got gut feelings about stuff- stuff you just didn't know how to process but made you act anyway. As I looked up on the Inn steps and saw Hobie wisely inches inside the patio to avoid the rain, I could tell exactly what he was thinking... "Moron."

The rain was coming down harder and the weight of my outfit was becoming cumbersome. I cut back through the intersection towards Quinn's in an attempt to go home. Still more people tipped up their umbrella's to catch a glimpse of Super Dog. I had suffered enough embarrassment for one day and as I approached the curb the weight of my drenched cape caused it to slip forward on me. My front paws stomped on the cape dangling off my neck and my forward momentum sent me face first into a mud puddle accumulating from the gully of water streaming down the Route 80 hill. I gagged as water gushed up my snout and I tried and tried to get my face out of the water but I kept stepping on my cape and flopping back into the puddle. Have you ever heard a dog gag or try to hack up anything? It's a disgusting sound. Finally the cape tore off and I arose with little dignity intact. Hobie, watching across the street, just turned and headed towards the Inn door. Customers in the Quinn's Market doorway laughed hysterically. Certainly Underdog would never have gotten himself in this predicament. This is not the doggie self-promotion that I was aspiring. The best doggie self-promotions occur when events lead to natural doggie reactions.

I gathered my fur-soaked self in need of some doggie damage control. So, I headed up the curb, calmly approaching the few hecklers of my misfortune. Nature did the rest. It takes less than a second for the weight of the water in my fur to send impulses to my brain and then down to my legs. Those impulses begin a quivering that starts at my paws and generates massive toque to my body. Bystanders seemingly safe in the Quinn's doorway were now getting a wash and rinse courtesy of my body's natural reaction to over absorption of water. And I was really over absorbed. They spewed profanity as Super Dog repelled the heckling evil with his super duper counter defense body spray. Who's laughing now puppy. Redemption doggie style is so sweet. I wish I had planned it. I pissed again on the fruit baskets for good measure and headed for home somehow knowing that those in town that rainy Saturday would not forget me. Assuming they could recognize the village's Clark Kent without his big red "S" and cape.

That spring I was so excited to be a free dog that I spent a lot of my days water drenched. Albeit from spring rains or exploring the village at hand which was bordered by a number of creeks and a swamp or two. The Chenango River is a much larger waterway, big enough for a canal in the olden days. It was mainly accessed by heading west outside the village and scooting down under the bridge where Sugar and Master Mark met. You could follow it South away from the village or North through Rogers State Conservation Center all the way to the end of the village. Eventually past the large mill and on off to the next town of Earlville about four miles away. The other main watering hole was Mad Brook or what was generally referred to as "the creek." It was south east of the village notably meandering the borders of the elementary and middle school fields, the village pool and Paddleford Park baseball fields. It was fed from a notable Sherburne landmark called Rexford Falls. About a half mile east up East State and Route 80, Rexford Falls was mildly impressive for a tiny village with its suspended bridge overhanging the cliffs of the falls. It was a great place to piss off of but falling over the bridge would get you to my current location.

I tended to frequent the creek over the river because the creek bordered all the "in" places to be. There was also much more brush and secluded scenery to rustle through and around. The village kids had the same tendencies. You could reach the creek on flat land at any of the mentioned locations but on the opposite side of the creek was a steep hill cluttered with thick brush and trees peaking at a long housing area called "The Heights." Any location along the creek was a great place to lose yourself in full childhood play. You could sink cans with rocks, turn stones for salamanders, play hide & seek or build a secret fort hidden in the brush. Sometimes the kids would even join in the fun. I'm joking, that opposable thumbs thing prevents me from throwing rocks at cans or constructing anything.

As a young maturing dog I had yet to find a comfortable demeanor towards the village kids. They all come in different sizes and temperaments. Some are scared and timid around dogs. Others are expecting some type of affection. Still others love to antagonize or even be mean to us. Let it be said that I loved being a part of the youthful exuberance kids display. The village streets and parks and stores were alive with kids showing the same appreciation of newfound freedom as I had. If you are in the eight to twelve year old age group, it's still a fresh accomplishment to be able to walk to school, spend your hard-earned quarter on a pack of football cards and be responsible enough to be sure you are home in time for dinner.

Teenagers, now they generally suck. You mostly would see them hangin' out in Gaines Park sittin' on the stone wall smokin'. They tended to be mean and didn't welcome my advances on them. It was hard at first because it was generally my park. I lived across the street and I spent a majority of my free time there. It was a big park and I eventually learned to keep my distance from certain kids. Over the years my antagonistic rebel reputation earned some amused respect from some teens but others saw me as a challenge just like I was a human. They figured I had a real human attitude like I was a tough guy or something and often used that rationale for cruelty towards me.

That's a reason I liked to get away from them down to the creek. The older teens in particular were too adult to be playing in the water and brush. I wish now that I had a greater understanding of how to be apart of youngster's activities but I tended to mostly disrupt the kids at play. It might have softened an encounter that would save me some nasty scarring years later.

Master Tom had been playing some sort of tag game at the Captain's on Union Street. For a small street, Union Street had an extraordinary number of kids. Even though the ages could have a six or seven year gap it was not unusual for them all to be engaged in some activity together.

Another usual occurrence was the eventual brutal outbreak of fighting between Captain and Little brother Cappy. There was three years between them so unless Cappy could land a cheap shot, and he often did, Captain would eventually pummel his younger brother. This would usually break up whatever activity the rest of the kids were doing so Master Tom made his usual three or four attempts at trying to catch me and bring me home. I eluded him and went on my own way.

From Union Street it was a two-minute trot to the creek. I choose to go through the parking lot separating the middle and elementary schools, past the band equipment out-building and over the blacktop basketball court where there was a wide-open entrance. A few feet down the creek there was a large deposit of clay. Some kids were making little figures and buildings with the fresh mud. I just wanted to see what all the interest was so I wagged my tail, splashed in the water and trotted in the shallow stream to the fun. I got about three feet from the clay deposit when one of the kids sucker hit me with a stone to my head. I didn't quite get that he was protecting his little "Michael Angelo", so amidst the pleas from the kids to stay away, I proceeded forward. Oh, they yelled and screamed and whined and moaned but I crushed their artistic endeavor with some carefully placed goliath sized paws. They were pissed and started splashing water and throwing mud at me. I was actually having fun trying to catch the mud balls in my mouth. One very angry kid got right up in my face to plaster me with a huge mud ball but I jumped on him in exuberance and I seemed to intimidate him with my playful aggression. That's when the tornado came in.

If there were kids at play in the creek or about the village, you often could find one dog who kept a protective watchful eye on them- Laddie. As best that can be determined Laddie had a mix of husky and sheppard but was most notably a Collie. He was a stray for a time but like

Sugar he simply followed his eventual Masters home and the family, owners of the Sherburne News, took him in. Quite frankly, I don't have the patience to list all the Masters in that family. Lots of kids you see. He mostly ran loose anyway. I think I can show the proper respect to his Masters by just saying "a Master of Laddie" at the appropriate time.

There were none of Laddie's Masters around when he came roaring out the brush like some lion of the jungle. I swear the dog cleared the kids in mid air from the top of the short embankment. I had about one second to be impressed because he clawed me across my eye on his way down. Damn, I got stoned and clawed in one stupid afternoon. Laddie landed directly between the kids and myself like he was protecting his own. He often waited after school by the band room for the kids to be let out. If he couldn't find one of his Masters he'd befriend anyone who gave him notice.

Today was a special treat for him as he rarely got to defend his pick of the day buddies from another dog. Laddie the good. Laddie the wise. Laddie the noble. Maybe if he had gotten to me before Sugar. Maybe if he would have tried to take me under his wing I coulda' appreciated another way of expressing my self-promotional needs. Laddie found the protector approach as his angle. The problem is that I wasn't out to hurt anybody. This would become a theme with him- the pious bastard. He took his do-gooder angle way too seriously. I say let the blind guides and drug sniffers and cattle rustlers live with that burden. This was a golden era to freely do what we do naturally, not what some bone rewarding slave driver trains us to do. So some kids got their little arts and crafts stepped on by accident. It allowed me to get them to throw mud balls at me. He coulda' joined in the fun. But no, he gets his attention by being the bodyguard. Did anyone train him for this? He was a stray for doggie freakin' sake so be happy you now got a home, a master and a bowl of chow every night and join in the great life of dog lovin' chaos. If he wants a job let him go sniff out some land mines for the military or maybe he can be a stunt dog for Lassie.

T o m   M o d y

Well anyway, that's Laddie for ya. And of course, we start to go at it. Laddie was in his prime and he had a definitive size advantage over me. It was a short whoopin'. I got the point and ducked out of there as soon as I was able to get his jaws out of my neck. I wish this woulda' been the worst of our fights. Maybe if I had stayed a pup or not grown so cocky over time but that wasn't my destiny.

Laddie was feeling extra studly that afternoon so he did the only thing any reasonably normal dog would do. He went and boned a local collie lass that evening. He boned her quite successfully actually and he and his future son Scamp would soon make double trouble for us all.

Revelation 6

The dogs of war never got their own holiday

Imagine, if you will, a brisk evening. Be it summer or winter, it's just one of those night where a little warmth brings you comfort and relaxation. Let's say that you're spending a rare night away from home. You're a little boy or little girl and you just need some snuggle security being in a strange place. If you are planning on spending this stay over at my domain, may I recommend you bring your own sleep security. That mischievous grin on Master Tom's face isn't because he's happy to see you.

Oh, it's innocent looking enough. Tucked away in the living room closet along side some cozy slippers, a few pillows and those treasured knit afghans grandma made while watching The Price is Right. There in lies the trap. The knit blankets appear a little colder because the yarn doesn't cover one hundred percent of the blanket surface area. You want something a little soft and maybe a little worn. You then spot some warm navy blue cotton with cool satin trim. It's perfect to secure your needs for the evening. I should know- that blanket sure got me through a few hundred evenings when my needs were very high.

I was a maturing dog, you know. Chemicals inside me were always changing, my brain constantly sending impulses to my body. I got hot flashes. My sense of smell tended to peak causing me to peak, if you know what I mean. Dog, I'd find some strange scent in a bush or back alley and I don't know what would come over me. I learned quickly that brush just plain scratches and garbage cans got no grip and no give. Yes, yes, I'm referring to mounting shrubs and trash cans. No need to read between the lines here, I'm talkin' about humpin' inanimate objects. Believe me, it's just a learning thing and I understood quickly that something wasn't right.

Gimme a break anyway. I didn't have an older brother around or the ability to understand cable television. Either of which is useful for explaining these urges. Walk around in heat all day without pants and you'd be surprised to find your thighs wrapped around anything that didn't require sharpening and wasn't dangerously motorized.

To be honest, I didn't start humpin' that blue blanket alone. Some catalyst, an innocent child on a weekend stay-over needed to be in the blanket sleeping on the floor. Master Tom's cousin Lew, little brother to Big Lew (and this is the last time I'm noting that), was the devirginized first victim.

Laddie had been roaming surprisingly late that night due to his family enjoying dinner at the Inn. As dusk drew to night he was pacing awfully brisk up and down the Inn's sidewalks. He seemed annoyed it was taking so long, like he had someplace to be. His Master Family is enormous so it's no small task to host them when they are all out together. Unfortunately, this logic escaped him, as it tends to do with all us dogs. But when you've just impregnated some lass, paternal instincts do surface and conflict with your instinct to wait patiently for your Master Family. He only wanted a quick check of his mate's condition but she was across town and he was impatiently stuck while dessert was being served. The curse of the guardian I guess.

I was returning home from the railroad tracks after trailing some skunks outside of town. Not necessarily the type of tracking that requires a lot of skills and still I couldn't hunt them down. That's a lucky break for my Master Family. As I approached the Inn, Hobie came out from the garbage area and ran across the road towards the corner post office. He caught my attention so I followed him to the other side where we stopped and engaged in a sniff-over. It was a complete diversion on his part to steer me clear of Laddie. I suppose it avoided an incident but Laddie did smell me and approached the curb though he was still bound to wait on his side of the street.

I was getting the feeling from Hobie that Laddie was not in a delightful mood. I could sense a real purpose in Laddie as if there were actual responsibilities affecting his mood. This is the type of weird shit that would happen when Hobie was around; sixth sense, doggie channeling, Cajun gypsy, back river Amazon, freaky mutt karma. I figured it had something to do with the pregnant Collie in the village. I had chased her down myself some weeks back and immediately sensed she'd been "had." I could also detect Laddie's scent on her and in my own way of comprehension figured she was Laddie's bitch.

I hadn't felt that sense of purpose and responsibility since Master Mother was pregnant. Lacking it made me feel a bit empty inside. As dogs we always have the urge. You know what I'm talkin' about- we'll hump anything. Had I not encountered Hobie my humpin' drive for that night would be no more than pure animal urge. It's a drive I understood and could manage. But along the walk home the urge felt cold and archaic, like it alone wasn't enough. I know we were evolving and domestication gives us unprecedented opportunity to grow but I didn't want to mess with the urge by adding purpose to it- did I? Technically being a virgin the urge hadn't served me well to this point but I had high hopes for it in the future. Like freedom I could sense its delights on the horizon.

At home I laid on my sill troubled that I couldn't draw those purposeful impressions out again. The later the night went on the more I sunk into a feeling of emptiness. Master Tom was asleep in the recliner and Lew had cuddled up on the floor, wrapped in the still pure blue blanket. The TV was left on as they slept. That music with the flag wavin' played its course and then the screen went white. I guess Humans in the 70's didn't feel the need to buy diet pills or face creams or real estate with no money down after midnight. Man could sleep in peace knowing he couldn't possibly miss anything with only three channels on the tube.

I wish I coulda' slept but I not only had the urge, I was hankerin' for a purpose. A purpose with a firm lump covered in a soft fuzzy exterior. That's what a female mutt-stress feels like- right? I hadn't been drawn to anything like this before. Like I said, I had control of the urge in it's pure form but now I was corrupted with purpose. I wanted to feel as the protector again. Maybe if I just satisfied that carnal urge that emptiness would subside.

The static buzzed from the lack of broadcast on the TV. It masked the sound enough to prevent anyone from hearing my approach. The tube emanated a glow, a sensual light upon the still lump. Curled in a fetal position, Lew couldn't have been more submissive. I suppose it's the equivalent of drunken sex with humans. I sniffed around his perimeter as smells often activate my glands. Nothing here set me off scent wise. I looked around, conspicuous only to God and my dead relatives. I approached the front of the lump but even I couldn't mount him on his defenseless face. I rubbed my head along his side and felt the softness of the cotton. A little shot of static electricity perked me up a bit. It also woke up Lew from his deep slumber. He muttered something about being uncomfortable from the floor and in a semi conscious state rose to his knees in a bent position.

BINGO!

I now had the urge, purpose and position. I rounded him with all functioning anatomical apparatus in the proper state. (You can thank me later for sparing you the blunt descriptive style of the previous chapter). I rose like a ghost in the night, lunged and clamped on to the startled lump. Lacking any experienced technique I didn't just thrust my hips but I thrust my whole body at every stroke. Lew was just a little boy a few years younger than Master Tom and he was trapped under a beast stronger and of equal size, bound in a blanket of lust he couldn't loosen. My forceful lunges literally moved him a few feet from the middle of the carpet to the edge of the defunct fireplace mantel. Eventually trapping his face against the cold stone. He still couldn't sort between his conscious and unconscious state. Eventually my heaving pants of hot doggie breath awoke him to a nightmare in reality. He was being victimized by beast and not beauty.

He screamed to Master Tom as his head smack repeatedly against the stone. Master Tom at first just mumbled, "Dallas go lay down," unaware in his half conscious state the extent of my activity.

Lew pleaded. "Tom, get this pervert off me"

More aware now, Master Tom threw his black and yellow pillow football at me but it deflected off without breaking my strides. After that feeble attempt Master Tom still didn't get his lazy butt out of the recliner to help his cousin. He just told Lew to get away from me. Lew, now able to get some bearings, being fully awakened, made steady progress at getting his hands free from the blanket and eventually shoved me off. Master Tom joked that it was obvious I "loved" Lew and rolled over to get some sleep. Lew began to scold me verbally but Master Father was now awakened and yelled at the boys to shut off the TV and keep quiet. I walked up to Lew a little stunned at my own actions but he kicked me hard in the hip and I backed away.

I personally was very satisfied. I knew it was simulated. Instinct tells me I can't impregnate other species. But it's also instinct and not deduction that gives me the urge. Let's be frank, I don't have palms and it's so freakin' frustrating. I know what you're thinking, I've got the spine to get tongue access but I can't bend and lick vigorously like that for extended periods.

Besides, being in heat isn't just about genitals; it's about the whole sorted, savage mounting and humping act. In fact, the whole act was so invigorating and self healing that all I could focus on was the rush of aggression and release of anxiety. The little seed of purpose planted by Hobie's voodoo was now overshadowed by the bloom of pure canine truth. I don't need no alcohol or cigarettes or soft kisses or any purposeful complications to expand and embellish my act. When the urge comes it doesn't need to be managed or suppressed or medicated away. As long as I can identify what's comfortably humpable, go with the flow puppy.

After a few years I wouldn't need no defenseless lamb in the blanket. I learned to just wad it up between my upper paws and go at it. For the most part the blue blanket was in

T o m   M o d y

public access because it was also the blanket I used to lay on around the house. Unknowing guests would often just grab it to cover up, much to the family's admittedly gross and juvenile amusement. Over the years it would become worn, torn... and stained many times over. The blue blanket would become almost as infamous as the dog who made it his bitch. It was another example of utilizing all available promotional outlets to permanently instill myself upon the conscious of my era.

I wasn't really as desperate as my fondness for the blue blanket might project. I had Master Tom to follow and pester which kept my mind off canine carnal desires. These were storybook summer days and snowy holiday filled winters. The very same ones that rotated with consistency for the past 100 years since the advents of the bicycle and the toboggan.

Back then it didn't take much to stir the excitement of kids. Something as simple as a new brand of candy bar could have all the kids begging parents for quarters only to find the shelves quickly sold out of the newest treat. Another nifty seller exclusive only to Bigelow's Drug Store was the "slush puppy". I don't know how us young pups got all wrapped up in the name of this device but I sure wish I had it's self-promoting draw. A pull of a lever would drop watery crushed ice in a cup and then you could select your flavoring to be mixed. Lemon, lime, raspberry, grape, you had to try them all at least once but ultimately the choice was to mix them all together in one grand splash of bitter sweet refreshment. Fortunately, humans don't have the same need to lick themselves as do dogs. Given your humility you'd be awfully embarrassed to have someone see your privates tainted with rainbow colors matching the syrup on your tongue.

It's almost absurd now to think of a kid getting excited over the cupped reinvention of the snow cone. Unless, of course, the cup adorned the mug of their favorite scam artist wrestler. This innocence which had spanned back to the introductions of soda pop, rock candy and bazooka bubble gum was like all things Americana about to get dork dated by the digital human. Kids still love sweets like the candy bar just as much in this new century but the days of them being a treat are over.

The candy bar had a good run of youthful significance. It made it through the industrial revolution, the sexual revolution, a couple world wars, a cold war, the baby boomer generation, the me generation- almost the entire twentieth century. The candy bar, despite all these societal changes, was still important to the kid. Until they became digital. Now even the coolest, hippest, rockingest, graphically explosive candy bar commercial couldn't motivate a kid to nag his mother for chump change.

And why do I care? Because the candy bar was important enough to get your Master out of the house. Any time Master Tom left the house it gave me an opportunity to follow. I love to follow! He'd hang out at the corner and get his sugar fix, actually excited at the newest combination of chocolate and fillings. The sugar would make him hyper. I love hyper! He'd run and be active. He'd be a boy and I'd be his dog because of the candy bar. I love boys and dogs! I love the candy bar! I hate change! Changes that strip the simplicity of boy and dog. Changes that complicate our simple pleasures. Changes that simply occur in such an effortless and expeditious manner that a century's innocence dissipates with as much resistance as a chain saw through butter. At least for my entire life, the candy bar, the summer day and kids that reveled in them carried on like innocence would last another hundred years.

They lasted only a bit longer than the picturesque village hardwood. On the subjects of chain saws and lasting a hundred years, during the last few years of my life the village upgraded the sewer system, which meant cutting down most of the century old curbside trees. In my prime the village was full and vibrant with stately timber to shade your entire stroll along the residential sidewalks. If kids were out summer strolling the journey usually ended at the public swimming pool. In it's day it was jam packed with swimmers and sunbathers. The grounds also had blacktop shuffleboard, swing sets, climbing apparatus and a pavilion with picnic

Tom Mody

tables and barbecue. The Paddleford Park baseball fields were conveniently adjacent and it all bordered the creek.

It was at the pool that I started to develop another nasty bad habit- obsessive barking. Master Tom hated having me follow him to the pool. I would just sit outside the fence and yelp intolerably until he had no choice but to come out and appease me. The reason it became a nasty habit is that I eventually would do it whether he was there or not often causing the personnel to call Master Mother to come get me. This is where our wires get crossed sometimes with our primitive use of conditioning and response action. The pool simply had too much activity overloading my drive of curiosity. I couldn't focus on any singular purpose of why I needed to be in there. Master Tom would be in there and I'd see him so I'd bark. Then he'd disappear in the crowd or in the water and I couldn't see him so I'd bark. To make things worse everyone was having fun and no one was paying attention to me just sitting there- so I barked. It was a vicious circle where no matter what the circumstances I barked and barked and barked. Over time that simply became my conditioning, go to the pool and bark. Between that pool barking and the car chasing I was really getting a nuisance reputation tagged on me. It's fair to say though that Sugar and a few other mutts weren't far behind.

On the contrary, one dog that always seemed to get the goody-four-shoes... ooops, I mean goody-three-shoes tag was Scooter. Everyone always gave a special loving sigh towards him and never assumed he was anything but an angel. This I'm sure was because of my first encounter with Scooter. A rather fateful day that could have been avoided if Sugar and myself weren't in prime form.

There was a dead squirrel outside the legion located on South Main Street a few blocks from Master Marks. Every year on Memorial Day the veterans march from the legion to the center of town and blast a few rounds. Twenty-one to be exact but who's counting.

Not me, I couldn't count. Even up here I try using the human finger method on my front paws but every time I expected to get to ten I only got to eight. Apparently when you get to heaven anything unnecessary of the body stays dust on earth so I kept forgetting to count in that little hook-stub-hoof-claw thing that use to hang about an inch above my paw. What the doggie hell was that thing anyway?

I ran into Albert Einstein's dog up here one day and he told me prehistoric humans use to have a sixth digit on their hand but since they couldn't count it became useless and withered. The reason Master Albert couldn't figure out pi was because he needed that eleventh and twelfth finger. I guess it would stand to reason that someone in America is destined to crack the secret of pi as long as we don't go to the metric system. I'm joking, I made all that up. It's not very funny. I'm a dog not a comedian so I hope you didn't laugh. Truth is, I know the answer to pi being up here and all. I'm just not allowed to tell you.

So anyway, back in the day it was perfectly acceptable to bring out your toy BB guns to symbolically take part in the ceremony. As barbaric as this makes the 70's seem, it was not okay to pellet defenseless happy go-lucky squirrel vermin from their seemingly safe perch, which some overly-engaged, fully-loaded juvenile delinquent had done. I, of course, in all my hypocritical glory could without consequence tear their flesh from their scrawny leap-happy bones. Assuming I could catch one. But since that hard part was already done, I was more than happy to dispose of the carcass. So was Sugar.

Ah, yes, my partner in dog lovin' chaos. Fancy meeting you there to deliberate over the last rights and funeral arrangements of that poor lice ridden soul. He argued that the body should be dragged to a sacred location of shrubs separating Master Mark's property from the school bus garage parking lot. There he could respectfully dismember it in dignity. I objected and countered that it's no different than road kill and should be immediately mutilated as such. Why stain the sidewalks of our beautiful village with blood and fur dragging this to his private dining area. I'm assuming that's what we wish we could have said but unfortunately we don't have words, only actions. Sugar got there first in time to snag the body but I pounced on him and we tumbled on the legion lawn in full aggression.

Those old veterans, once brave, courageous and strong, looked like a bunch of buffoons trying to meddle in our fight over this inheritance. They mostly just stood around and muttered obscenities, taking a few swipes at us with their boots and muskets. I believe the final casualty report read two pulled groin muscles and a stiff neck. I'm of course, referring to the veterans. Sugar and I were fine. He knocked me around. I knocked him around. It would become just the same old shit, different day. He was able to regain control of the carcass and run off towards home. Catching him was not a problem. Truth is, by now I was the quicker and stronger dog. He was wiley and used it well, which is why he always seemed to be a thought ahead of me. I engaged in pursuit and harassed him the short distance to Master Mark's. I'd had enough of the rough stuff for now. I just wanted him to know it ain't over and that I could take him if I wanted to.

Sugar ran into his little brush area with me on his tail-pursuit speaking, not literally. He dropped the mangled fuzz ball and nipped at me. We then started a growling standoff which escalated to significant barking. Once again we're locked in. Eye to eye. Snout to snout. Heaving waves of doggie breathe at each other. So focused on what the other dog may do we couldn't notice anything else. Sugar better not show me that fang! Don't show it! Don't show it. Uh, he showed it. I snapped and lunged at him but as we made impact we were startled apart by some unexpected activity underneath us.

It was Scooter the beagle. He had just waddled in and was sniffing over the dead squirrel right under our noses. He musta' been use to Sugar's attitude and secure enough that Sugar's conflict wasn't going to endanger him in the least. The whole thing just went right over his head. This was a dog who habituated with cats so he definitely had a high tolerance level.

Scooter was undisputedly Master Mark's dog. He wasn't a stray like Sugar and he actually lived with and relied on Master Mark's family for food and care. In the spring of '73 the cat-lovin' family went to the kennel to balance out the house by getting a dog. They actually snagged two pups. One for them and the other for some friends also on the south side. They both were kept at Master Mark's overnight and studied for any slight advantages in making their choice. Seems Scooter pissed less on the floor than the other pup so they kept him and the other beagle went on to be Barney of Chapel Street

Scooter and Sugar were pretty tight despite Sugar infringing on his Master rights. Oh sure, in that first year Scooter was a bit put-off by Sugar's street hooligan mentality and blatant self-promotion but that never threatened him. Sugar, once an outcast, had taken so to Master Mark and he quickly became aware that any aggressive banter towards Scooter would not win him favor. As a big brother and mentor there were acceptable circumstances for a skirmish but Scooter was no match for Sugar and he was expected to respect those limits.

At the time of this carcass battle between Sugar and myself, Scooter had yet to warm up to him in a brotherly way but he was starting to learn that Sugar's many dramas were highly entertaining. Which explains why he just planted himself inches below our savage regression. He didn't get it, it was just more entertainment. He figured it had something to do with the dead squirrel so he stuck in his own nose with oblivious curiosity. Just like any beagle really.

Beagle's noses are excellent and they've evolved a great domestic demeanor but I find their intuitive senses to be sub-standard. It's their nature to just kinda' walk in to a situation with that half-happy, half-dopey ear floppin', tail waggin, careless, old fashioned charm. It must be the dopey and careless adjectives that makes them the most likely canine to get treaded by their own Master's metal beast.

Let me flat out state that I would never wish another dog to get run over. Well, one dog maybe, but that's an upcoming issue. Having said that, I'm also not going to take responsibility if my actions are too distracting for the dopey and careless. It's a dangerous world out there for animals.

Despite all the sensory advantages we hold over humans we simply can't account for the unnatural. As I stated early in this memoir, cars, buses, trains and such, are not adaptable by instinct and senses alone. What about our super sensitive hearing, you ask? Look, we can detect piercing highs and bowel busting lows but humans have developed some very unnatural sounding noise. I can hear a train coming well before any human but it also is so unworldly that it can occupy what little functional brain cells I have and render me one dimensional in focus. Kinda' like a deer in headlights.

Poor Scooter simply couldn't account for the chaos of Sugar, myself and the school bus garage. I quite frankly was insulted that this rug mutt dare even approach us in ferocious debate. I let him know it by giving him a lung lashing, just unleashing a round of vicious barks down on his head. Opportunistic Sugar took advantage of my distraction and headed off with the carcass through the shrubs and into the bus garage parking lot. I was still in verbal assault when that disrespectful oversized wiener took off in tow of his brother. That pissed me off.

Again I chased after Sugar and caught him two-thirds of the way down the lot on the backside of the bus garage. By now the squirrel was nothing more than a coonskin cap but doggie hell if I'm going to give up any gains. I was able to secure my jaws on a section of the carcass skin and we proceeded to tug-o-war in circles. Scooter, in naive jubilation, just nipped and yelped at us both. It was fun to him. He felt protected by Sugar and didn't see me as a threat with him around. Even with our jaws clamped and our eyes in laser-lock stare across the carcass we still had those few extra functioning brain cells to account for the school bus that was backing out of the garage bay. As it moved towards us we both dropped the carcass and parted. Scooter had all of his functioning brain cells focused on the opportunity at hand which was to finally get a piece of the booty. For all that he gained in the two seconds of his possession, the price was high.

I'm not minimizing the situation by saying he was fortunate, but he was. The bus finished it's backward motion doggie hairs from treading on his torso. His right hind leg, though, got a Firestone tattoo. Scooter certainly didn't have the lung capacity of us bigger breeds but the sheer pain and panic in his cry drummed up any hint of emotion I have hidden deep in our evolutionary potential. Beagles are just a breed of innocents maneuvering through a world where things happen fast for animals. Things that harden your heart and potentially break your spirit. Imagine hearing that cry of pain that could cause such a creature to be thrust upon a side of life darker than his soul could comprehend. That was Scooter's cry. Had we dropped the carcass two inches further back he would have escaped with just a shit and piss incident. A mentally recoverable close call.

The bus, square on his leg, had finished its backward motion and headed out to pick up some kids for an extracurricular trip- unaware of the harm it left behind. Scooter wailed as the wheels dug in and lifted away. I just whimpered from what ever was drawn out of me by his cries and ran off. In a daze I almost got treaded myself crossing the roads for home. Sugar, disillusioned, picked up the squirrel carcass in his mouth and stood silently. He gained his prize but the victorious taste of blood had long run out its veins. What little meat was left had been tainted with the dirt and pebbles of the pavement. Flies buzzed around his head but their nuisance could not penetrate his state. It was a shocking and momentarily sobering incident.

When you don't really know what's happened to you and you don't know the grim possibilities for further pain and death, it's amazing what the survival instinct can achieve. Scooter dragged himself across the pavement, wailing at every lunge forward. Ten, fifteen, twenty, thirty lunges and he still couldn't anticipate the pain that was coming at each push. Sometimes it takes a lot for conditioning to sink in. We don't comprehend what has just happened. We don't know what will happen next. We only know that some force is pushing us to a certain point. A spot to rest. A spot to be found. A spot to die.

Scooter hadn't quite reached that spot when the conditioning set in. He had just crossed the shrubs to the back border of the family yard. At that point he had learned that if he pushed again pain would strike. It wasn't the spot

T o m   M o d y

for him to die but it was close as he was heading for some grass and flowers near the back door. He made one final attempt but he now knew the pain was coming and it scared him into stopping and submitting. Though it wasn't his spot it was one extra lunge and one extra cry enough for his Master Father to hear that cry and investigate.

Scooter received prompt attention and was rushed to the veterinarians. The eventual outcome would be the loss of his right hind leg- and his innocence. As I stated, he was very fortunate. He could live without his innocence. When the car whisked away taking Scooter to his animal healer, Sugar stood in the dust of the tires- carcass in jaw. Moments later dropping his day's wage because the flies were simply too bothersome to enjoy it.

Revelation 7

The Grim Reaper
is not efficient in a crowd

If there's one thing that can be said about humans in any century, they love their ride and what they "think" it says about them. Getting carted around on a canopy by a dozen slaves let's people know you're the reason they built that big triangle in the sand. It also lets future people know you weren't smart enough to invent the wheel. A white horse lets the bad guys know that by an unspoken rule of justice, you're likely going to have a half-second faster draw out your holster. However, they also stain a lot more noticeably when you were shittin' through your pants while the seemingly calm duel was being played out- fortunately, dead men tell no tales. The stretch limo with the jacuzzi let's the ladies know "you's a playa'." Sadly, the real truth is the Bat Mobile was already rented for the weekend and this was the only ride available from the car museum. But it's okay because you were able to procure the Bat Suit. You know how the ladies love that?

So what does a banana yellow, monster-treaded, steel-bar-soldered, jumbo-spring-shock loaded bicycle say about my young Master Tom? In the summer of '76 I'm sure he thought it said he was the "baddest" ten-year-old in the village. What it really said was you're the only freak mental enough to ride that steroid-stuffed, two-wheeled mutation. Dirt bikes weren't in vogue back then so in his defense, the normal childhood bike was still a banana seat purple low ride with soon-to-be hundred dollar sports cards flapping in the spokes. He was too young to get a ten-speed so you can imagine his eye-bulging, daddy-begging enthusiasm for a bike with spring shocks they pulled off the set of a Frankenstein movie. Nobody in town had seen anything like this. Be it silly or cool, you could tell who was coming half a mile away.

A bike was life in the village. Almost every activity revolved around them. If you were "bookin'" through town it was an expression born of the bike. If Master Tom wasn't embarrassed by his bike, that's fine with me. I loved following him on his daily rides. That bike really was a workhorse. It could take any curb, tear through any terrain and survive any crash. I stayed fit and moved fast because of that bike. What a pair of savage beasts we were bookin' down the street. With my bark and his bike we sure thought we were cool.

The bike probably saved me from a few unnecessary scraps with the dogs around town. If Master Tom had been walking the pace would have been slow enough for me to be distracted by anything in my peripheral vision. The occasions he was on his bike would, by doggie rules of engagement, require me to continue following him rather than leave and pursue a conflict.

I remember one day coming down the East State Street hill and seeing Laddie escorting some girls along the sidewalks. He always seemed to be on the grass between the sidewalk and the road and would physically push kids off the curb away from the road. Problem here being that Master Tom and I were cruising down hill on the sidewalks. The tire treads on that bike were huge and you could hear it rumbling along like a runaway train. Laddie's attention drew to us pursuing towards his little protected hoard.

I swear his bark sounded more like a little mother hen as he cackled them off the sidewalks to a nearby lawn. As we came by he lunged at Master Tom forcing him to make a sharp screeching break, almost causing him to topple. It was unlike Laddie to do that and in fact, he often would nip after other dogs chasing bikes or cars through the village. If he wants to be "Mr. Guardian" then fine but it was really starting to get on my nerves. I guess the human term is "fed up". Seems whenever he was around I just wanted to lash out and knock him down a peg but circumstances kept us from coming to blows. In this case, Master Tom just continued on down the hill and I was by nature obligated to follow him.

Laddie's son Scamp had been born a year earlier and this would only fuel his need to act obnoxiously protective. Though Scamp wasn't with him on this day they usually roamed together. Since Laddie's bitch collie couldn't run free, Laddie was responsible for Scamp's tutelage. It was a job he relished with pride and Scamp was eager to learn.

Scamp had much of his mother's features. He had a longer snout and a white ring of fur around his neck. He got the white fur from his father but Laddie's was just a tuft of white on the back of his neck. Everything else about Scamp was all his dad. He was really up his ass those first couple years and it was presenting a problem.

At this point, us village dogs didn't bond. We were left to our devices of promotion and to fight our own battles. Laddie and Scamp upset this balance. When Scamp was young and wide-eyed, Laddie was overly aggressive about making an impression. Not just in training Scamp but he was overly aggressive towards us in his protection of him. Once Scamp matured they simply became a two-dog gang with an aggressive righteous demeanor. They didn't think much of Sugar and myself but we weren't a team by any definition so they were able to admonish us without consequence.

Fortunately, in the summer of '76, Laddie was too occupied with Scamp's development while I was becoming the king of my domain. I was all over the village- you couldn't escape me. When the kids were let out of school, I was prowling the school's large stone terrace. If you were in church and heard car horns blasting, I was likely chasing someone down the street. No baseball game was safe from me running off with the homer. And the pool- well, as I stated earlier, I was a certified public nuisance. If you strolled up East State Street daydreaming your mind away, I could put about a thousand volts of wake-up on you simply by throwing a barking rage from my balcony.

Usually I was up there just resting in the warm rays of the sun but certain stimulus could set me off. Dogs being the number one trigger. Particularly dogs I hadn't encountered before. I just felt I needed to project some domain warning in their direction. If they were in view from my balcony then that would extend to my turf. Loud noises like mufflers turning that Classic Street corner were another trigger to my ranting. Simple pedestrians were more of a random trigger to my tantrums. You can imagine how many walkers and bikers went by the window every day. I developed a knack for identifying the feeble, the timid and the oblivious and could project a stunning assault on them even though there was thick glass and yards of ground between us. Yeah, it was bully tactics but they were the most impressionable and that's show business, puppy.

Public gatherings were generally the forum for which I excelled in my pursuit of self-promotion. You plant the seeds throughout the year by getting paw marks on Sunday dresses and stealing pantyhose off clotheslines. Then the humans come out for some gathering and you bring forth your best showstopper of dog lovin' chaos.

Every year the village celebrated the Fourth of July with a quaint display of fireworks at the Paddleford Park baseball fields. For most of the day you did your own thing with picnics and summer activities as blue and white-collar workers alike enjoyed the day off. But this wasn't just any old Fourth of July. It was the country's bicentennial. Two hundred years of freedom. Two hundred years of snubbing your nose at kings and dictators. Defiantly and triumphantly telling them that this is how to build power, industry and intellect. Two hundred years of unparalleled exploration across continents, deep into oceans and to celestial bodies humans once debated were gods or cheese. This was pretty cool. This could be me we're talking about. It had been two years since I declared my rights to freedom, my desire to explore and my need to ascend to power. Two years, two hundred years- the parallels are there. Dallas and America were both at the same jubilant sigh of ascended evolution. We could loosen our collars for a day and celebrate.

Actually, it was my collar, which was responsible for my attitude that day. I just happen to have gotten a brand new red collar with round metal studs. It was a little thicker and a little heavier. I know the collar couldn't really do anything to make me a better runner or chaser but it was a fresh sensation that tends to perk up your attentiveness. Maybe it's like getting some new piece of clothing that makes you strut a bit more adventurously. With my new collar I was ready for some adventure.

The village was planning a number of activities for the bicentennial with parades, games, food and all sorts of public fare. By mid day the downtown was already a bustle of activity, much of it passing before my eyes as I rested from my balcony. I could sense the activity in house was in preparation to leave so I descended from my perch and headed towards the kitchen. Master Father was already in the act of calling me as I strode confidently past him towards the back door. Baby and I waited impatiently for everyone else to gather their needs for the day. I guess we both were at the same intellectual level where we could sense we were going "bye bye" but were wondering what the doggie hell was taking so long. We bantered a little, her swatting me on my snout and I wiped my cold wet nose across her face. It was nice to not have to look up at someone once in a while.

Finally everyone was ready to go. I needed to get on out and celebrate with America. Celebrate our hard earned battles, our pains, our gains, our unwavering faith in freedom. I was sensing a very special day. The freedom I would enjoy, at least on this day, I would not take for granted.

Sadly, that was truer than I possibly could have known. Master Tom opened the door and the family filed out. I nudged my nose in front of Master Father to be sure I didn't get left behind and suddenly I went species transcending from dog to fish. A big hook, Master Father's hand, snagged my studded accessory and led me out the door. I kept my head down in some attempt to try and play dead. Maybe if I'm calm he'll let me go. However, my ears heard the dragging of oppression long since silenced by my will and aptitude. Master Tom handed the once defunct relic of a bygone age to Master Father and the rusted chain, an old nemesis, was now given renewed purpose.

This was the Fourth of July, the bicentennial for doggie freakin' sake! "Throw me a bone, you can't do this to me. I'm America! I'm freedom and exploration! I'm the embodiment of all this day represents. Okay, okay, forget all that crap. I'm just a dog and there's lots of people runnin' around out there. Please, let me off this leash" I know this all sounded like "ruff, ruff, ruff" but couldn't someone hear me? Couldn't God understand?

It seems tales of my exploits and whispers of my nuisance had funneled back to the family and the thinking was that maybe this was too crowded a day for any dog lovin' chaos. As the family faded down the driveway, I must have been in shock. I ceased my barking. I didn't try to run after them. I just sat there in hopeful patience. This behavior was completely beyond my normal profile. For about five minutes I just sat and waited on the pavement. They had to be joking. They had to be coming back.

Mature dogs usually bark based on response action as they are accustom to certain situations. They associate that familiar situation to barking- like me being fenced outside the swimming pool. Barking is often the accustomed response of a chained or confined dog. You humans always wonder why we just don't understand the need for being chained and grow out of it. We often don't grow out of things, we need to be reprogrammed.

Strangely, upon being chained, I didn't bark at all. I was so use to being free that I could only assume that I was. Yeah, the shock of my renewed leashing made me that delusional. Part of me knew I couldn't travel more than ten yards but the freedoms of the past few years had reprogrammed my brain to assume otherwise. I guess I wanted to believe I was free so I just sat there and hoped my brain wouldn't figure out that I wasn't.

Eventually, my ass started to itch so I bent down to nip and scratch it. As I turned my head the chains rattled against the pavement breaking my imposed trance. "Son of a bitch in heat, I'm chained up! I'm really chained up! Where the doggie hell are they!" The silence was broken. The realization had surfaced. The shock turned to anger. I spewed doggie slurs too profane to print. Besides, it was all in bark. I stretched the chain as far as it would go and howled when my progress was stopped. I wanted to whimper but that would mean I had resigned to this confinement.

A car pulled into the driveway- it gave me hope. Lew jumped out and headed towards me. "Dallas, you been a bad dog," as he commented on my enshacklement. He petted me and walked into the house only to return moments later presumably learning Master Tom wasn't home. Again I got a pity pet and he got back in the car. The car did a three-point turn in the driveway and headed out. I could see in the rear window two poodles in muffled yelp. It was Tuffy and Mitsy, hyper at my presence. Secure as their happy mobile safely escorted them through our dangerous little world. Yeah, their ride say's it all about them- prissy little rug mutts. I don't know much about physics, but if I did, I'm sure I would have been calculating how bloody flat their smug mugs would be if a Mack truck rear impacted their cozy "Jag" at 60 MPH, catapulting them into the windshield.

Deep down I was envious. It's obvious now because my normal dislike of poodles would have me calculating the Mack truck impact at only 30 MPH. Their pathetic free ride irked me enough to completely double the impact speed. Maybe a little release is needed here. Maybe a little ditty.

> There are oodles of poodles boiling like noodles
> stewing in a Chinaman's Pot.
> They were sent from the states in little brown crates
> 'cause their Masters learned dogs they are not.

Okay, we've eliminated comedian and now poet off the list of reincarnation match-up candidates. I'm hoping the telling of this memoir will eliminate dog from that list as well. As much as I love being a dog, I don't want to come back as one. Not in this century! Even if I had an opposable thumb and extended length digits to type keypads, press remote controls and manipulate joysticks. It's a fat ass society under the false assumption that walking your dog a few blocks constitutes a fitness regiment. I'll tell ya what, unclasp me for a second and give me fifty yards to dash towards the interstate. Now, in fear for my life, haul your sorry butt in maniacal pursuit. A three times a week regiment of fifty yard dashes laced with panic, fear and anxiety can compact your workouts from two hours a week to two minutes a week. And for us dogs, I'd rather live two free minuets a week on the edge than a shackled lifetime of watching your asses grow. Have you noticed the gradual increase in seat sizes of recliners and office chairs? It takes five hundred and eighty thousand more dead cows a year to comfortably seat you people than it did in 1986.

Nope, if I'm coming back I'm not digressing. The evolutionary clock on dogs finally stripped its gears. Sure, we're still lovable, trainable and integral to Master but what's in it for us. Like I've commented, farm dogs got all the freedom now but a goat and five cows lack the capacity to be offended at my self-promoting antics. I'd rather just stay up here and work on my dead poodle poems.

> There once was a poodle named Tuffy.
> And another named Mitsy, so fluffy.
> Tossed in the woods they were hunted by hoods.
> Now they sit on a mantle all stuffy.

If I had this crude yet effective outlet for my tension back then I could have avoided stupid and useless behavior. Human's engaged in smoking and drinking during their times of tribulation; also stupid and useless behavior. So, maybe there's no relief in bad poetry but if it coulda' prevented me from barking at rocks I prefer reciting bad poems.

Yes, barking at rocks. I took up barking at rocks. It was just so dumb. It's a freakin' rock, even I knew that. The inanimate of all inanimate objects. It's not lauded in story and song. It's got no value, sentimental or marketable. There's nothing you can pray to it or say to it that will make it any more than what it is. I'm not talking about landmasses worth fighting over or shore side boulders to mark your place of arrival. I'm talking about the stubbing your toe kind. The kind that makes you jump every time you run over it with the lawnmower blade. You know... rocks.

It all started because I was so damn pissed off over being tied up and having less freedom than the rodent-dogs of Beverly Hills fading out of my driveway. I thought things had changed. I didn't have Nixon to crap around on anymore. I didn't have walls confining me from my dreams. I didn't have birds thinking they could get within ten yards of me without consequence. I lacked the ability to debate the permanence of my enshackelment. I only knew that moment. I assumed that moment was how it would always be- chained again.

I hated all things; trees, grass, sun, clouds. I stretched the full tension of my leash across the yard cursing in bark at every object in my view. Then my nails grazed across the solitary granite peaking above the grass. A simple stone in the yard, maybe three or four inches long with a robust body. I grazed my nails over it again. The scraping annoyed me like humans to a blackboard. Stupid useless object, even it has more freedom than myself. Even it is pursing the full scope of its abilities by just sittin' there. I hated it and I barked at it because I could not pursue and strive to my potential. I barked relentlessly taking out my anger at this rock. I continued for minutes, not as a mad dog but as therapy. I became focused on barking the rock into movement. Wanting to push it outside its comfortable little place in rock Nirvana. Channeling all my pent up frustrations to this purpose became enjoyable. It passed the time with a purpose.

Sure, you could debate the greater intelligence the rock possessed over me at this point but I loved throwing my anger and expectations at this rock. I suppose you carve at a piece of wood for hours, even days expecting in the end there will be a ridiculously small payoff- a little object to set on your mantle with pride. All that work simply because you needed to pass the time. It was the same here. That damn rock was going to do something beyond it's potential and I was going to pass my time and channel my anger to that end. I was out there a good hour just screamin' at the thing. Unfortunately, when you're a dog and you do something enjoyably repetitive, it becomes a learned habit. That's what this incident quickly became.

If I was angry or bored I'd find me some rock and bark uncontrollably. I did this all my life- hundreds of rocks. Where did they all come from? I mean, they'd just be in the yard. How'd they get there? You find a rock in your yard; you pick it up and throw it in a corner. A few days later your walking around and there's another rock. Do they grow like mushrooms? Are they meteors out of the sky? Personally I think they liked me barking at them and at night they'd secretly roll back into the yard. Was I that intuitive? Did I sense something about rocks humans couldn't. Did God have empathy for the dull life of a rock and was using me as their instrument of pleasure and self-awareness. I sit up here and wish that was true. I hope there is a rock Heaven because barking at inanimate rocks is the balls out dumbest activity bar none of any tailed species in history. If I had included non-tailed species it only would have been the 47th dumbest activity of any species- with humans accounting for 45 of them. But this is only limited to tailed species as I don't want to insult my audience.

I didn't care what was going on around me. Master Tom could be playing kickball in the yard and I'd sit right in the middle of it all barking at a rock. He'd throw it in a corner and I'd go drag it back to its previous spot. He'd throw it in the shrubs and I'd fish it out and drop it back where I had found it. He'd throw it on the roof and I'd find another one in the dirt. When I got my rock barkin' flow goin' you simply had to grab me by the scruff, if you could, and toss me in the house. I honestly don't think I ever just stopped barkin' at a rock out of exhaustion. Usually other stimulus or sheer force broke the spell.

Think about it though, you humans understand therapy. You understand that there's a time for it and a duration with conclusion for each session. Once completed you then move on to other purposes that fill your day. As a dog becoming engrossed in humanistic therapeutic outlets, it would be very hard for us to stop. We have a very limited number of emotional states to sort through every day. A simple pleasureful, purposeful release of barking would be hard for us to want to turn off, nor would we know how. We're in an enjoyable trance dealin' with sensations of release that have no other outside stimuli to compete. To use a human reference it's like that mongo Cheech and Chong "doobie". The never ending high. Who gets tired of that?

I know what you're thinking, "Dallas, it's a freakin' rock." Oh, you think it's dumb, do ya? You think I'm matching wits with an object equal to my IQ, do ya? I've already admitted its rank among the stupidest things of all time. But before you judge me consider this. My rock barking may be first on the tailed list of dumbest activities of all times. However, if I add non-tailed species to the list do you know what was first on the list of dumbest activities of all times?

#1. HUMANS BUYING PET ROCKS!

Yes, you people know who you are. You in your plaid pants and polyester sport coats crowding gift shops and flea markets handing out cold hard cash for ROCKS! Oh sure, I understand, you needed some company while you sat two hours in line waiting for gas and the AM dial hadn't caught the wave of talk radio yet. As if you rock ownin' humans were intellectual enough to listen to talk radio. What's the matter, your pet rocks not stimulating enough? Well I'll help ya' out here, try barkin' at 'em. They seem to enjoy that.

I definitely had become oblivious to the sounds of the village all hyped up for the bicentennial. That rock barking was entrancing. Much to my surprise I apparently didn't account for everyone who left the house that day because a barrage of the Lord's name in vain came screaming out the back door. It was Grandpa. Not my Grandpa- do dogs have "grandpas"? Master Tom's Grandpa.

"You gosh damn crazy dog, what the hell have you been barking at all gosh damn afternoon. I've had a gosh damn 'nuff of it."

T o m   M o d y

He didn't really say, "gosh damn" but I'm not allowed to express the Lord's name in vain up here. Anyway, Grandpa was highly agitated trying to watch the afternoon baseball game on the tube.

"It's a gosh damn rock for cryin' out loud. What the hell are you barking at that for? All gosh damn afternoon, I've had enough. Back in my day someone would have shot you by now."

As soon as I saw his hand reaching towards me I knew I was village free. Arthritic hands and weak eyes got all they can do to concentrate on working the leash clasp. I would have at least a two second window of opportunity to escape. I only needed one. As soon as I heard the scrape of the clasp against my collar ring and the snap of it sliding off- I bolted. Grandpa groaned a few more expletives at me to come back as I kicked up a dust storm in his wake but he probably could care less where I went as long as I wasn't around to bark.

As I headed towards the center of town I realized I was damn thirsty. It was a warm summer day and I had been exhausting myself in therapy. Try licking slate and screaming at the top of your lungs for an hour in eighty-five degree heat. Unless you got a hump on your back, you need water. I reached Quinn's Market and tried to piss on the apricots but just a few drops leaked out. I needed water bad. Ah yes, just across the street on the Congregational Church corner was the public water fountain. It had a top fountain for drinking and a lower spigot to fill containers. Even on a dry day there was usually a puddle from spigot overflows and it's slow drip.

I headed across the street and noticed a little activity near the fountain. Two kids with balloons had been trying to fill them with water but they seemed scared to approach the fountain. They had good reason. General was making use of the available water pouring out the open spigot. I had never seen General before. The gray tinted German shepherd was guzzling water directly from the spout after bullying the kids away from their attempt at making water balloons. They tried to access the fountain again but General growled them back.

As I looked across the street I could see Hobie limping badly towards the Inn steps. He was ruffed up and shaken. I don't know the nature of their confrontation but the bicentennial festivities had moved towards Paddleford Park so no one would have been downtown to break up any potential canine disturbance. Knowing General as I do now, it was likely divine intervention, which saved Hobie severe or even fatal consequences. Knowing Hobie as I do now, I'm almost certain of it.

I was only a few feet away from General when I reached the fountain corner. I was close enough to somehow comprehend from Hobie's body language that crossing the road may have been a mistake. I backed up towards the kids who were now standing on the first level of the Civil War monument. My problem was that my instinct and Hobie's karma tended to conflict. Plus, I was thirsty. Animal gut reactions are that there's an unfamiliar dog in my presence and boundaries must be established. I also have an instinctual perception of bigger and badder which is what it appeared I was facing. But those presumptions must be tested. Still, Hobie was clouding my mind with doubt and caution. One of the boys made the actual decision to test General's boundaries again but General was still thirsty, probably trying to clean Hobie's fur out of his teeth. General turned menacingly at the boy who ran back to the statue.

It was ironic that the boys sought safety upon the slim and sloped statue base. During most chasing type games Master Tom would play in that park, the statue was "home safe". Now myself and two boys were testing that assumption outside the bounds of childhood law. If we were wrong we wouldn't catch cooties or that other temporary branding called "it" which tended to prey upon the slow and timid. We were stranded on an island with a predator on the loose. That's how the boys saw it. The fact was that General didn't care about attacking boys that weren't directly in his space. Even if they persisted towards him the chances of them getting bit were slim. However, myself and any other dog would never be safe, even if childhood law states otherwise.

When General turned and gave that menacing glare which scared back the bravest of the boys, he didn't expect to see another dog. Dogs don't like to unexpectedly see another dog in their vicinity. If the environment is chaotic, like the village fire, they become startled and frozen before engaging in bark or bite. If the environment is calm there's no outside stimulus beating down the territorial instinct. I know in my case if I'm relaxed upon my balcony and a dog unexpectedly passes my view, the bay window gets immediately splat with saliva. I'm instantly giving notice of my territory. General lunged towards the monument with equal intimidation in his bark and his glare. The boys ran losing all faith in the monuments jurisdiction of their rules. I had no choice but to meet General's advance with my own posture of aggression. It was a bold enough move to freeze him about fifteen paws from my snarling face. Hobie barked from across the street, which annoyingly reminded me that I should consider his fate. He's no fighter though, but then again, that's what made General all the more dangerous. If he would attack Hobie then the rest of us were undoubtedly fair game.

In an instant I realized that was the decisive point. To dogs like Sugar and myself, much of it was a game. We fought and acted out in competitive promotion of all that is beloved in dogs. We were the professional wrestlers of Sherburne. Love us or hate us. Cheer our antics but don't call our bluff because we are capable of real harm and we do have pride. To General, this whole confrontation wasn't a game- I was the game. I was no different than a pheasant or a turkey. But those hunting dogs have training and discipline from their Master that I can respect. General was just an angry dog with no care of the freedoms we've achieved. So in that instant using the same reason and extra percentage of my brain which allows me to cross streets without getting treaded... I bolted outta' there.

Using a human point of reference, did you ever notice in a number of movies where the good guy getting chased is running his ass off but the cold blooded killer just calmly walks briskly in pursuit. I don't know if it's psych-out posturing or if he's just saving up his energy but I can tell you from being on the pursued end of this scenario that it's damn intimidating. I ran past the library towards Gaines Park as fast as I could. When I reached the monument and flowerbed I turned to check my distance. But General was still there just trotting my way. I probably shoulda' just crossed the street and went home but I didn't want to take a chance that someone would be waiting to chain me up so I continued deep into the park. I turned and there was General calmly trotting in my direction.

I didn't make sense for him to be tracking me. I didn't have anything he wanted. I wasn't in his space. I had never been pursued in this capacity before. How long and how far would I need to go to make my point that I want to be left alone? At the end of the park there was a chain link fence but I could slip around the edges and enter the back of some residential yards. I did just that and stared back through the fence. General upped his tempo but it was still a trot. I ran through the nearest residential lot and on to Chapel Street. There were streams of people walking up Chapel Street heading to some festivities about a half-mile up at Paddleford Park. I blended in the crowd and headed up the street with them. Once I reached the old high school I moved out from the crowd and peaked down the road. There was General parting the masses, calmly on my trail. Parents grabbed their kids and lifted them out of his way as he menacingly approached.

If he was human he would have been one of those no personality international henchman that pushes people down escalators in pursuit of the guy with the microchip hidden in his jacket. Do you humans really buy that scenario in your entertainment plots? Don't you ever wonder how these goons can get away with such blatant disregard yet if you J-walk in a crowd on a back alley street, you're the one who usually gets a ticket. Just once wouldn't you like to see some old lady trip the guy up with her cane so he tumbles to the bottom of the subway station floor? Then in classic urban fashion everyone just walks over the top of him as if he's not even there. The innocent young lad he's pursuing slips onto the train and whisks to safety.

Maybe that doesn't make good fiction but it would have been convenient if it was good reality- my reality. Couldn't some old person driver get disoriented and weave onto the sidewalk miraculously missing all pedestrians before fendering a tree- making a General sandwich in the process. Okay, how about a golf ball size asteroid ripping through the atmosphere right to the very spot that... okay, just drop it already, that's not even good "B" movie fiction.

An interesting thing about dogs is that we know what the other is capable of. Maybe if I hid in a bush or under a porch he'd just pass by me. No chance though, I knew he could snuff me out of any hiding spot. German Shepherds are the top pick for police and security canine units. But while those dogs have bark, bite, intelligence and discipline, General only has bark and bite and intelligence. Oh, he's a naturally discipline stalker but without the proper tutoring and environment, the intelligence lashes back.

The actual German Shepherd breed has only been around a little over a century if you can believe it. Only one of the pups from that original German farm dog's litter showed the intelligence and work ethic they are noted for today. But that one dog impressed some ex-military guy, Max Emil Frederich von Stephanitz. Sounds like some freak who was interested in breeding the Master race, doesn't it. I guess in his mind he was because when he came upon General's great great great great great great great great great great great, great grandfather, he was so impressed that only a pawful of the finest bitches were allowed to breed with him. I think the dog's eventual name was Adam Likz von Stukup Tail but the original farmer called him Skippy. Just kidding, the original name was Hektor Linksrhein but rechristened immediately upon purchase to Horand von Grafrath. Neither name is registered up here in Doggie Heaven. I suspect he changed it when he arrived. Probably to Skippy- smart choice!

But these pure breeds you know, things need to be done a certain way or they get twisted. German Shepherds need to have a job and to feel useful. They also need to protect. Messin' with these breeds by trying to draw out Doberman viciousness and keeping them too confined just makes them angry when they do get out. Laddie had just the right mix of Shepherd with some other lovable dog breeds and it was manageable to the best qualities- in some folks view. General just had too much old school German in him. Raise him wrong and eventually he's growin' a stub of a mustache under his nose. Now I've got the leader of Sherburne's canine Third Reich stalkin' me.

I recognized some of Master Tom's older friends, Beaner, Oggy and Abby in the crowd so I kept pace with them towards Paddleford Park. They weren't moving very fast but I felt safe with the familiarity. Both Oggy & Abby had lived back in the old quarter near our apartment. They played in the back lot daily with Master Tom so they tended to be much friendlier towards me having known me as a puppy and not as the village nuisance. Like me, they enjoyed teetering the border of hooligan and prankster but nothing hard-core in their intent. Beaner's collection of fireworks he purchased at South of The Border on his family's annual trip made him the juvenile equivalent of an arms broker. No doubt he was wired from his socks to the inside of his plastic baseball helmet. Firecrackers, jumping jacks, bottle rockets and of course, cherry bombs.

The boys stopped by the swimming pool to light up some of these festive accouterments. This was not good. We needed to keep moving- to blend in. I waited patiently with them as the crowds began to grow. I couldn't determine if this was to my advantage. As they sat on the bordered log fencing and sorted Beaner's arsenal I paced nervously behind them. Oggy shoved Abby off the fence dropping him on top of me. I was nervous having to keep my attention at a three-hundred-and-sixty-degree eye level perspective. Humans falling from above were not something I wanted to account for. Knowing better than to direct any expletives at Oggy, Abby directed his frustration at me being in his way while he tried to get up. He pushed at me as he tried to make room for some leverage but then froze solid as his eyes bugged outta' his head.

"Holy Shit" he screamed and ducked for cover. This was no old person driving mishap or golf ball from the sky coming at us. This was the calm calculating persistence of all those hit men, terrorist, and demonic evildoers rolled into one canine antagonist. This was General who had saved up all his energy by not over exerting his tracking until he had me spooked, cornered and distracted. He hit me like train driving me back onto Abby. Blood was shed right from the first strike. I struggled to get to my feet but I was tangled up in Abby. General's teeth sunk into my upper hip yet he still managed deep intimidating growling from his jaw. Beaner and Oggy dragged Abby by his feet out of the fray. He escaped with a scratch or two from my claws and his spindly body quivering in panic.

I was now able to get my feet under me and wrestle out of General's grip. I managed a few paws of space between us but he rammed me like a cannon ball again with the whole force of his power pinning me up against the pools chain link fence. I was able to use frantic jarring movements of head and legs to keep him from getting a solid grip on my neck. I utilized this desperate tactic for a few seconds but it seemed like minutes. I was still without water for most of the day and weakened in dehydration. I was tired from the anxiety of the pursuit and in shock at the force of his presence. Still I fought back and wedged out of my entrapment.

Again he rammed me into the fence scraping his claw across my face gouging a tear above my eye. My blood and his spit poured into my vision. In retaliation I may have cut him or bit him or something. I don't really know; I was just reacting as any trapped animal would. He took the brunt of my defense as simply a minor resistance to the inevitable. I'm sure at some point he woulda' let me go- once he had obtained my jugular for his charm collar!

A third blow into the fence sent me sliding down its links to the ground and under the weight of his being. My teeth raked against his several times in self-defense of my neck. It was a sharp hideous crackling noise that even caused some spectators to cover their ears. Finally his body shifted over my head pinning and suffocating my best defense. My paws flailed with no purpose and my spine twisted and turned but still my head was trapped under him.

It was all happening so fast, I didn't have time to contemplate my fate or reflect on my life. One moment I'm dodging falling people and the next I'm suffocated under a cold-blooded predator. My body just gave out and I whimpered but my cries went unheard, absorbed into General's chest. They vibrated through his body searching for his heart and his soul but they most likely just reverberated in the emptiness of his chest cavity. I knew I was exposed in the most critical of ways when the afternoon breeze blew cool across my neck from the saliva splattered upon my fur. In an instant the refreshing air was gone and hot breath bore down on my neck.

RAT TAT TAT TAT TAT TAT TAT TAT TAT BANG BANG BANG BANG BANG BANG RAT TAT TAT TAT TAT BANG BANG BANG.

The weight lifted off me but my body was attacked with quick sharp jabs only trumped in pain by the thrusting percussive explosions in my ear.

It continued...

RAT TAT TAT TAT TAT TAT TAT BANG!

I howled in disillusion jumping to me feet, both blind and deaf, stumbling against the pool fence. Whatever force had caused to separated General and myself was unlike any continuously abrasive assault on my senses I had ever experienced. It was like being strapped to the Congregational Church bell as it strikes midnight with car mufflers backfiring in all directions around you. It was every sudden jolt of hammer-smackin', door-slammin', foot-poundin', chain saw-blazin', thunder-cracklin', heart stoppers all released in a seven second barrage. It was in fact a full pack of firecrackers tossed directly on top of my potential gravesite. Beaner to the rescue, thank you very much. Fastest lighter in the east I would say! My hero, first dragging Abby out of danger then tossing a blast of life saving explosives on to my soon to be extinguished existence.

General was even more startled and disoriented than myself. The gunpowder had stung his eyes and his ears were painfully ringing. Beaner snagged my collar and dragged me a few yards away while Oggy tossed stones at General sending him off to recover. Beaner looked me over and searched the oncoming crowd for any signs of Master Tom or family. Aside from my pride and some blood I was actually okay. I'm a dog, it's not like I sat around and cried. I didn't need to be mothered or coddled. Had a poodle ran in front of me in that moment I'm sure I would have been almost as heartless as General. It's just animals being animals. We take our licks and move on. You are soon to find out I've done some nasty, murderous things towards other animals all in the name of natural selection.

Was General's attack on me any different than my nasty, murderous episodes? It was, if you believe as I do, that our evolution is about self-promotion of our doggie spirit and the expression of all that's heralded in canine lore; and not about bloodthirsty power. We constantly battle this new evolution with our savage past but for most village dogs during this time the balance has been achieved.

More fights are to come but not in the name of survival of the fittest but in the pursuits of our passions and drive for dominance. You know, good ole' acceptable human race agendas. To this point, most village confrontations had been nothing more than personality conflicts. Even Laddie and Scamp never made me insecure about my daily routine and agenda. General, however, was just a cancer to us all. And like cancer there seemed to be no full cure to the disease except prayer and the power of good. Had I known about Doggie Heaven I would have pounded the prayer therapy but fortunately we had Laddie who was an awfully strong advocate of good and a mean son of a bitch when tested. This added some countermeasure to General thinking he could rampage unscathed through the village.

I limped to the creek to wash my minor wounds and get a freakin' drink- finally! Eventually I hobbled around Paddleford Park as the afternoon turned to dusk. Embedded deep in the crowd I was now free and relatively safe. For almost two years I had enjoyed unprecedented doggie freedom and lived the dreams I formulated upon my balcony. I was a player, a promoter, a fighter and a blanket lover. When this day started it was all unencumbered, all taken for granted despite my intent to be sure I didn't treat it that way. I planned to celebrate along with America this easy street life of freedom and the power to will all your worries away in its concept. As the fireworks shot through the sky I couldn't help but look over my shoulder on occasion. Afraid the glow from the sky would compromise my cover. Freedom meant I was exposed. Taking freedom for granted meant I had reached a point where there was potentially no place to go but backward. In one fateful day its liberties were dulled by chains and challenges to my life.

General was not a dog that was let loose often so out of sight out of mind helped in my mental recovery. Grand and glorious days were still ahead but I had learned that freedom needs to be maintained and continuously fought for. I would need to be stronger and wiser- we all would. I would have to accept that on occasion it's Master's prerogative to keep me grounded at home. I would have to accept that there always seems to be a bigger fish in the pond. That wouldn't stop me from ruling my domain. I needed to be able to defend myself but my dominance in the village wasn't about being the toughest dog in town. It was about making lasting impressions that would mark me forever in my era. As I stated early on, I believe my time was the last great boy/dog era and by being the most notable and quotable of my generation, that keeps me ahead of the pack. I eventually would have to die of something and leave my legacy to the great debates. I just needed to make sure I wasn't done in by a cancer or by indifference.

T o m   M o d y

Revelation 8

*Playground justice
requires proof of innocence*

I was stuck- Literally!

How in the doggie hell did this happen? I could see the large recliner rocking back and forth so I knew I wasn't alone in the room. I tried barking for attention but no sound would come out. I tried clawing forward with what little room I had to move but I'd swear it all seemed like quicksand. I kept hearing my name called out in the room. "Dallas blah, blah, blah and Dallas yak yak, yak". There were no other recognizable words to my limited understanding of the English language. I couldn't turn around to see who was calling me.

It was the Sunday before Thanksgiving, 1977. The usual aunts, uncles and cousins couldn't be here on Thanksgiving Day so the traditional dinner was celebrated the weekend before. It was the same people every Thanksgiving and every Christmas. The same people that prefer I stay outside while they visit. Can you believe it, actually kicking me out of my house? So, I'd go out for a while then bark and bark at the door 'til I was let in with the promise I would be kept shut in the den. Then after dinner someone would go to the little room and I'd sneak through an open door to the living room and lay inconspicuously in some corner.

Well, here I was inconspicuously stuck under the living room end table. It's not really an end table. It's a solid oak furnishing placed between two chairs. The shape was square with the corners angled off. There were three levels. The top level for the phone and drinks. A middle level with current magazines, pens and paper. A bottom level with a few old papers and such. Every puppy the family ever had would make use of it to hide when they were in trouble. It was the best place to avoid a rolled paper swatting. But I was a grown dog and confused why I actually went under there.

Ah yes, it was that cat. That damn white striped one-eyed cat. And I don't mean the cat lost its eye, it only had one to begin with. Practically centered on its face like some type of Cyclops. I didn't notice the eye at first but the white stripe slid down it's back like a skunk. I had been given the traditional Thanksgiving boot during dinner and caroused the yard for some entertainment. Then I saw that cat scram under the spiked iron fence separating the neighbor's property. The fence ran the whole border of the back yard. It was a few feet high. A bit shorter than my balcony so I could traverse it's height easily. However, any lapse in judgment could be perilous. The spikes were fairly dulled so it's not like it could impale me but I suppose it would be an undesirable way to get neutered.

I leaped the fence into the neighbor's yard but the cat easily escaped under the garage. I did a little barking therapy to try and get it to come out but as usual, barking accomplished nothing. A while had passed so I headed to our front door to participate in some useful barking. The kind that gets me let inside. The odd routine is that I go to the large front doors and bark. Once I hear some rustling of doorknobs I jump down through the shrubs to a side door where I'm normally let in. The purpose being they can hear me at the front door but they prefer to open the side door entering the den. So I followed this normal routine. I heard the knob noise and jumped to the other door. Then things started getting weird.

I leaped to the steps of the side door but nothing opened. This is when I started hearing, "Dallas blah, blah, blah and Dallas yak yak, yak." It was kinda' faint, kinda' muted. I ran back under the shrubs to look up at the front doors and for some reason Master Father had opened the damn front door. His head was sticking out and looking around for me. I tried barking and this is where that no sound problem began. I figured I better leap up on the small front porch so he'd see me, but damn, it was a long ways up. Maybe I never noticed it before. Maybe I never had to jump up- only down. I felt sluggish. I knew I couldn't get up there so I sprung my front paws up to the stoop ledge. Leaning upright my head barely could see over the ledge but I had be noticed now. Still, Master Father seemed to be looking far into the distance and not under his freakin' nose. I tried barking but I couldn't. I tried hoping on my hind legs but I couldn't. Then that damn black striped one-eyed cat hoped up on the porch right in front of my ledge peering face.

Wait, did I say black striped? Yeah, it's black striped. Did I say white striped earlier? I'd swear it was white striped when it was in the yard. But no, it's black striped and it's starring at me with that freaky one eye just inches from my death vices. I tried to bark at it but I couldn't bark. I tried to leap at it but I couldn't leap. Master Father was still just standing there waiting for me to coast in from space on a magic carpet or somethin'. I don't know where he was lookin'. The cat nudged even closer to me and its big freaky eye opened so wide I could see its eyeball veins. It hissed as evil as a thousand serpents and ran into the house. Nope, Master Father didn't see it but once the cat was in he turned back and closed the door.

What the hell just happened? I dropped back to my evolutionary four-pawed stance and ran to the back of the house. When I got there Master Tom was playing nerf toss with Lew in the yard. When did Lew get here? Normally I'd try and chase the ball but there's a white striped... I mean black striped one-eyed cat in the house. A one eyed cat in my house! I ran up on the back stoop and then Lew made a helluva throw from the back of the yard, right over Master Tom's head and smack into the back door, miraculously pushing it open. Sweet throw puppy, I'm in!

I ran through the kitchen but my progress was stopped at the dining room door as I was shut out during dinner. That didn't matter as there are two routes to the living room. I took option number two through the play room when out of nowhere that one eyed, black striped rat cut in front of me and zoomed into the living room and under some furniture.

Wait a minute, black striped one-eyed rat. Yeah, it was a rat, not a cat. But that eye, it was huge. Dog, that's gross. There's a one eyed rat in my house. Probably recently escaped from some secret scientific mutation experiment. Maybe they transplanted a big cat's eye on this black striped rat. Maybe they are creating a new race of black striped cat eyed rats to exterminate the free dogs of the world. Maybe this was the prototype mother of all black striped one cat eyed rats and it's loose in my house. For all dogs I must stop this rat cat thing before it can be cloned. But I'm just a dog-too big to be chasing this mutation under sofa's and chairs. Barking it out didn't work in the yard and plus, I can't bark now.

Suddenly it ran out from under the couch and was doing intricate movements around the room. Obviously it's had specialized maze and cheese training. I tried chasing it around but I kept bumping into the furniture. Bumbling into the furniture was more like it. There was furniture everywhere; chairs, tables, lamps, ottomans. The damn black striped one cat-eyed rat zigged and zagged around it all. Had I never noticed all this furniture before? Every time I had a clear shot at the bastard rat cat thing some fine piece of craftsmanship and comfort fell into my path. Finally we got into open space in front of the television. I had it now and it knew it. It turned at me with its rat face and it's big cat eye and hissed again so piercing that I stumbled in my tracks. It then dashed for the three-tiered table. I had to lunge now or I'd lose him in the curtains if he got through the table. I lunged- yes, now I can lunge for some reason. I made the desperate heave in full trajectory sliding right along the lower polyurethane oak base and suddenly stopping fully wedged between the lower base and middle level shelf.

I was stuck- literally!

So that's how in the doggie hell that happened. I'm stuck under the table and the black striped one cat-eyed rat is nowhere to be seen. Suddenly, family start moving into the living room and placing their dinner fattened asses in the comfortable craftsmanship that kept bumbling in my path. I could see the recliners going back and forth but no one saw me. I tried barking but I couldn't. Yeah, you know the deal. I was stuck and couldn't get out. Then I kept hearing my name again, "Dallas blah, blah, blah and Dallas yak, yak, yak". What's up with that? Who's calling me? What do they want?

Finally, I hear a scream; it's one of the cousins. Did she see the black striped one cat-eyed rat scurry across the carpet? No, she noticed the damn dog is in the house. She's not comfortable with me around and makes her case. I wish I could tell her I'd gladly leave the room if she'd get me unstuck for doggie freakin' sake. I wonder how she'd feel if the black striped one cat-eyed rat ran up her dress. She'd sure wish I was in the room then. She's adamant though; she's not coming in the living room. Maybe she was bit as a kid or something, I don't know. I'm distracted for a moment as once again I hear, "Dallas blah, blah, blah and Dallas yak, yak, yak".

Then that sound is broken by the auditory trigger of fear almost all dogs learn early in their domestic life. The violent, unnatural, unholy, inhumane, corner-clinging, womb-reentering, sucking roar of the vacuum cleaner. Drop me in a vat of fire ants. Stick me in a dark room for a week with the constant serenade of the fire whistle. Put me to work as a twenty-four hour watch dog at the Gaines Dog Food factory but do not get that damn vacuum cleaner near me.

I remember once Master Mother leaving that thing running while she left the room to attend to a Baby accident. I always cower in the corner when that's around and still it eventually gets pushed over to my corner forcing me out with all its freaky sounds and vibrations. This one day I decide I'm going to check this thing out. I figured I could deal with all it's rumbling and vibrating as long as it wasn't moving. I nudged around it a little. There was the smell of rubber heating up and dust was leaking out its center. I stuck my nose up to that center bag sack and with a little tap it tipped over from being top heavy. Well, drop my bone, I completely freaked and jumped back startled by its unmuffled screams and furious blur of its spinning teeth. I wanted no part of this anymore and grabbed the blue blanket in my jaw and ran past this demon in search of a corner to hide. With quick and cautious steps I navigated past the open mouth of the beast with my security in tow but it suddenly ripped the blue blanket from my jaw. It's got the blue blanket and it's making this God awful sick gagging. I think the blue blanket is chocking this thing and it's rattling and quivering on the floor. Its pure evil, pure evil I tell you. We dogs don't have the type of vivid imaginations that make us panic over extreme future events but I could imagine getting what little counter balance I have ripped away by that thing.

So, now I'm stuck with my ass hangin' out in this death trap of a table. I hear it getting closer but I can't move, I can't turn my head. The sucking is coming! The sucking is coming! Oh, the inhumanity!

THHHHHHHHH-WHUMP! "AHHH! It's Got Me! It's Got My Tail."

You have no idea the panic, the terror. My own distant family member has decided the only way to extricate me from the room and to unwedge me from my situation is with the most sinister household appliance ever conceived. And keep in mind we had a trash compactor back then as well.

My claws sunk into to the oak base leaving gaping nail marks as my body slowly drudged into the turning cylinders of death. I tried to bark, nothing came out. I tried to scream, whimper, cry, maybe even pray as best I could comprehend. Still no auditory function existed. It was all dry heaves. The sounds from this black hole of an appliance got louder as I was being sucked in. As my head dragged away from the front ledge of the base, guess who reappeared? The black striped one cat-eyed rat opened its eye wide and again I could see the blood pulsing through the veins. It again began hissing- so piercing, so evil.

The vacuum, still louder and louder, kept drawing me in slowly to a hell known only to lint and dust. That clogged sucking sound seemed to overpower any thoughts of pain my coiled and shattered spine would eventually encounter. The suction power was so strong it tore the collar from my throat. The metal studs clanging around the motor like it sucked up a hundred pennies heightening the unbareability

110   T o m   M o d y

of my terror. And through it all I could still hear, "Dallas blah, blah, blah and Dallas yak, yak, yak".

I awoke to the sound of my own yelps. Thank God! My yelps. My sounds. My voice. I could be heard- at least by me and that was good enough for now. Everyone else in the room seemed to be directing noises at the television. Maybe it was their sounds that woke me up. They freed me from my nightmare, my doggie nightmare. Oh my, it was horrible. My heart was still fluttering. I laid on the cool slate base near the fireplace and yet it was two hundred degrees inside me. I was burnin' up. I really wished I could sweat. I'd never wished that before 'cause some of you people stink... bad! I should know, I'm a dog and I like smells but some of you people give odor a bad name.

So there I lay, startled yet in obvious relief. But then I heard it again, "Dallas blah, blah, blah and Dallas yak yak, yak". I thought it was a dream, I though the nightmare was over. I looked around frantically for the that black striped one cat-eyed rat. I cowered in fear of the vacuum cleaner. But all that was familiar was something similar to that cat rat hissing sound.

Oh, it was the new baby in the house. No, not Baby but the new baby, Nat. Master Mother had a new baby a month or so ago. All she does is cry so maybe that explains some things streaming into my subconscious. But what's with the "Dallas blah, blah, blah" stuff. Well, heavenly revelation tell me it means... Dallas 13, Pittsburgh 28. Ah yes, Sunday NFL football invading my unconscious state.

This dream was one that seemed to stick with me most of my life. Kinda' a haunting imagery that would spook me in remembrance. Doggie dreams generally don't have the creative imaginations to venture far beyond what reality might possibly hold. A car chase may end up a bit too close or we might get locked in the car but never anything too far removed from what we know. We do have the usual human type anxieties of can't bark or move too slow, but on the bright side, we don't have to worry about suddenly being in public naked.

Now in Doggie Heaven, I took the opportunity to talk with Freud's dog for some dream analysis. Apparently the black striped one cat-eyed rat was indeed Nat. Things around the house had been a little different. A little more stressful. A little more crowded and I had been feeling a bit displaced. And she cries like no other baby hence the thousand snake hissing. The "Dallas blah, blah, blah", I already knew was from sleeping close to the TV during the football game and every time the announcer's said "Dallas this" or "Dallas that" it snuck into my dream. Had I been a little more open to heavenly revelations I would have realized, as "Sigmutt" did, that the overall tension the relatives directed at me caused the whole vacuum drama. Yeah, I called him "Sigmutt" even though I think his real name was probably Weiner Schnitzel or something like that.

Freud's dog made most of my dream seem reasonable until he surmised that Lew appearing in the back yard had something to do with my desire to hump my mother. A vestige from our little tryst in the blue blanket. Hump my mother, what the....? I told him he was full of dog shit and should stop shaving his head bald like his earthly Master since the warm heavenly environment pulsing on his unprotected brain is making him delusional. What kinda' psycho-barking analysis crapolla is he yelpin' about.

From now on if I want answers I'll go directly to God. I just wish someone would tell me where he hangs out up here. I understand all these revelations are his doing but once in a while I have a question, you know? I'd at least like to thank him for the nice spread of human foods and shag carpet fields.

Yes, we do indeed have some pleasant accommodations in Doggie Heaven. As for the Upstate New York winters, its familiar approach was the dread for almost all creatures alike- except for dogs and kids. It was the time of flopping without consequence, crashing without injury and sudden impacts on crystal feathers. We dogs share so much in common with our Little Masters. Our bodies always runnin' and jumpin'. Our hearts always pounding staying constantly active. Always warm inside. We utilized every opportunity to take advantage of God's seasonal airbag. When we exhausted our enthusiasms we could return to a warm, lazy and relaxed haven.

Home was never cozier than those few winters where Master Tom was still on the path of boyhood heading to teenager. I knew that when I was home at night, everyone would be there. Dusk would come around 4:30 or 5:00 in the evening. Master Father and Mother couldn't go out golfing plus they had to attend to Nat. Master Tom was still young enough to have curfews and restrictions on weeknights. There were only three choices on that television so everyone tended to hang out in the living room. It was a family season. I absolutely loved laying next to the floorboard heat. It was right below my balcony so if any curious noises came about outside I could be up there in an instant.

That probably was the best time of year for "caged" housedogs as well, knowing that people would always be around. By housedogs I mean dogs who are leashed or actually have a place to crap in the house. And I don't mean poodles either. They're not dogs, they're poodles. Beaner's family dog Alec, now that's a housedog. I'm not going to diss them because I hardly think they could survive in the dog free world. No dog should be running loose that might be considered dinner by the average large bird. For seasonal concerns, a little short haired Daschund like Alec would suffocate in just an average accumulation of snow.

Master Tom held fond memories of Alec as Beaner would let him loose in the parlor and they'd chase him from corner to corner; never ever being able to catch him on the run. They'd laugh hysterically as the little speedster barely escaped their dives and lunges. It was a few evenings of good clean fun for all involved. The dreadful end being that Beaner was summoned to the school principal's office in anticipation of punishment for some odd prank or misdemeanor, only to find out he was being let home because his mother backed over the dog in the driveway. That's why they're called house dogs my friends. Until some breeds can genetically advance in size or some other form of natural selection they will only survive a handful of slip-ups and escapes. Master must be diligent.

On the other end of the spectrum, I happened to be strolling down Union Street one wintery day to witness a very odd occurrence. I took a leer into Captain's and Cappy's front window and what did I see? Poodles flying in mid air. At first I was impressed. Is this the type of evolutionary necessity that comes from being locked up all day? Equivalent to the geek who stays home and reads all those mad science books to one day invent the pill that skyrockets muscle mass and eliminates acne in three easy to take doses. As I got a little closer I noticed Tago and Pierre weren't exactly wide-eyed over their little triumph against gravity. In fact, they were bug-eye scared. Silly me in thinking anything positive in their plight. It seems the boys were just playing a little game of house football... Tago and Pierre were the actual footballs!

Freakin' poodle nerfs, that's hilarious. I do have a heart you know. I hope those boys weren't kicking field goals. I'm tellin' ya though, they just aren't the same species. Only a poodle could get in that kinda' situation. In all my theory of the house dog enjoying the family winter down time, I guarantee Tago and Pierre couldn't wait for summer so those beastly boys would get the doggie hell outta' the house.

I enjoyed Captain and the gang when they were out of the house in the winter because I was usually more involved in their high impact low-tech activities. A favorite was "king of the hill." The elementary school parking lots would be plowed with mountain high piles of snow. The very person at the top, usually Captain, would have to defend all comers with tackles, pushing, shoving and snowballs. The gang which consisted of Cappy, Master Tom and a block of kids ranging in age from about eight to fourteen would make relentless charges up the hill and Captain would normally tumble them all harmlessly to the base. I would be like some hyena jumpin' and howlin', bobbin' and weavin' through the maze of on-commers. When one little kid would get knocked on his ass I'd bury them with insult by mountin' them and dry humpin' their faces into the icy cold snow. Their cumbersome snowsuits totally limit mobility allowing me to keep them down a good ten or fifteen seconds. I'd have to take a few stinging snowball bullets after the fact but it was worth it to get my groove on numerous times in an hour.

Eventually, some older kids more to Captain's age would show up and things would get a bit more physical and activities tended to end in the same manner. One time Captain got nailed in the ear with an ice ball and ran home insisting he was deaf. Then a subsequent time he got pegged in the face and ran home in tears insisting he was blind. All this happened under my radar of course. I only knew everyone was leaving and I was still horny.

Sugar and Scooter lived right down the street from the snowplowed mountains so I usually sniffed around their turf when I was in the area. We didn't sit around the front porch and drink beer like Master Tom and Master Mark would in later years but we were dog cordial. By that I mean no blood was shed. Sugar and I usually stuck our noses where the sun doesn't shine and we'd take some nips at the other but it was the same old hello-back-off shit. Scooter would try and get involved but we'd snarl him back and he'd go scratch his stump against some tree.

Sugar was still doing his best to get noticed but his location in the corner of the village obscured him from much of my audience. Thus I had become the most notable and quotable dog in town. His proximity to the elementary school did give him a twice a day opportunity to maximize his exposure in front of a captive group. In the winter of '77-'78 both Master Tom and Master Mark were on safety patrol guarding the younger kids from the savage metal beasts. It was a dreaded early rise year-long duty known for its rewards of daily hot chocolate and the annual trip to our nation's capital.

Master Tom never cared to have me around at his post. I tended to chase cars, dry hump a few kids and follow him to school barkin' the whole way. It really wasn't that safe for me as well. I had a number of close calls with fenders surprising me around a corner as the stagnation of our

The Dogs of Sherburne **115**

position dulled my alertness and the continuous stream of kids distracted me.

Master Mark, however, made the most of Sugar as his companion by often placing his orange patrol belt around the dog. This was a great "PR" tactic as the kids really took to him as their guide and protector. While I was getting noted and quoted for my village menacing, Sugar was building up points as the brave loyal mutt. Then to have Scooter, the now lovable tripod by his side, this only added to Sugar's favor among the coveted 5 to 15 year old doggie demographic. Sugar was now a second rate Laddie and I was starting to notice some subtle differences in the way kids responded to us. Subtle if you consider sneers, jeers, snowballs, rocks and even books being tossed at me whenever I was around. Subtle if you consider, petting, fawning, laughs and courtesies addressed in Sugar's direction.

Pleasantries can only get you so far in the new order of this doggie free world but to lose the admiration of the coveted 5 to 15 doggie demographic was a huge blow to my cause. These would be the ones someday telling stories about me at the local pubs. These would be the ones eventually so uncomfortable in their forty-something skin they would prefer to think of me as still alive with my hoarse bark and grey muff still dragging my arthritic hind legs after any car that wasn't goin' over the speed limit. This type of legend can't grow if they prefer me dead! One dog alone in despicable doggie self-promotion could be viewed as a sad, undisciplined, desperate ploy for attention. Without Sugar backing me up there's no precedent to set for acceptability of dog lovin' chaos. The 5 to 15 doggie demographic actually love dogfights and car chases and dry humping if it has entertainment value.

Picture your local high school wrestling match with those clean-cut farm boys in fair and honest disciplined competition. Now picture some kid on the opposing team taking the mat in gold spandex pants, knee high army boots, sunglasses and a black silk robe with a skull on the back. Spewing insults and proclamations at all that will listen. You'd hate that guy right? But what if every team had one of those guys, then they'd be the guys you love to hate. If all the wrestlers were self-promoters you'd even find a few you absolutely loved.

So what's happenin' here is that these non-village kids are being bused in to school and they don't know about us village dogs. They're use to their fun lovin' pets that are practically the only friend they've got because they live in the boonies. When they get off the bus they turn one way and see the familiar comforting sight of Sugar runnin' around with some badge of importance and they think it's quite sporting. He's snowjobin' 'em with that safety patrol belt. They turn another way and I'm tryin' to cause some commotion and they find my antics just short of a bully and now I'm treated as such. I mean, I loved catching snowballs in my mouth but even I began to realize they weren't thrown with love.

Sugar may have been reveling in his new role as "Laddie come lately" but I can assure you that bright orange was not his color; at least not his true color. Can a robber stop robbing? Can a cheater stop cheating? Absolutely they can but there's no stinkin' way a liberated dog like Sugar was going to stop creating chaos because one things' for sure, a promoter can't stop promoting. The world works in certain absolutes so if you insist on fooling yourself that you are something you're not, circumstances (and conniving dogs) will test the flexibility of that assumption until it bends full circle.

Winter had kept the kids at school bottled up in recess activities relegated to the gym. For twenty minutes every morning and afternoon the kids loading onto buses or crossing at Master Mark's post were treated to our traitorsome mutt practically in training for a noble seeing eye job. In revelation I now salute Sugar's earthly instinct to act appropriately when that patrol belt was around him but at the time I was losing ground with my own agenda. Activity and public fare downtown during the winter was low and it limited my opportunities of promotion. I also sensed a distance with Master Tom as he tried everything he could to keep me from causing trouble at his post- including leashing me up some mornings. As the spring of '78 approached a window of opportunity was sure to present itself in my favor.

The kids could now recess outdoors at the playground which was practically in Sugar's back yard. When the patrol belt was off our muttley friend wasn't quite the same samaritan. Some circumstance would hopefully bring that to light as he caroused the child filled grounds without his inhibitions in check. I couldn't plan anything being that I'm a dog. I couldn't drag some kid down to the creek and write a forged ransom note signed by Sugar. I couldn't payoff some other dog to dress up in a gorilla suit and terrorize the kids as I came along and scared him off. Even here in Doggie Heaven that's the best set-up I could think of so imagine how futile I was back then. But just like the time I licked Baby's face and utilized that random diversion for my first escape to freedom, circumstances well within the doggie realm of possibility could occur. I could initiate an unplanned action and then sense an intuitive outcome by adding a sequence of events.

Consider what I do know to this point. I know how to make Sugar adversarial. I know there's a growing general annoyance towards me. I know as dogs we are protective of certain territorial gains, be it land or lass. I know Scooter and Sugar function like kin with Sugar being the older brother. I know I love to create chaos. I can't add all this up but I do function by instinctively progressing what I sense and learn. If I've learned something I enjoy propagating and reinforcing that action. It's good stimulus.

So, one early spring day I happen to be browsing the village when I came across an approachable female of the purebred beagle persuasion. A persuasion for which I had a decisive size advantage. I hadn't encountered a situation to this point that was so amicable in her willingness and my potential to simply take what I wanted. In other words, what I didn't know was that she was just tired. There was no ritualistic dance or the tiresome outdated etiquette. She saw me coming and grunted the doggie equivalent of, "not again." I still approached the situation knowing that this

118   T o m   M o d y

potential bitch could turn bitchy. As I moved my nose in close one thing became very obvious- Sugar had been there. More to the "been there done that" category and he hadn't been gone long. In the simplest capacity a light went on in my head. Mountin' his bitch would really piss him off. I made sure it wasn't my usual "wham bam thank you ma'am" routine. I rubbed myself all over her. She was tired and didn't resist so I took my time and let her full aroma work into my fibers and my pours. When we were done I even offered to spend some time with her and snuggle up close, maybe have a smoke or two. She declined so I took her dog tag number just to let her know there was a slight chance it wasn't a one-time thing.

Yeah right!

I wasn't just a blanket humper anymore you know. I was the real deal. Stud, Casanova, playa', whatever you want to call it. Oh yes, you humans are politically correct now so I guess the proper term for my behavior would be sexual harassment. Sticks and stones as your statement goes. I was gettin' some action and don't care what you call me. Although in analyzing your saying, I wonder how many of you who use that phrase would actually prefer getting your bones broken to standing up to your beliefs. Wouldn't you love to break someone's arm with a rock just once when they spout that comeback at you?

It was nice to have the time and the willing (tired) partner to savor the act, as you will. Usually I spend most of the energy on the chase and the effort to hold down my bitch. Other times you've trespassed into some yard and you're trying to get the deed in before the owner responds to all the heavy howling. That's what happened my first time.

Master Father was having a dinner party for a few clients. This meant that they folded up the blue blanket and set it in the closet. That's a lonely feeling. The wives at the party were both wearing mid cut dresses so there was a lot of leg exposed. There's something about that, something species transcending about the human female leg. I've noted my preference for a hairy ass but the smooth cut of a bare skin woman's leg exposed in the proper sitting position- it's a trigger. I think we tend to respect her because the urge usually ends up on the husbands pant leg and a humpin' we do go. Then there's the unfortunate instance where we've picked up a scent off the woman's leg then discover it again on a coat draped over a chair in the den. It's a bit embarrassing when Master Father escorts his guest to get her coat only to find me romantically engaged with it. Sadly, I had just started when this occurred and my ass got booted out the door before any satisfaction was gained.

I was getting very tired of the artificial stimulation the world of fabric was offering. I needed a release and in the cool of the night I could imagine what it would feel like to strap up against something warm, something warm blooded. The thought made me howl uncontrollably. I decided to inspect a small corner of the village near my domain. I went left down the sidewalk and left again one house down onto Classic Street. A couple houses down Classic Street I took a right onto Summit Street. From there I wandered into the creaky village cemetery.

It was a good spot to try and get some smells from the area. I stuck my nose high as the breeze was coming down the streets slight incline. I picked up a definitive scent that seemed awfully fresh and prime. That being in heat thing sure could enhance my woeful tracking skills. My mind became very acute to the particular direction of the scent and its ability to arouse. I howled again keeping in the spirit of my environment. I'm sure a number of nightlights were flicked on by the children in houses bordering the cemetery. A howl came back from a few yards away. Now I had a scent and an auditory response. I needed only to head up a few residents to sneak a peak at my warm-blooded vixen.

I strutted up the driveway of her domain to find a lonely and leashed Irish Setter patiently waiting on the patio for her Master to return home. She had been on alert since hearing me howl a few yards away and seemed awfully defensive about my approach. Her profile was quite striking and she had a sumptuous ass of red hair. Frankly, her face coulda' used a bag over it but it's not like I'm some judge at the Westminster Kennel Dog Show. At the time I really didn't have a preference for particular features and I wasn't going to be looking her in the face anyway. I moved in close but she got uptight and started barking. A neighbor enjoying his evening on a back porch peered over with his flashlight which calmed her down as I waited by some shrubs.

That little incident made me realize that I needed a forceful and quick initiative if this was going to happen. At home I could wad up the blue blanket and work myself into a lather as I got groovin'. But now I was most definitely in heat so I had moved beyond any potential of doggie foreplay mating rituals. As a female she would have to have been quite a bit bigger and meaner to keep me at bay. I woulda' needed to have been a little tike like Scooter. I couldn't imagine his dopey demeanor and three-wheeled caboose trying to get a mount on such a breed. I guess it's poodles for him.

In my presence this lass was a bit intrigued but mostly guarded and reserved. I moved out of the shrubs with a brisk step. She froze right up like headlights were coming at her. Damn, there were headlights coming at her. Her Master had pulled up to the front of the driveway to grab mail from the mailbox. When he opened his door to exit the car she turned her head in his direction and I leaped three giant steps to her backside and put a mount on her like I'd just escaped from prison and the warden was virtually seconds behind me. Had I thrusted like this with Lew in the blue blanket he woulda' had a concussion. I knew my time was short but there would be no resistance from her. It's kinda' how nature works. Once the male ascends to the biologically correct formation it's her nature to be submissive. It's usually after he's released and reaching for his cigarettes that she goes for the decapitation.

So I'm thrustin' away and I can hear his footsteps leading back to the car like the tick of a play clock. The door shuts and the engine rumbles closer to where now the headlights are on us. Her Master sees what's happening and lays on the horn in disgust but I'm not stoppin'. He slams on the horn again and exits the car screaming some profanity. I know this show is coming to an end so I thrust even faster determined not to leave the premises before I'm satisfied.

Her Master dashes over to his garden and grabs a shovel. The poor girl realizes something violent may happen and she could potentially be in the middle of it but I'm too far embedded for her to make any sudden movements. I'd say at about this point the play clock was down to mere seconds. In human sports lore you could say I was dribbling the ball up court as time was expiring. The clock was now in tenths of a second, the defense was bearing down on me. I ducked under the defender (and his shovel) got my shot off and bolted to the locker room before the home crowd had the chance to razz me. Truth is, I don't know where my shot landed, I don't know if it was good or not. In this game just getting the shot off is the most important thing. Isn't there a lesson in this philosophy somewhere?

I was pretty lucky actually. Her Master was smart enough to not take a real crack at me or he could have hurt us both. Still it was quite the rush this whole warm blooded experience. Almost all encounters would be like this. Being forced to perform under pressure. Working against the clock to get your shot off. Fun game this basketball you humans play but I'd say I prefer my interpretation of it.

Back to my current conquest. It was nice to have an opportunity to play against the "B" team and enjoy a blowout. My encounter with this purebred beagle was an easy romp over a tired and overmatched opponent. Now that I had my "Scent of Sugar's Bitch" cologne all over me I headed towards South Street to make a point. It was mid day when I strutted up Sugar's driveway. He was nowhere to be seen so I headed for the back yard and peered through the shrubs. As I gazed across the school bus parking lot onto the elementary school playground I could see Sugar in all his pseudo pious reverence engaging large numbers of kids out on recess. He didn't have that stupid belt on but the kids knew him from his daily duty.

If I charged out there I'd once again be the bad guy because once he smelled his bitch on me there was going to be trouble. Even if he started the fight I was the invading dog with my menacing village reputation. Then suddenly, opportunity knocked.

Something was poking around at my ass. Down that low it had to be fleas on a ladder or Scooter. It was Scooter. He was sniffin' me over, curious that he had smelled my bitch cologne before. I figured since he seemed to like it so much I'd give him what he wanted. I turned and started mounting him. I was all over him. Mouuntin' his face, rubbin' my balls all over his back, sticking my nose in his groin. You might say I was bit more demonstrative than the perfume sample lady soliciting at the mall department stores. After pinning Scooter down for a good minute I let his startled bitch smellin' body up and off he ran to the playground and the safety of Sugar.

Scooter waddled his tripod on to the field and the little kids all noticed his vigilant handicapped steps striding towards his big buddy Sugar. They thought he was the most innocent looking mutt and cheered his staggered progress. Sugar was enjoying his own adorations until Scooter got to be but a few yards away. Like a trigger, Sugar's nose lifted to the air and pointed in Scooters oncoming direction. Scooter was hoping to be some type of messenger of my harmless accosting. The problem with being the messenger as you humans say is that they often get killed. Particularly when your species lacks any communication skills beyond three yelps and a whine.

Scooter approached Sugar slobberin' at the mouth to tattle on me. He stopped mere paws away as Sugar's eyes turned a savage stare towards him. Sugar was getting some awfully conflicting scents in his direction. Scooter peered behind him hoping those looks were directed at something else. He saw nothing to indicate Sugar's intent was past him.

Sugar lowered his nose and slowly leaned towards Scooter. One of the kids yelled out, "look dog, it's your three legged friend", anticipating Sugar was happy to see Scooter. Sugar moved in closer and began a sniff-over inspecting every inch of Scooter's now quaking body. The kids were innocently amused by his thoroughness. As Sugar approached Scooter's head he quietly growled in his ear. Scooter began quaking more noticeably and one little girl tried to calm Scooter by telling him, "it's okay, he's your friend". Scooter didn't know why Sugar was intimidating him. He tried to back off but Sugar growled again causing the kids to really take notice that something was wrong.

If only your poorly developed aromatic senses could detect what Sugar was detecting. How many more crimes could be solved? How many felons could be apprehended? How many more wrongs could be righted? None I tell you. Your world would be total chaos. The sense of smell is the most powerful sense of them all. It's an arousing, corruptive, manipulative force that intoxicates the brain debilitating reason and judgment. In the cutthroat world of emotionless wild animals they can respond to its singular trigger and act with a definitive purpose. Sometimes the actions may not be based on the whole truth but there is no fairness in the wild other than the strongest will survive. Doggie society truth is that Scooter is holding the smoking gun and he's guilty despite the fact I placed the gun in his possession.

I shutter to think if human society might someday evolve a more advanced snout. You are already so quick with judgment based on what your eyes and ears take in. Do you have any idea how condemning your judgments would be with the nose of a dog?

A highly developed aromatic appendage would absorb stimulus deep into the brain secreting chemicals to your furthest emotional triggers. Your conscious would be all encompassing to what emotions first burst forth and reason would not be controllable. If you smelled money on some guy you'd uncontrollably call him a flaunting snob. If you smelled garbage on some guy you'd label him a bum. It would just come out, all your deepest petty thoughts and emotions on public display. And forget about anyone walking within close proximity to anything. Accusations would fly through the air like influenza in a fan testing factory. You'd only be innocent until you smelled like something suspicious.

It was in fact, the perfect set-up. A total frame job. Finally, I was thrown a bone. Scooter smelled like Sugar's bitch. The line had been crossed. The doggie justice system of guilt by associated smell was about to be enforced. Some of the teachers noticed the kids suspiciously crowding around the dogs and began to move in for an investigation. When they got to the scene Sugar was already poking at Scooter, knocking him back on his stump then growling. One teacher ordered the kids to step back while another tried to shoo the dogs away. Scooter had no problem with that command and agreeably began to waddle away but Sugar hadn't made his point. Scooter backed away about three steps before Sugar pounced on him and pinned him down. The Kids couldn't believe that Sugar had turned this aggressive towards his buddy. Sugar wasn't going to seriously hurt Scooter but the dominance of his scolding and the viciousness of his barks had the kids fearful for Scooter's well being. They yelled at Sugar to get off him but Sugar continued his aggressive enforcement of doggie code.

I could sense it. The tide was turning against Sugar. The true colors of this street tough mutt were now showing through. The pedestal he had been sitting on for so many months was now up for grabs and it was time to crank up the old self-promotion machine. I made a gallant dash across the bus garage lot barking all the way. Oooh's and ahhh's were heard throughout the playground as kids on the verge of tears now saw some hope.

I came crashing into Sugar in an obvious show of support for Scooter's predicament. Sugar rolled and flopped back on his feet. One young boy tried to push Sugar back further but Sugar nipped at him. A very, very bad "PR" move. The teacher's came upon us like banshees and for the safety of the kids made it clear who was in charge. We scattered then held ground. For the record, I didn't get any preferential treatment based on my defense of Scooter. Any dog lovin' chaos was considered a threat no matter the intent. It was Sugar though whose bubble was burst. Attacking poor Scooter, nipping at kids, causing the teachers to have a shit hemorrhage. The final insult in a dramatic statement came as a young boy flung a rubber kickball smacking Sugar square in the head. The whole crowd erupted in cheer.

I tried to escort Scooter off the field but he wanted nothing to do with me and went off himself across the bus garage lot to home. I began to head in my own homeward direction off the playground between the tennis courts and school. I didn't even reach the end of the tennis court fence when I detected paw steps behind me. Sugar wasn't going to let this go.

During this whole fiasco a number of little girls were drawing silly stuff with chalk inside the tennis courts. A teacher called them to exit the "cage" before we got too close to them. It was too late. Sugar caught me at the end of the fence near the gate but I wouldn't let him simply ambush me. I turned and snarled back at him but he was angry and intent on lashing out. Once again we smacked snouts and rose to our hind legs just scratching and clawing for the upper position. Having already achieved satisfaction for the day I wasn't into making any aggressive moves so I let him come at me and used my size to combat him back. It worked momentarily but I was a bit too passive and Sugar got the upper advantage and seemed intent on doing some harm. Particularly since he could smell his bitch on me as well as Scooter.

He was positioned well atop me forcing me to match his aggression. The whole display became very ugly as the saliva was flyin' and the volume of our growls hit ferocious levels. The girls in the courts made an attempt to slip through the door but the teachers screamed at them to now go back inside. Our little battle had us pushing and shoving right up against the fence and the teacher's concern now made the girls panic and they began crying. A custodian even started running over from the bus garage to assist. From a distance many of the kids were experiencing anxiety at seeing such a savage display of violence. I'd like to think this was a good situation because it further demonstrated that Sugar wasn't the benign little goody-goody he had been projecting. This was however, a minor trauma for all witnesses and it would only be remembered that way. The kids now were scared of us both. That grand pedestal for appreciation amongst the 5 to 15 doggie demographic was still open for occupation. Then outta' nowhere Laddie Showed up.

Well, drop my bone, the original do-gooder doggie citizen rushed us a few steps ahead of the custodian and broke up our little fight. Sugar almost appeared to be ready to go at Laddie but the custodian was now on the scene waving some wrench at us. I can't say he really scared any of us away but the kids sure got a laugh as he tried to hold up his pants from exposing his butt crack while he whirled his little tool around. Laddie wasn't intimidated at all and actually stared the butt crackin' custodian back a few steps then calmly backed us off as the girls scurried through the gate to safety. Once they were out Laddie lunged at us to be sure we stayed apart and order- the real order of things- seemed to be restored. Laddie was up on his pedestal where he truly had been all along. Sugar was again just a mutt about town. I was still a menace but with some redeeming quality. And Scooter... well, he got his first humpin' but came out of it smellin' like he got laid.

 # Revelation 9

Karma is very inconvenient
in a dog eat dog world

The butternuts were flyin' like bullets. Aimed at the young and weak, the fleeing targets suffered stinging and bruising welts. It was acceptable to run but only out of range. Running home would label you a wimp, pussy or baby in the eyes of your peers. For Master Tom, having the park so close to home made it difficult for him to escape unscathed. Everyone would see where he was runnin' and those labels could hurt more than the welts. The golf ball size spawn of the park trees lay scattered in large quantities throughout the grounds so it's not like you could run out of ammo. Butternuts were reusable projectiles unlike Beaner's preferred gunpowder laced arsenal.. I still haven't determined which is more traumatic. I've witnessed assaults with both numerous times

For example, late one evening I had followed some potential warm-blooded prize to the playground when glows of light flared across the field. A few kids were laughin', a few were beggin'. The beggin' few were lined up like carnival booth targets against the bus garage wall duckin' and bobbin'. Colors of light and heat were bursting from a dark image's extended appendage making a spooky popping sound that kept me from investigating closer. I didn't need to get any closer to know who the dark image was. I knew it was Beaner. I could smell that sharp chalky smoldering odor which seemed to reek from his hands whenever he'd reach to pat me. The residue was burnt into his pours from the minor explosives he often pulled from deep in his pockets

I also could sense what was becoming fairly frequent. The continuous mild hazing every boy goes through when most of his friends in the village are a few years advanced. You're on equal ground only until boredom sets in and then you must be the court jester for the royalty know as "the older kids." In this situation, Master Tom and Abby had to be targets for Beaner's roman candle accuracy demonstration. I could sense Master Tom's position in "the pack" just like I would if I was in the wild. He had no leverage to defuse the situation.

If you humans only knew the subtleties your canine companions can detect, you'd show even greater appreciation for our attachment to you. We know when you've had a lousy day at work. We feel your anxiety. If you ever wondered why we often misbehave during these times, it because that's how we react to an environment of anxiety. It's not about us wanting to be bad. We want you and our environment to "feel" better. We get nervous and we act on that nervous energy.

We know where you stand in the grand scheme of things. We know who you control and who controls you. We're nice to the people you like and cold to the people that make you uncomfortable. We can read your eye contact or the eagerness with which you greet a person. We can determine your vocal inflections and note the distance you accord certain people. We watch your expressions when certain people arrive and prepare for your moods when they leave.

We respond to you by the type of music you play. We know your patterns when certain sounds and images come out of the television. We can smell when dinner that night will give you lots of energy or make you too stuffed to move from your lounge chair. We can hear the danger in your voices and act upon the panic in your eyes. And though I never got to experience this first hand, we often know when you are dying.

God knows the roller coaster of emotions we live every day with our Masters. The frustrations of internal realizations yet having no intellectual way to formulate and consciously understand. Thus, our reward is here in Doggie Heaven. And though on earth I could sense Master Tom was a pawn in Beaner's ten minutes of amusement, I now know in revelation that it's an amusing memory to him and nothing more. Besides, he knew it was a short test of endurance that would flame out quickly when the roman candle was exhausted.

The butternut wars were inexhaustible. If you weren't strong enough or tough enough, you'd better be fast enough. It was quite the minor skirmish as I watched eagerly from my balcony. This was the type of outbreak of chaos I needed to see first hand. I leaped down and dashed with great grip along the living room and dining room shag carpet. My pace was too eager and as I hit the kitchen linoleum I slid into a spinout against the cupboards, knocking over my water dish in the process. Master Mother knew I wanted out and quickly opened the back door in a race to get me out before the pool of water leaked across the floor to Nat's immobile position.

I ran to the road and waited impatiently for the traffic to clear. I didn't get but a few paws into the park when I got my first welt. There were about a dozen kids either attacking, running or hiding and it was hard to clearly see from where the next projectile was launched. I made a few passes through the battle field but settled near the stone wall bordering the library for a semi-safe view. It was apparent that Master Tom and a few others weren't as whole hearted to the conflict as kids like Big Lew, Captain and Beaner. Those kids weren't afraid to dish out and take the punishment while the others occasionally grabbed a butternut in a semi offensive posture but mostly just ducked and hid behind trees.

Eventually this battle was not ended in a victory or peace negotiation. It was stopped by some fun-sucking adults. In fairness to them, not because of their safety concerns for the kids but because they needed to set up temporary fencing for the annual Sherburne Art Society Park Show which was being held the next day.

Most of the bruised and battered kids walked off over to my area near the stone fence. Some of the older kids took up their normal posture of sittin' and smokin'. I hung out by Master Tom as everyone cooled down and found other ways to harass each other. A few of the kids sittin' and smokin' along the fence never did warm up to me. In particular was Master George, General's Master. He started bustin' on Master Tom that his dog was a pussy just like him. Master Tom tried to pay him little attention and stood up for me when he got tired of Master George's put downs. Master George knew he had the trump card though and decided to play his hand.

"We'll see how big a pussy Dallas is, I'm going home to get General."

He just called me a cat. I never realized it until now. He didn't say I was lion or cougar or something respectable in the genus. He called me a pussy. I've been called many things- menace, bastard, animal, even degenerate seed of the devil. All but the latter being true of course. Being called any type of cat slang is barely above being called a poodle. This is the down side of heavenly revelations. Finding out the bitter truths long after you can't do anything about it.

How would you feel if when you got the Heaven you learned that the lottery ticket you lost was a winner or that your spouse was unfaithful or that had your dad's sperm impregnated your mother's egg thirty seconds sooner you woulda' had the genetic make up of an NBA basketball player. I suppose when humans get to Heaven you don't fret about this stuff. It's all good, no problems, let it slide, yadda yadda. How benign! Seems to me that's the pussy way out. I don't have that luxury here. Alls I get is the gut churnin' unsweetened truth. There's no angels powdering us with magic stardust as we glow in a higher state of reverence and acceptance. Me and my attitude gotta' lump it if I want full heavenly revelations.

Even now it's hard to let go and impart forgiveness knowing Master George made good with his threat to get General. Knowing he wanted his dog to rip me to shreds. As Master George hopped off the fence, flicked his cigarette butt to the air and laughed down the street, Master Tom made a panic move. He lunged quickly to grab my collar but I just couldn't be corralled that way. I didn't know the threats or the danger for which he was trying to protect me. I just knew he was trying to grab me and that only meant one thing; he was going to drag me inside.

He could try a thousand times to make a sneaky quick move for my collar but he'd be lucky to get a fingertip on me. I loved to hang out with Master Tom and follow him around town or play in the park but I could just sense when I needed a couple paws distance between us in fear of being caught. I'd go home when I was damn good and ready, not a moment sooner. Usually help was necessary to snag me in the open but none of the kids hangin' out that day would assist. They wanted to see a fight.

Master George lived in the village just a few blocks away. The clock was ticking as Master Tom did everything he could to first catch me then beg me to follow him home. He ran across the street and stood by the open door yellin' my name but doggie hell, I wasn't comin' in. A lot was happenin' in the park; I might miss something- (Yeah, like my funeral). Master Tom ran back to the park and tried to play nice.

"Dallas, come her boy, come on, come on. Lets go for a walk boy, come on."

Nope, I just sat in the middle of the park and stared at him. He knew it was futile. He hadn't ever caught me or convinced me to come with him yet- I wasn't starting now. The kids made Master Tom even more nervous by sarcastically stating the obvious.

"You better get him inside before General kills him. George is serious, he's really gettin' his dog."

Enough time had passed where Master Tom knew General was on his way. All he had left to try was to get demanding and desperate with me, but- nah, that didn't work either. He screamed angrily. He made threats- it didn't matter. I knew he wanted me inside and I wasn't goin' inside. As he stood on the edge of the street he could now see General and Master George rounding the corner of Quinn's Market. At that point there seemed to be a convergence of fate upon us. Master Tom looked up East State Street to see

Laddie and Scamp headin' down to the village. Across the street a car horn honked which was the brown Cordoba of Master Mother letting Master Tom know she was leaving. Suddenly options were available.

I was oblivious to it all, of course. I just sat a distance in the park waiting to get the sense that the bounty was lifted from my head so I could hang out with everyone unthreatened. Master Tom considered that Laddie and Scamp could foil Master George's plan for a dog showdown with me. But my safety wasn't guaranteed so he opted for the sure thing. He quickly ran to the driveway and told Master Mother the situation and that we had to get me in the house. Master Tom then hopped in the car as it backed out of the driveway into the street.

In the mean time, Laddie and Scamp were close enough to the park to see General approaching. Appropriately, their mood turned drastically nastier. Still, I sat distant and alone in the park center until I heard the one trigger that tends to override my freedom protecting sensibilities- the click of a car door. Master Tom opened the Cordoba back door and yelled those magic words.

"Dallas, wanna' go for a ride?"

"Doggie hell yeah" I did. "Where we goin', where we goin'" I excitedly pondered and sprinted out the park, across the road and took a good ten paw leap into the back seat. How does the saying go? "Fool me once shame on you, fool me twice shame on me." Well it should be extended for dogs. "Fool me three times shame on me, fool me ten times shame on me, fool me a hundred times shame on me... etc, etc. The ole' "let's go for a drive" routine is full proof in its results and fool proof in it's duplicity.

I just wanna' stick my nose out the window and fly. Every dog loves a fast and free oxygen-snortin', bug-suckin', tongue-flappin' ride. If our Masters leavin' was a rare occurrence we may not fall for the ole' routine. It's just that our Masters get in that metal beast so often and just leave us whinin' and whimperin'. We feel a sense of accomplishment that we somehow managed that rare opportunity to not get left behind. And the confined assault on our senses is titillating. The low hum in our ears, the rumbled vibrations. And every car has a distinctive smell. It could be new leather, polished vinyl, pine or coconut scents, gasoline, washer fluid, coffee or the odd garbage residue. And of course, the anticipation of the previously noted arrival high.

By now I've had plenty of experience going for rides and I know that when all those titillating movement sensations stop I'm just one door handle click away from arriving someplace. Maybe someplace I've never been. No matter the destination the car's confinement makes that burst out the door the most natural high we can experience. Combine the anticipation high with the fact we don't want to chance being left behind and you can understand why there could be a family of grizzly bears in the back seat- if the door opens I'm jumpin' in.

But pup of a bitch, we didn't go anywhere but thirty paw strides into the driveway then Master Tom clamped my collar and literally dragged me into the house. Laddie and Scamp arrived at the park in time to see me run out the park, leap to safety and then get escorted inside. As best they could determine, I fled the scene in fear.

General had been leashed but Master George set him free when he saw me make a break for the road. The line of cars at the traffic light had obscured his view to the fact that I had run to safety and was not loose to do battle. General needed about a split second of freedom to determine that there was "fresh meat" in the park and he bolted towards it. Master George jogged behind him soon to realize the inevitability of General's battle. It would be two against one.

Master George yelled to the kids, "Where the hell is Dallas?"

"Tom got his chicken shit ass in the house," someone yelled back.

Now I'm a chicken for doggie freakin' sake. How many animals can I freakin' be? I know what they mean though, that I was scared but that's not a fair assessment. Fortunate as all doggie hell, yes. Scared, no.

You could still smell the smoke from my nails being dragged across the pavement as I tore through the house and

134

leaped to my balcony. Sure, I was pissed at being car ride duped but curiosity is my overriding drive and I desperately wanted to look out and see what I was missing. In mere seconds I was in full bark attack as the free dogs caught my attention. A heavy drip of saliva was running down the large bay window as I projected the force of my frustration outward. I was scolded for my continued outburst but that was a mild woopin' compared to the conflict I was diverted from.

Scamp, though doin' most of the growlin', stayed half a length behind Laddie as they approached the Gaines Monument. Laddie had taken a quick peer towards my window to note my safe and protected distance. When he turned his focus back, General was past the Library steps bearing down on them both. Scamp started to nudge forward but Laddie flicked his head back to keep Scamp in place.

Many of the kids stood up on the stone fence to excitedly get a good view of the impending blood bath. Laddie held Scamp's ground as General was upon them but Master George had now become uncomfortable and ordered General back. General was the type of dog trained by consequence to mind his Master. He fought every aggressively bred instinct to momentarily mind the command and even managed a brief pause. Momentum, though, was working against him. Not just his forward motion but the rush of testosterone and adrenaline that was charging his brain. The smell of dog upwind. The exuberance of being off the leash. Too many forces to tame and he couldn't totally break stride. Master George's command was just a pebble in the path of a boulder.

General crushed the pebble and bore into the front lines of battle. He pummeled Laddie as if he were another pebble in the path; knocking him to his back pinning him down. General's forceful blow was impressionable enough to shellshock Scamp to momentary submission. Laddie tried to roll left and right along his back paddling his paws at General's oncoming jaws. General got a nip or two of fur but when he attempted the full lunge to make the big strike it threw him off balance and Laddie was able to roll to his feet.

Laddie's escape broke Scamps trance and they bore down on General. Three growling, snarling and hissing regressive animals smacking heads and slicing flesh. The kids loved it.

Scamp managed to get up on his hind legs and ride General. He gauged his distance to Generals flesh with a series of pinching nips waiting for the right moment to take a deeper bite. With General's movement slowed by Scamp's grip and weight, Laddie could engage General with sharp head butts and teeth smacking attempts to wear down his energy. It appeared to be working, particularly having to drag Scamp's weight on his hind legs every time he tried to make a move or defend himself. General couldn't turn his head aggressively towards Scamp or Laddie would have a clear shot at his neck. In under a minute General's hind legs began to give out and slump lower making it impossible for him to make any aggressive play. Scamp then made the play for a chunk of his neck and was able to secure a large jaw lock to his upper back. A jaw lock that shot pain through his nerves and out his snout in a loud savage cry.

The pain carried on the wind to the ears and heart of Master George. A Master whose pride was now in deep doggie doo doo. Master George was not among the cheering crowd lined upon the fence but a closer concerned spectator. He would be that no more. He grabbed a few butternuts and started pelting the whole doggie can of worms. A few other kids joined in, not out of concern for the dogs but for the sheer fun of throwing the projectiles. It had no affect on the fight so Master George entered the fray himself with broken tree branch in hand.

He clumsily swung his branch striking all three dogs to some degree. The distraction helped slow down the escalation of violence but it didn't calm their heightened aggressive state. A few more swings of the branch loosened Scamp's grip on General's back but both General and Scamp turned on Master George and nipped at his legs out of sheer anger. Master George kicked at 'em both but that just diverted their attention back to each other. All three started up again kinda' spinnin' in circles until Master George just had enough and cocked back his size ten Buster Brown

Tom Mody

hiking boot. He swung full force into the fray and struck Laddie square in the right hip. The kick was jarring and penetrating, forcing him to the ground. He yelped and cried on his way down and his fall was fortunate enough to keep him out of line for the next swing.

The second swing missed everything but it was enough of a distraction to put some space between Scamp and General. Undeterred, Master George grabbed General by the scruff and collar and yanked him back keeping Scamp at bay with his branch. It took a closed fist punch to the side of General's head to get him to stand down then Master George picked up his leash and secured control of the situation. Laddie had since gotten back to all fours but not without a severe loss of strength and balance. Laddie was fortunate that Master George didn't initially realize how bad he was hurt or General, after potentially disposing of Scamp, woulda' had no problem feasting on the crippled father.

I watched the whole incident from my balcony, stupidly envious of the combatants. As Scamp and the limping Laddie headed back up East State Street I barked once more catching their attention. It was an innocently normal bark I always put forth when objects of interest pass by my window but I wish now I had let it go. As dogs, we may not know how to interpret seemingly innocent stimulus responses but Laddie and Scamp were retentive enough to notice my departure from the scene. My innocent barking only served as an unfortunate reminder that I left them to be attacked.

I woke up the next day to the continuous sounds of slamming car doors muffled through the bay window. The park was busting with activity early as the area artisans unloaded their works for sale to the park fences. I was extremely hungry and forced to eat the crusted warm slop of Alpo I ignored in my dish the previous night. It went down hard. There was no snortin' and tongue slobberin' most associated with us as we push the bowl across the floor. We're a finicky lot us canines. I could drag three day old lice-infested, pebble-imbedded, pavement-warmed road kill to a comfortable corner of the yard and pick the bones dry but twelve hour old Alpo makes me wish I knew about religious fasting.

The conventional thinking is that we get accustomed to human food and that spoils our taste buds for dog food. Well, conventional thinking is pretty smart because that's exactly what happens but that doesn't explain why I prefer day old carcasses to specialized nutritionally-enhanced, genetically-perfected chow. The answer is that it doesn't smell dead and it doesn't taste dead. The fact is you try and keep it alive with your preservatives and flavor additives. To be fair, I'm way too familiar with the process of your processing. Remember we have a dog food factory in town.

You've heard of the LeBrea Tar Pits of prehistoric times, haven't you? Well, we have the Sherburne Goo Pits of processed dog food times. Off the railroad tracks in the far corner of the dog food factory grounds are pits of preservative goo. Seems to me there were like three or four different colors. If you ever opened a can of Alpo and dumped it in a bowl you'd get about seventy-five percent "meat" and about twenty-five percent of this jelly substance a kin to afterbirth. I'm assuming these pits were the afterbirth of the afterbirth- a dumping ground for this goo. The kids would take B.B. guns and shoot pellets into the goo, wait about five seconds and watch the air bubbles rise and make this gurgling sound. It's an amusing opportunity to kill about a half hour of your day.

One day I happened to be menacing around the Goo Pits when this chipmunk came flying out of the brush and carelessly went head first in the day-glow green pit. The pit swallowed him whole. Seconds later this Basset Hound named Peaches appeared in stomping pursuit. When she cleared the brush and saw me she stopped. She looked left, then right, then left again but there was no chipmunk. She gave me the most annoying glare and barked at me real mean. In doggie terms, accusing me of being responsible for her game's disappearance.

That stupid Basset Hound was way too slow and fat to catch a chipmunk but nonetheless she's really mad at me. I'm actually thinking I might have to defend myself against this dumb ass but in amusing delayed reaction a larger than normal air bubble and gurgle rose from the depth of the pits and the guilty party belched up its confession.

Peaches was one of those dogs caught between the sizes necessary for freedom aspirations. Scooter had the guide of Sugar and the casual nature of his Master's Family to be allowed free despite his modest size. Peaches was just slightly larger but unfortunately the victim of a stricter household. She had just made a bold and daring escape through a carelessly abandoned open door and was about as giddy as is capable for a dog. A dog of any smaller size would be looking over its shoulder with all fear senses on alert but Peaches was stout enough to realize her relative safety in the free world. She could enjoy without reservation the euphoria of limitless exploration.

She was a housedog desperately trying to transcend to a higher level. A level enjoyed by the Labradors, Collies, Shepherds and Mutts of the free world. Had another Master taken her, she potentially had the ability to make the permanent leap to our world. As we stood a few paw paces apart, I felt no need to make an aggressive first impression. I had no desire to mount her for pleasure. I just kinda' minded my own business and went on sniffin' around the area. She only got about a dozen moments like this a year and I could sense somehow that I was infringing on her time- making her cautious. I was going to just leave the area but Hobie showed up and Peaches became uncomfortable and ran back home. Hobie just looked around a moment and strolled off to his own business. The Inn was a very short walk to the pits yet it was still out of the norm to see him in the brush. I can only assume he was making sure I didn't spook Peaches into not wanting to make the outing again whenever she could manage to get loose. It musta' been Hobie's sixth sense channeling voodoo shtick that kept me from jumpin' on the hound and mountin' her.

So anyway, back to Saturday morning. I got some food in me but I didn't bother to lick the bowl clean. I just couldn't stomach it. Hopefully, Master Mother will wash out the dish before she dumps another mound of Alpo in there. I found the first available human, Grandpa, and made it evident I wanted to go outside. He obliged. I couldn't have been out the door more than couple minutes when some mother nailed me in the head with a stick. I don't mean the derogatory slang "mother" but a mother. I was just cleaning up some crusted chocolate off her "little one's" face and she whacked me good. Well doggie hell, I had to get that damn day old Alpo taste outta' my mouth.

Little incidents like that just gets me thinking- now that I can. Why is this mother giving her child chocolate first thing in the morning? Why is the child saving perfectly good chocolate on his face for later? Why can't the mother be happy I cleaned up her child? Why is there always a stick around when necessary? I've been ranting this revelation stuff for a while now and these little random contemplations are starting to drive me nuts. How do you humans let it go? Aren't you curious? Don't you want to know who killed Kennedy- nah; many of you weren't alive then. What happened to Amelia Earhart- nah, she probably landed safely in Tibet. Why the dryer keeps eating one of your socks- yes, now that must drive you nuts. All the little common sense stuff that just seems to make no sense. Doesn't it build up after a while? Is there a point you just can't take it anymore, you just gotta' know?

Ah, I know how you handle it. You think your Heaven will answer all the little curiosities and trivial questions that accumulate over your lifetime. This is the grand comfort in which you live your lives. "No problem, someday I'll know it all", is what you think. We'll, I'm up here, and I don't know why flies always land on my nose when I'm trying to get an extra hours sleep in the morning. I don't know why tennis balls always seem to roll one paw nail too deep under the furniture. I don't know why my flea collar simply moves their infestation party from my neck to my ass.

Oh sure, I know the meaning of pi, a big doggie freakin' deal to that revelation. You think it's going to be all grand questions up here and that's great, wonderful and all that. Just don't expect God to tell you why your car keys kept disappearing. He won't tell ya' that because I believe it was

God that was hiding them. His way of saying he didn't appreciate his name being used in vein or maybe you spent too many Sunday mornings sleeping off a hangover.

I know. I know. You think I've got no grounds for a gripe. I'm learning all the important questions now I couldn't comprehend when I was on earth. The car chasing, the fetching, the need to roam free. But get whacked on the head with a stick a few times and you'll wonder why they keep falling from trees right in the spot they are needed to club me. These little questions add up and there doesn't seem to be any answers forthcoming.

Well, I had some doggie profanities to grumble at that "mother" of a mother then went on my way- mission accomplished. Though, facial salt and chocolate had cleared my pallet. I strolled down the sidewalk past the park and library but my eye was irritated. I had a small spec of bark in my eye and I tried to keep pace yet flip my front right paw up to my eye on the off steps. I was heading for the village water fountain but this walkin' and rubbin' routine made me look drunk and I clumsily bumped into a display table knocking over a ceramic piece a local cartoonist had on display. And I'll be go to doggie hell, the cartoonist picked up a stick that had fallen next to the table and smacked my ass. Well, fetch me a bone, dog, not again! Don't you wonder why?

Okay, I'll make sense of it if no answers are forth coming. I'll take the high road and believe that God is just helping me out here. God felt bad the "mother" of a mother got bark in my eye so he sent a little angel to snap off a tree branch which fell near another little angel who shoved me into the display table. The cartoonist picks up the divinely fallen branch and smacks me on the ass. The sting was so sharp it made my eyes water thus flushing the irritating debris from my eye. High road taken- Thanks God!

So this day was starting out rather ominous. To make matters worse there was no puddle next to spigot of the corner water fountain and I've got crusted Alpo and chocolate facial salt drying out my mouth. I coulda' headed back to the house but I decided to stay where the action was.

Artists and vendors were lined up all along the sidewalks of the Congregational Church and Library while the competitive pictures to be judged were hanging along temporary fencing in Gaines Park. I weaved through the vendor area making a few attempts at stealin' a lick of refreshment sitting on the ground but everyone either had soda bottles or a thermos. I grudgingly headed back to Gaines Park where there was a snack trailer dispensing drinks.

A handful of cups laid littered around the garbage cans but there was barely a drop of soda or lemonade left to consume. I lapped up what I could with my head down deep in the cups. When I looked up, there was Master Mark. "You Hungry Dallas" he asked, and tossed me some popcorn. If I could talk I woulda' said, "No, I'm freakin' thirsty, but thanks for the free chow... and where's your gangly mutt?" He tossed about a dozen butter drenched pieces on the ground which I snagged one at a time. As I headed for the last piece Sugar butted in and took it. I should have known the gangly mutt wasn't far off. It was just one piece of popcorn but I don't have to share one piece of garbage scrap with anyone. This is doggie etiquette and it's well understood I don't have to play well with others.

I mighta' started something right then and there but I noticed a stick lying nearby and I'd gotten whacked enough for one morning. Coulda' been a sign to let things go. Nonetheless, as Sugar headed into the park I followed him, hoping he'd do something else to piss me off. Not that I needed any instigation- I'm a dog. I coulda' pounced on him, pissed on a fire hydrant, stole a hot dog and been well within my behavioral norm as a species.

Sugar stayed a couple lengths in front of me sniffin' along the contour of the temporary fencing. The fence was annually stored in a dank utility shed and the consistency of its scent was worth investigating. He didn't seem to mind me trailing him and truth be told, I actually felt a bit safer hangin' near him should General or Laddie show up. We often weren't adversarial in each others presence but that popcorn stealin' thing was still sticking with me. Kinda' baiting me to look for another instance of annoyance. I definitely caught the fascination of the fences scent and how out of place it was. Like Sugar, I kept my nose down to trail it through the park. A short time later, a meager, insignificant breeze eased through the park but its affect on us both was instantaneous.

Sugar and I went nose up in synchronous motion and turned to the park center to witness an intimidating sight. A pair of horses had made the trip from a local farm to the delight of numerous onlookers and curiosity of two conspicuous dogs. I'd seen a horse go by my window on occasion but never while I was loose. The two deep brown studs were mounted by their local owners and surprisingly gentle to the touchy feely humans for such large beasts. Unlike a cow, which we could run circles around, these horses oozed strength and power and Sugar and myself were no less gazed than the hoards of humans in their presence. The odor alone from the horses had us practically standing in line waiting to get a close up sniff. Our reputation for dog lovin' chaos musta' preceded us because a few in the crowd did their best the nudge us away with a knee to the head.

We had no intention of making bad with these horses-what could we possibly do? Before that question could be answered the owners directed the crowd away and the horses turned tail and started towards the road. But not before one of them dropped a monster load dispersing the crowd in pungent disgust. Sugar and I just kinda' looked at each other- ya know, that hmmm look. Maybe because we're dogs and we're attracted to manure. Maybe because those horses stole a bit too much interest away from us. Either way, we both were thinkin' the same thing- lets roll in the crap!

We both ran to the pile and snarled at each other trying to secure the first dip. I hadn't forgotten about him stealing my last piece of popcorn so I gave him the ole' growl and shove then rolled my back through the fresh dung.

Okay, I've tried to call it a few different terms to be creative in my descriptions but screw that, it's horseshit and I was bathing in it to the stone-stiff faces of bystanders. I wiggled back and forth with my legs in the air getting the horse shit deep in my fur then I rolled off. Sugar just dove in head first kinda' slidin' across his belly then took one big roll for a more dispersed coverage.

The smell was just glorious to us both. It was fresh and sweet, conjuring up a summer's day in the country. The coverage was thick and there's the primitive odd sense of security knowing you've masked your natural odor from predators. It just brightened our mood and we ran through the park like best pals with the crowds parting a red carpet path. We were truly refreshed and acting pesky. Little girls dresses, argyle socks, bell bottom jeans- all stained with horseshit as we approached people to share our enthusiasm. Once we circled the park we headed towards the snack trailer to look for some liquid. As we stood there panting, food sales dropped off as if someone had opened up an outhouse door. The human groans and gagging were beginning to become noticeable to us both but it was nothing we could comprehend. We just sensed we weren't wanted. Especially when a snack trailer worker came jousting at us with a broom. By now I had gotten horseshit in my mouth and I was really thirsty. Sugar followed me back up town towards the water fountain. We didn't get very far when some friendly little boy left his mother's side, ran at Sugar and gave him a big hug. The boy was now covered in horseshit and Sugar was kind enough to give him a tongue washing in return.

Well, the mother went ape in front of everyone and acted like her boy had been assaulted. No one really had been paying attention at this point but her ranting made us appear to be more dangerous than we were. A group of bystanders had become concerned Sugar had hurt this boy and chased us off the sidewalks to the grass of the Congregational Church park. Now keep in mind, I was headed straight for the water fountain but these people chased us off my route and well, it was becoming apparent that maybe this horse shit on me was causin' some trouble.

You know, you can't have an art show without someone making country quilts. No doubt the hours and hours of heart and soul and labor it takes to sew each patch makes them much coveted. Most were displayed on a vendor table but a customer had laid one out to see the pattern in all its intensive labor. So it's sprawled out on the grass and I'm sensing I gotta' get this horse shit off me and before I know it I'm paw deep in the middle of this quilt. Screams worse than the little boys mother are coming from all directions and I'm really, really, concerned this horseshit is an issue so I drop and roll around on this quilt to the horror of the vendor and buyer. The vendor begins to charge at me but Sugar follows right behind and does the exact same thing. We spread so much horse shit on this heart felt mosaic that I'm sure plants were already beginning to grow when we rolled off and ran to the fountain. The whole village is in an uproar now and to make matters worse there's still no excess water to drink.

At this point Sugar and I decide to split up. Sugar heads down South Main Street towards home and I cross the street towards Quinn's market. I stop at the other side to look back and I can see glares and dismay from many in the park so I lift my leg, piss on a crate of apples and head for home. Doggie self-promotion to the end!

I don't know where the family went but I waited out back all afternoon. I just wanted to go inside and get a drink. Being a dog I'm not always thinkin' ahead and I spent a good hour of my day barking at a rock in the yard. I don't know why I do that when I'm so feakin' thirsty but it's just my therapy, you know. The park had cleared and by late afternoon when Master Tom came up the driveway on his bike, now a more adult ten speed, I'm thinkin' finally I can get inside and get some water. Well, he took one whiff of me and my dried horseshit and ran tail in the house.

I was bone raging angry now. I wanted to just go inside as bad as I wanted a drink. He came out minutes later after changing his clothes and turned on the water spigot to the hose. Yes, some water! He hosed me down good to my quenched delight for a solid five minutes. Now I was feeling a bit hungry and just wanted a quick snack and rest in the cool of the house. No doing, he wasn't going to allow a formerly horse shit dog all wet in the house. He went back inside leaving me out to dry. I was pissed.

Now, I'm not going to blame my upcoming actions solely on being shut out of the house. In truth, there is no blame to place. I'm a dog, instinctive, animal, primal. I don't need to defend myself but I understand how you humans see certain helpless creatures and maybe you expect more from an enlightened domesticated go-getter like myself. Be fair though, as I explain. I was a bit hungry and in this new century you don't seem to have too much of a problem with hunting as long as it's not solely for sport but for food as well. So my hunger completely justifies... Ah, who am I kiddin', I was angry and I don't give a poodle's ass what you think.

I'm wet. My stomach's grumbling. I'm ornery. I feel mean. I also see a curious sight. Two young girls seem to be coddling around something in the park. It was just the two of them sitting in the large void between the rows of empty temporary fencing. All the people who were aghast at our earlier antics were gone so I decided it was safe to make a friendly saunter to their location. The moment I crossed the road they saw me coming and became awfully panicked and guarded. So panicked that they didn't know what to do with whatever had caught their interest. A few steps into the park I could see what all the fuss was about.

A bird's nest had fallen from a tree. Two eggs were intact and assumably unharmed. There also was a freshly hatched chick which had warmed the hearts of the young girls. Yeah, yeah, it was probably the cutest little thing they'd ever seen but unfortunately being cute and meek never spared an animal in the wild. Those poor young girls, they couldn't have been more than 12 years old. Probably were still sleeping with their favorite doll and dressing their Barbies and caring for their pet bunny rabbits. They were just doing what comes natural to them- loving and fawning over an innocent displaced creature. And I was only going to do what comes natural to me.

They tried to lift the nest but it had become splintered from the fall and they were concerned the eggs would roll out. The eggs and the chick were also too fragile for their unskilled hands to scoop to safety. I would also presume the chick may still have been a bit too gooey for their timid constitution. All they could do is yell at me like I was their pesky little brother and hope I understood the rage in their tone and the tears in their eyes. I didn't.

It's curious how distinctive instinct can be. I suppose domestication has helped somewhat in that regard. If they'd been holding a sandwich I woulda' ran up and begged for some morsels. In the olden early days when I was supposedly some wolf type beast I woulda' killed for a ham sandwich on rye. The same holds true for our current day bears and beasts of the wild. Domestication seems to have soothed our savage nature towards processed and generally dead foods. I doubt I even woulda' attacked if they had been protecting roadkill.

As misfortunes would have it, they were mothering a live creature that falls low on our food chain and high on our ideal kill chain. We watch those birds, like the crow, fly and drift high above our slobbering fat tongues. So free. So unattainable. So desirable. Now one lay helpless in it's crib, well within my sights. I'm not going to mince scruples over the fact that it's freshly born and can't fly. That's not my problem. I'm only responding to what I'm capable of and that's my instinct to finally get one of those high flyin' worm-eaters in my teeth. The thrill of the chase is of no interest to me, I just want a prize to help absorb some of my pent up anger.

It was a full on charge. I doubt any adult or child would have boldly stood their protective ground. Whether I'm killing an ant or a deer, at my current state the vicious growls and fang exposed frothing is a prerequisite. The girls maybe had three seconds to think they could dissuade me with screams and cries but I was a mad predator knowing there was no doubt to the outcome of my kill. One of the girls made a last second attempt to at least salvage one of the eggs and it's too bad she failed because I didn't care about the eggs.

I was airborne and drove my paws down on the defenseless. I may have crushed the chick to death, I don't know, but its body was limp and lifeless within seconds of entering my jaws. It's torso and feet were dangling as I writhed my head back and forth. My exuberance trampled both eggs exterminating the close to completed life which had laid dormant inside. The nest was now held together by the sticky embryonic fluids of the unborn. The kill tasted sweet to me and though I didn't swallow my prey I savored the variety of flavors that climbed from my tongue to my nose. I was damn happy Master Tom didn't let me inside.

The same couldn't be said for the two inconsolable bystanders. The young girls were sobbing uncontrollably and cursing me beyond their years. Well maybe not beyond their years for this century but surely the pre cable TV post "Leave It To Beaver" era.

I really didn't notice their despair being in my delight but I can honestly say now I wish it never happened. No, I'm still a cad up here so I'm not regretful due to their trauma- they got over it. We'll, one girl had to get some therapy, but really, she's fine now. My regret is in the pain it eventually caused- to myself.

If there's sobbing little kids then sure as a stick falls conspicuously in my perimeter, Laddie is soon to appear. And oh goody, It's Scamp too! Yes, there they were, Sherburne's own "Justice League" arriving right on cue to thwart the evil villainous scum. But I didn't do anything wrong, I just did what I do. What both Laddie and Scamp would do if they came across some helpless prey. I doubt they knew or even cared that I mowed down on some helpless chick. The fact is that some little innocents were very upset and I was the presumed perpetrator. They also had it fresh in their minds what they perceived as my cowardly exit in General's presence the previous day. This was more than enough fuel to stoke their rage at me.

Scamp really took the lead on this one and came charging at me immediately upon sight. Laddie wasn't too limber from his scuffle with Master George's boot the day earlier. I doubt he wanted to fight that day but we animals do what we do and damn the weather or sickness or injury. Besides, these little girls were devastated and his duty was clear. He dragged behind Scamp towards my position.

Scamp intruded on my spot and laced me up and down with some ferocious verbal abuse. I snarled back with my eyes wide and nostrils flaring. Problem is, I didn't want to drop my bird. Its carcass hung out the side of my mouth like a wet cigar and I'd rather been the distinguished gentleman enjoying a finer moment than slugging it out with Scamp and dad. I turned and headed to the back of the park but Scamp jumped me. His jaws sunk into my back with a lucky first lunge and the tearing of my flesh caused me to clamp down on my little dead birdie severing it's head from it's body. The little head got caught in my throat and I gagged dangerously as it lodged deep in my windpipe. I couldn't clear it and I struggled for air while Scamp continued carving up my back. It was the excruciating pain of his third jaw-tearing grip that finally forced the birdie's head out as I writhed aloud.

I was still trying to get a full lung of air in me when I literally tore myself away from Scamp and managed to turn and face him. I fought back hard as we jousted for position but Laddie was soon upon me forcing me to defend myself against two foes. It was apparent a limp Laddie wasn't a concern to my physical well being but the mere distraction of accounting for the two of them made any offense on my part ineffective. The situation was that I was trapped deep in the park, bloody and outnumbered. The pain hadn't settled in yet and I set my mind to making a bold aggressive thrust to break through their entrapment.

My plan was irrelevant, Scamp just continued to attack and Laddie made every effort to push me around while Scamp clawed and gouged me. I fought back valiantly but the level of danger to myself was becoming critical. Saliva and dirt were streaming into my wounds as the three of us wrestled for position. Scamp was hounding me with great speed and agility while every movement away from his attack was blocked by Laddie and his lame hip. It was Scamp's aggression that finally gave me the light of day. As a moment of separation between us was closed down by

Laddie's positioning, Scamp burst at me forcing me back into Laddie. His injured hip couldn't support the impact we both put upon him and we all collapsed to the ground. I rolled over the top of Laddie while Scamp got caught up with his father. It was the split second I needed to break away from the situation. I ran towards home while Scamp, satisfied in his effort, stayed behind to assist his father. The young girls threw sticks at me as I ran past them and Master Tom who had witnessed it all from the bay window was at the front doors to let me in.

I retreated to a corner of the playroom and laid on the cool linoleum for the rest of the early evening. I couldn't rest very well. The fur on my back had covered up the severity of my wounds but underneath it looked as if a chain saw had hacked away at me. Later that evening I got up for some toilet water and heard the usual artificial sounds which came from the den. Over the years I could often relax to the continuous and soothing blips that came from the television. The simple beauty of "Pong" and its back and forth mono-toned sedative nature worked like a hot toddy for my tense doggie muscles. I ached into the den and collapsed in a corner. Unfortunately, life's simple pleasures had now been super charged. The old standard was obsolete and the doggie ear grating, unsettling blips of "Atari" were all the rage now. How could I be expected to relax when the damn blip bounces all over creation and then that one target hunting game with that fake duck quacking drove me straight to the doggie sanitarium. I retreated back in pain to the cool of the playroom floor and suffered through the rest of the night.

Anyway, even though I couldn't lick my wounds I gutted it out as animals do. Being summer everyone in the house was pretty busy and not a lot of attention was coming my way. A few more days passed with no attention paid to my wounds. However, on the third day after the fight I woke up to some real tender pain issues. You know, we dogs don't get anxiety over these things, we cope and move-on because we quite frankly don't know what to do about it. I just knew no one was going to touch my back lest he lose his arm. I strolled by Master Tom as I got up and he just freaked out screamin' for Master Mother to attend to me. My wounds which had been concealed under my matted fur were now infected and swollen open with puss and mucus. They both were startled and did the anxiety thing for me. It was quite nasty and disgusting from what I'm recalling. Immediate plans were made to take me to the vets and I recall the urgent nature causing some pretty unsteady driving which occasionally jostled my balance smacking my back against the back seat door- OUCH!!!

Sterile environments seem to bring upon the same uncomfortable tensions in all creatures of heightened awareness. Try as they might to put a picture of a sunny rainbow on the walls or color the room in calming tones it's a half-hearted and surprisingly ignorant choice of decor. Shag carpets, flowing floral drapery and a few lazy boy recliners would go along way in making everyone a bit calmer. Yeah, I know, my idea is a germ trap but so wasn't my puss oozing back at the moment- what harm could carpeting do. Back in my day everything was so clinical looking- the desks, the chairs, the filing cabinets. If it can be hosed down and cleansed without being ruined then it's an anxiety trap not a germ trap.

I'd been to the vet's before for shots and minor stuff. It's ridiculous, the waiting. Dogs don't wait in unfamiliar environments. With our heightened senses, we're aware of all the tensions around us. You put us in a room with a group of worried Masters and the issues of the other leashed creatures- the tension is suffocating. How relaxed can I be with cats and rabbits in the same visual space? Then I'm forced to sit there and sort out all the smells from ammonia to urine to rubbing alcohol to farm stench. We were there a good hour and you can begin to understand the effects it has on us. I know it's the same for humans too but isn't there a better way. Pump some trace sedatives through the ventilation system or something.

The advantage of being a dog is that most of the procedures like shots and stitches are minor annoyances. The attention from the vet is kinda' nice. I could deal with all the procedures if you people around me would just calm down and relax. With all your worry you made me feel like he was planning on killing me or something- how sadly clairvoyant. The assistant shaved my upper back and all the infected wounds were irrigated, medicated and stitched up.

How freakin' weird, the cold air on my back, the tightness of my stitched skin. All annoyingly unnatural but most annoying of all was my natural drive to cleanse my own wounds and not being able to access them. I spent a good week experiencing new sensations of the modern sparse haired homosapien. I often wonder if the evolution of the dog will be as dramatic. Scant patches of hair styled over exposed skin. Having two legs on the ground during urination instead of three. And of course, clothing for our newfound humility. Sounds like a good movie- "Planet Of The Dogs."

I really wonder about this stuff. We've come so far in this small little village and it seems by the end of the 1970's we'd peaked as a species. We'd had all the freedom yet because we didn't need to hunt or scavenge for shelter it seems maybe our free time was working against us. Instead of runnin' and fetchin' and playin' in pure evolved bliss we had become territorial and adversarial. Always looking over our shoulders. Always guarded even in our most frolicking adventures. The scars were adding up as well. Scooter lost a leg, Laddie's hip was kicked in and arthritic and now my shaved back was a sewn up infection factory.

We were puppies no more. Our Masters were becoming man-childs. The free-spirited, unbridled enthusiasm and natural way of life embodied by the baby boomer era was now giving way to order, lawyers and technology. The global community was dictating our community. You wonder why we're concerned with these petty human issues? It all effects us. We didn't know it then but it's that curve in the flow of life I mentioned at the opening.

Man incites dog in Tucson. Dog bites man. Lawyer sues city. Judges blame lawmakers. Insurance companies panic. Small Town USA tightens its belt. Oh, I guess we're to blame a little. With all the dog lovin' chaos we've instigated around here it's no wonder all the kings men start worrying their relaxed little town is too lax. But what about the other shoe. It used to be that a dog was the funnest and most interactive entertainment a boy of any age needed. But now the onslaught for a parent's dollar and Master's constant attention will hit a new peak. More TV channels, more commercials. Cooler and faster blips. Smarter and smarter chips. I remember when kick the can or tossing the ball required some skill in navigating around the pesky dog. I was part of the game.

A new decade was upon us yet still not enough technology to allow me to jump in the TV screen and chase that dot-munching ball. Anyway, there aren't earplugs big enough to allow me to exist in that world. The odorless, one-dimensional, brain-sucking boxes of the digital man was out to stop our evolution in its tracks. Yet we carried merrily on 'til the arthritic end.

Revelation 10

Dogs are wolves in sheep's clothing

The collision was violent. Invoked by a force of such strength and speed that was completely out of control. The perpetrator, in such a hurry to get to a destination that any weak and unfortunate creature in its path would fail to register- until impact.

The victim's brain was underdeveloped to anticipate this fate. No matter how many times this passage was traversed successfully, it only takes that one incident to rock some hard reality into the innocent victim's world. The careless and unconcerned perpetrator would barely be impeded as the helpless creature was tossed airborne to a painful landing. A hit and run is something us dogs must learn to avoid or live through as best we can. This, however, was my first, yet, unfortunately the residual pain wouldn't be enough to keep it from happening again in the future.

I couldn't help it. I loved Milkbone brand dog biscuits. Master Mother would toss them across the linoleum and in my hyper state I'd struggle for several seconds to secure the treat as it slid away from me time-after-time. Once it was trapped in a corner I could flip it up and snatch it in my salivating jaws and I'd barrel outta' control through the dining room to the living room.

An innocent two-year-old toddler still green to this world, short of balance and anticipation, was no match for a grown dog in hyper-happy mode. As she made her way babbling through the dining room she met my charge and I tossed her aside like a dead flea enroute to the living room. I never stopped to look behind. I paid no matter to the smack on my head. I never considered that Nat wasn't strong

Tom Mody

enough to brush herself off and carry on. I just wanted to get to my slab of slate near the fireplace and chow down. Oh, I guess I wasn't clear- I was the careless and unconcerned perpetrator.

Nat landed somewhere under a dining room chair, maybe with a bruise or two but hurt and startled enough to cry in a psychologically immobilized state. Master Mother ran to her aid and pulled her from the wreckage- so to speak. Master Tom was sitting in the living room recliner quite amused at the convergence. In the past, Nat seemed to enjoy the rough play as Lew and Master Tom use to call her across the room back and forth tripping her up at every pass. She'd fall flat on her face and get back up laughing only to be duped again. So, I wasn't concerned for her well being based on what I'd previously witnessed.

Okay, let's be honest, I didn't give a Nat's ass about anything other than getting to my destination as fast as possible and chompin' my Milkbone brand dog biscuit. Fortunately, some time was needed to calm her down and I could enjoy my treat in relative peace. There were but a few crumbs left when Master Mother entered the living room with a yardstick. She usually was more enlightened to doggie discipline and chose to spare the rod and use the rolled up paper as a scare tactic, swatting it inches from my nose.

I've gotta' say, I love you doggie psychologists out there spewing intellect at the complex world of animal rationality and behavior. It had saved my ass a number of times. Maybe your chatter works well on the meek world of poodles as their hair is trimmed and their balls snipped but let me tell ya', a wad of paper struck by my face a few times makes its point just fine. Point being, after a few times it tells me you're not gonna' hit me when I piss on your doggie training book. Master Mother took three good "real" whacks at my ass. Only one landed as I bolted outta' her path with knowledge and fear that I was bad. Pundits are true to the fact that this type of "real" punishment may be ineffective if I was oblivious to what I'd done, and that's often the case. I kinda' had a clue though that the blur in my memory of Nat lifting off the ground and the small knot in my head were related enough to Master Mother's rage.

I never did come to a more subdued charge when I had a Milkbone brand dog biscuit in my clutches. I get too excited over treats. Hyper-happy as I called it. I did learn the few other times I sent Nat airborne to not stop and enjoy my bone but to find the furthest secluded corner and quickly chow what I could. After a while it became a non-issue as she simply outgrew the potential for further hit and runs.

There seemed to be a number of hit and run type activities lately in the village perpetrated by Master Tom and his peers. Keeping up with the newly-anointed teenager was now becoming a day and night chore. His freedom had become very nocturnal as the village kids tested the borders of clean fun. The pace of their bikes and boundless enthusiasm made it difficult for me to chase them around safely.

Beaner's arsenal of fireworks had been mostly limited to a PG rating of blowing up inanimate objects and a few insignificant and dispensable creatures of God. The problem was a frog couldn't chase you with its guts blown out. They wanted to act then have something react. To up the ante, they tested a few locations to find an "R" rated antagonist. If there was an open house window or old fogie driving too slow, they'd blast a bottle rocket or some accelerated charge to try and enrage the unsuspecting goat.

One night they managed to get chased clear into the creek behind the old band room by a home-owner, shot gun in hand, who had simply gotten fed up with packs of firecrackers detonating under his window. Another night they miscalculated and antagonized one of the meanest bastards in town as he sped by in his Trans Am. I had to keep my distance when these antics were going on because should they get bored I could be the only antagonist in their sights. Master Tom was amongst the youngest in the group so he'd have no say in Beaner or Oggy turning their bored eyes to me.

I happened to be ahead of the group which had congregated on the corner of Union and Chapel Streets.

When that Trans Am approached something was detonated and the boys dispersed as the car came to a screeching halt and hit reverse towards the intersection. With no perpetrators in sight he continued in my direction and turned into the old middle school driveway. They all knew the guy they pissed off had no reservations in beating them up and a few of the boys like Captain and Cappy were smart and headed into their house which was just a few yards away from the intersection. Some of the others, including Master Tom, assumed the danger had passed and returned to the intersection. But I saw headlights deep into the school lot.

I charged towards the boys quite frankly scared of the metal beast due to the startling sounds and smells of full-on screeching tires. Seconds later the Trans Am burst out the school driveway and rounded the corner. All the boys freaked and scattered again. I followed Master Tom as he headed for Captain's house. The front porch wouldn't be cover enough for him. He ran down the back driveway and leaped upon the stone stoop only to forget about the tin doors to the cellar which lay flat across the stoop corner. His full weight came down on the flimsy metal and he collapsed through, fortunately grasping the outer rim and hanging by his fingers. It was a radiant forceful sound and Captain's whole family rushed to the back door as if something had crashed into their house. Master Tom sheepishly looked up, dangling in the cellar passage and was assisted out by Captain and his father, the latter who didn't seem amused. As I peered up I was able to get a live peek at the mangly poodles Tago and Pierre shaking in the arms of the two Sister Masters from the disturbance. Their startled unsettledness seemed to make Master Tom's embarrassment worthwhile to me.

When I wasn't keeping my distance from the bored guys with explosives, I was tirelessly chasing bikes by the glow of streetlights and the dim lamps of back yards. Ditch was the game and most of the village was the playing field. At night the boys would split up into teams and play a high-speed version of tag. There were outer borders in the village but nothing was off limits inside those borders as long as you stayed on your bike. Streets, parking lots, creeks, back yards-all in play. A lifetime of experience was your guide as you navigated at break neck speeds through dark terrain. Knowledge of which yards had fence borders, which driveways had potholes and exactly how fast you could transact a candy bar purchase at the convenient store before the other team hit mid village were important factors. In some of the great pursuits there was generally no time to stop at intersections and check for traffic. You had a split second to check for headlights before the decision was made to round a corner.

As many of us dogs were so commonly seen running free in the village, it was wondered how we never got waxed more often. I find that observation very hypocritical as many of your very children were playing Russian roulette on bikes. I just think we're due more credit for our intellect and intuition than to simply deduct we were lucky. Call it luck or an advantage at reaching this evolutionary peak; we naturally still had to chase our Masters in this dangerous pursuit. One dog who came close to paying the price for that loyalty was a south side dog named Sam.

I haven't spoken of Sam to this point as I didn't really hang out in his territorial yards, and frankly, he was too well respected for my taste. He was also quite a few years older than me and for a time didn't tend to get caught up in all the other doggie chaos. Oh, we'd sniffed around each other on occasion casually making contact in the village but he seemed clear that I should just mind my own business. He'd probably had enough of Sugar's antics being situated in the same part of town and one ego-eager dog was enough.

Sam came across as your average good dog. He didn't try to promote his noble stature like Laddie. And though he wouldn't be easily bullied by General, he preferred to avoid the confrontation, secure in his own skin. Outside his skin he was shaggier than myself though part black lab with a setter mix. He possessed a lot of the same qualities as his Master Jimmer- Strong, silent, amicable, and a closet juvenile. As Master Jimmer began to spend more time with the village kids on their nightly carousing, it was becoming clear that

Sam was not the straight-laced honor dog keeping his nose clean.

He came to Master Jimmer through a relative that was having trouble controlling the young pup. Sam looked exactly like a dog the Master Father owned as a boy and so they took him in despite his penchant for destroying neighbor's newspapers. He grew up to be the consummate family dog, accompanying his Master on fishing and small game hunting trips. Those enjoyable, quiet days walking railroad tracks and investigating the nearby swamps and waterways are boy/dog nirvana. The two sisters in the family loved him equally well and he did good by them as companion and protector. Without my heavenly revelations I'd almost feel guilty dragging him into our little circle of dog lovin' chaos but from what I know now, he fit right in.

Sam was more of a scrounge than one might have known. In fact, one family in the village could keep a clock by him showing up for meal scraps on a nightly basis. With all the stalkin' and humpin' goin' on now that many of us had fully matured to the urge, it was Sam who quietly had the knack of identifying many of the dogs in heat and inconspicuously camping out below the radar of other suitors and the dog owners. He notched a lot of village tail over the years and with all the posturing of us promotional types, it was Sam who actually had the warden's rap sheet and fines for his amorous transgression.

Sam's need for privacy in these pursuits was tested on a particular night. A few back yards away it wasn't often that the owners would let their golden haired lass, Brandi, out for "public domain." I guess that's my term for "fair game." It was getting past dusk and the teenage girls of the house were home alone with some friends in the yard enjoying what you call adult beverages. I mean, adult human beverages.

Under this influence or with a certain sick curiosity you often mistake us for guinea pigs. There's a few of you out there, don't bother raising your hand. I'm in Doggie Heaven so I know who you are. You think it's a real gas to give us special under-age privileges to your illegally-obtained beverage and see if we act as pathetic as you. We're dogs, we don't need alcohol to entice our fightin' and humpin' like some species. However, when forcefully tanked up, we'll puke just like you. Isn't that a revelation. What, you couldn't live without knowing that? You had to test it for yourself? You get all pissed off when we puke without your help, why is it so funny with your assistance?

So Brandi had a few nips of brandy and she's wandering all dopey around the yard. Sam waits quietly in a neighbor's yard hoping maybe she'll wander off or the kids will go away. After about a half an hour he gets his wish and they head inside for a refill or to make-out or whatever inebriated humans do. Brandi kinda' stumbles over to the edge of the driveway near to Sam's location. It's a circular driveway that can be entered from either side of the house but where Sam is lurking is away from the garage side and under little light except for the moon and glow from the streets.

For some dogs we prance around and sniff and show some dominance to our intent. Other times we spring from the bushes like savages. Actually, it's the latter that's the more evolved approach. You'd think the savage primal surprise mounting would be that of our brutal ancestors but really it's more of an enlightened realization. We've finally desocialized sex- at least when the female breed is smaller. You have to admit; it's not a lot of fun tryin' to woo your intended in dance when your loins are really achin'. With a smaller and weaker mate, the outcome is generally inevitable anyway so why waste time and energy- and in your case, money, buying beer after beer. Animals at a lower evolutionary state tend to need some mating rituals. Those can still be necessary, particularly when the female is large and bitchy. In hindsight, I can see the positive effect alcohol would have on easing the advance on these types. Still, I prefer to revel in our ability to move beyond rituals and make better use of our time.

I make this point to illustrate the oddity of Sam's approach. It was very human in the modern cad celebrity sense. He liked to slip under the radar of scrutiny yet was very casual and comfortable in just sauntering up to his intent and saying, hey puppy, we're going to do this now. He didn't leap all stiff crotched from the darkness. He didn't howl love songs or sniff around for an odor of permission. Sex was simply implied now that he was secure there would be no interruptions.

They'd become familiar before so he had no hesitation in making his way towards her. Brandi showed some curiosity herself but was a little too liquor-suppressed to exhibit any real preference either way. Sam basically nodded the equivalent of "hello" and headed for the rear, conscious to the gains of his patience. In his mind he administered a doggie self pat on the back.

In the secluded corner of Brandi's driveway his hind legs lifted and his front legs rose. However, he came down upon thin air. At his very moment of lift-off a group of boys on bikes and one tired dog, me, came barreling down the driveway. It startled Brandi out of her stupor and she ran towards the house before Sam even hit the ground.

I'd been following the boys clear across town, a group of five including Master Tom, Peaches Boy Master, Spazy and Brandi's Boy Master, Rett. Fortunately for me they weren't traveling too fast as they wanted to be cautious in avoiding being seen by the other group of boys on bikes. Otherwise I'd have to do what I often do which is wait near the village intersection for a group to pass by so I can tag along until a chase breaks out and I'm left in the dust. They made a rather brisk dash from the Legion intersection to Brandi's driveway having spotted some enemy activity near the intersection of Chapel and Union Street. I was panting hard when they came to rest at the back of the driveway. A few of the boys got off their bikes and went inside for a drink as the others posted a watch.

I was too tired to snarl at Brandi, which would be my usual action, when suddenly encountering a dog, but she quickly followed her Master inside. Sam apparently moved off into the brush unnoticed. I'm sure he was licking himself vigorously for some relief. Not so much for the self-pleasure but to help calm things down after such a close and frustrating encounter.

After a few minutes the boys came out, as did Brandi. The watch was clear and they cautiously headed up South Street towards the middle school grounds. I continued to tag along but we passed by Master Mark's and Sugar distracted me. I stayed behind and we postured a bit, you know, the usual snarl and sniff.

Brandi escorted them off the driveway but returned to the yard. She really wasn't suppose to be loose but fortunately the alcohol made her more subdued to not wander off. Sam possibly lucks out again. Still dopey, she walks back down the driveway as Sam peers for potential interruptions. Comfortable in their privacy he again approaches from the neighbor's yard. This time Brandi isn't so amicable. Typical women, right, you human males? Can you relate? Five minutes earlier it's okay but a little diversion, a little pondering and well, they're not in the mood. Poor human males, it works a little different in animal society.

Sam, who is normally so successful in picking the right moments where it's simple and easy for all involved to capitulate, is now forced to- well, be more forceful. He approaches her in his usual casual manner but she ignores him and walks further up the driveway. Sam takes a brisker stroll in her direction but she snarls back at him. She heads towards the grass of her yard but Sam cuts her off and gets a bit more insistent. She turns to head towards the house and he finally just jumps her. Annoyed, she doesn't bother to resist and lets nature take it's course. Unfortunately nature is halted again by boys on bikes.

This time they are in a flat out retreat and whiz by the two dogs deep into the back yard behind the garage. Sam tries to ignore them and continue but Brandi breaks away and rushes to follow them out back. I happened to have seen them seconds earlier pass by Sugar and myself so we followed them but as we arrived to Brandi's yard, all we saw is a pissed off Sam licking himself. With no one else to blame he immediately turns on us to get a little release- and no, I don't mean sexually.

Sam rose to an aggressive posture and bitterly snarled in our direction as he moved at us in guarded steps. Sugar and I mirror Sam in our response back. Eventually we build to full on barking and a series of vicious jabs and snips ensue. Concerned that Brandi is amidst a scuffle, her Girl Masters with friends in tow rush out of the house. They were quickly relieved that Brandi wasn't involved but then went into a full panic that they couldn't find her.

We were beginning to make quite a scene in the yard. It was tame by dogs of the wild standards as no flesh was torn or blood dripping. It was just a good aggressive, chaotic fracas between fun-lovin' and grumpy dogs. With the dog banter and the girls screamin', the hiding bicycle team and Brandi made their way out from behind the garage. Everyone joined in to try and separate our mess by throwin' balls or runnin' their bikes between us. We did our best to fight around the human effort but they did quickly make some progress. It was short lived however as no sooner did our barking cease than the second team of bikers, the "it" group, came rammin' up the driveway. From there everything went into chaos again.

The quiet teenagers who simply wanted to enjoy a cool evening of relaxed unsupervised drinking were now in the middle of a double war. Master Tom's gang split in all directions as they fumbled and bumbled to quickly get their wits and escape. Some of the older teenage boys at the small party intercepted the oncoming "it" group assuming there was going to be some kind of rumble, ignorant that it was just a simple game of tag. They managed to stop a couple of the boys but a few sped by them in pursuit of the closest adversary. We dogs just started barking again at all the hyper activity.

Everything was chaotic- it was great. Deep in the nearby yards you could hear the chases taking place as the "it" group was directing its bikers to the locations of those in retreat. The boys who were stopped were now allowed to continue pursuit and we dogs just kinda' jumped around waiting for the next bit of excitement to erupt. Seconds later, as we looked down the driveway, Abby had escaped the confines of the yards and zoomed by Brandi's driveway with Oggy and Jimmer in pursuit. That looked like it could have yielded some chaos so we charged to the road but only in time to see the faint wheels of Master Jimmer burning up South Street. They were out of our reach but Sam headed into the road anyway to be sure.

Screechin' burnin' tires just about scared Sugar and myself outta' our skin. And it just about knocked Sam outta' his. Sam's shoulder met the bumper of a squat sized blue Pinto spinning sideways in full-on brake. The impact was still forceful enough to send him two full rolls onto the curb. That squat of a car never did come to a full stop and continued on while its hit and run victim got back on his three good legs immediately. In a total state of shock, Sam just whimpered and stumbled in small circles for about a minute with his right front leg dangling limp. Once some sense of cognitive brain function was restored he made an extremely painful charge for home. Once again, Sugar and myself were left to ponder the gruesome fate of a fellow brethren maimed before our eyes. It does leave an impression.

I followed Sugar to his home on South Street and we were confused to see Abby sprawled on the far end of the street with his bike laying near by. As we approached him he slowly sat up and had the same look in his eyes as Sam did moments earlier. Apparently Oggy and Jimmer caught up with him in their own version of hit and run. We immediately turned around and headed back towards Sugar's house. Maybe because we'd just seen enough chaos for one night or maybe intuitively we knew Abby was now "it."

A few days later I happened to be heading down South Main Street when the ole' brain chemicals nearly had a human response breakthrough. Sam approached from his driveway and snarled a bit at me. He had a cumbersome cast on his bone shattered front leg. He was in no condition to berate me with threats and I paid him no attention. I kept an eye on him though as he backed off towards a flower bed and lifted his leg to piss. Because of the weight of his cast his whole balance was off and he fell right over into the flowerbed. It took him a moment to gather himself but I'll tell ya', inside both of us were sittin' on the edge of human emotions.

In my way, I was laughin' my ass off and in his way he was embarrassed as all doggie hell. I could feel it in my head, my brain screamin' "this is funny, do you get it." It kinda' tickled. It caused the muscles in my face to tighten and my gut to vibrate. No, I didn't understand it at my doggie level of earthly comprehension but I found myself recalling the incident throughout the day and having the same physical responses.

Sam and I shared an experience together at that moment. It didn't bring us closer together or make us buddies but it does speak volumes about the emotion of laughter you humans enjoy. Maybe we tapped into that extra one percent of brain usage I spoke of earlier. We were able to make more of the incident's strange sensation, to recall it and it would disarm us at many future encounters. It helped that Sam and I didn't run into each other too often and though we had some minor skirmishes in the past, the chemical imprint of our one comical incident was by far the stronger impression. Sugar and I had created far too many snarlin' impressionable moments to let one incident like that change our behavior towards each other. But then again, we didn't need that moment, we learned over time to tolerate each other.

I have a hard time understanding the tolerances of the multi-dog household. Coexisting with another dog or any other animal doesn't seem evolved to me. You humans love harmony. The birds singin', the squirrels playin, the butterflies flutterin'. You want it all to exist in concert without conflict. You particularly love the concept of a dog and a cat tolerating each other as one with the family. To me that's not evolution- that's suppression. Your logic would say it's moving more towards the human state of community but most of us animals had that. My ancestors ran in packs and had social orders. I'm not looking for a group hug. I don't consider perfect manners and temperament to be the ultimate state of evolution. I don't consider coexistence with all of nature as my goal. Comfortable freedom is my goal. Freedom without the days of starvation and the cold damp caves and the freakin' ticks. Freedom yet having a bond to a place and a creature I can trust- my Master.

I guess my real problem is the concept of sharing a Master, a legacy and all the family love and free food. Yet there are large numbers of animals coexisting in households all over the world. More so in this new century than ever before. But as I've so earnestly stated with clear vision from above, our evolution as a species reached a peak during my lifetime only to be halted by lawmakers and societal etiquettes of humans. As we ran free, safe from vicious, fang-toothed predators and soup-starved Asians and imprinted a lasting impression on our time without risk of fine or confinement, we peaked. When we share our Master with other creatures it divides our legacy. We're expected to expend energy and a good portion of our learning curve by getting along rather than promoting our agendas.

Maybe if I could share the moments more. If I could laugh or love in a chemical bath of brain-secreting emotions I could comprehend your concept of evolved harmony. What ever it is that Sam and I experienced did smooth over our rough doggie demeanors towards each other. But even here in Doggie Heaven where I can now grasp the concepts of human complexities, I have very little want for them. As was my attitude on earth, so it is even greater in Doggie Heaven. I never wanted to kiss and make-up. I never wanted to share and share alike. I never wanted to do unto others- blah, blah, blah, ruff, ruff, ruff. I had what I wanted during the best time to have it.

And I most certainly never wanted egg on my face. But that's what I got during Halloween of 1980. Halloween in downtown Sherburne was something I could really appreciate. There was bedlam, hooliganism and chaos. There was revelry, camaraderie and treachery. There was a big mess. As I look upon life in this new century, I know I was livin' at the best possible time because these days there's no way in doggie hell, human hell or any other unfortunate species hell, that kind of controlled environment war would be tolerated.

For the early evening hours Grandpa and I would eagerly greet the costumed youths looking for some freebies. The doorbell would ring and I'd jump up again and again, tail waggin' and overly-hyped at the constant flow of new visitors. I'd stick my nose in the littlest ones bag and bark at certain costumes that would spook me. I especially hated those flimsy plastic facial facade masks. I didn't get it. The whole body would have normal movement but the face was just ill looking and total rigor mortis- (cool word!). The head would just bob down at you and mumbled slurs would emanate from their dead faces. Very spooky indeed!

Once dusk passed you could feel a tension starting to move across the breeze. I usually got let outside after all the young kids did their beggin' so I wouldn't scare them- isn't that ironic. Like the zombie nations of your classic horror movies, bodies would get summoned to town. You could look up the streets and see the flow of teenagers descending upon the village square. Every so often screeching tires would round a corner and drop a payload of rotten tomatoes on anyone in open view. The sidewalks were marked with streams of shaving cream and toilet paper as if a directional trail for the possessed to follow into the pit- that being the village center. Some dark influence must have determined the gang groupings as equal numbers grew at the corner monument and across the street at the inn. Hobie was usually dug in below the patio near the garbage bins to avoid the edible mortars.

I don't know how it was decided who would throw the first egg or even what provocation would signal the onslaught but it's fair to say if you get two large gangs of humans to congregate on opposite sides of the street, some type of riotous confrontation will take place. And so it would begin, hoards of 20, 30, even 50 juveniles per side in a village-wide food fight that could feed a small nation. At first it was more celebratory to the season. Kinda' freewheelin' like a mud slingin' battle. Some brave combatants would venture into the street amidst the fire to get a more effective shot at the opposition only to be repelled back by the hoard. Just kids enjoying their loose reins. Ultimately, as the evening grew on, the climate got more personal- more intent to injury. The projectiles stopped being of the "splat" variety and more the "thud" type. Rocks, bottles, bruises and blood would mare the situation and eventually concerned adult humans would try to intervene but it really wouldn't end until all the rotted farm picked edibles were expended.

Most village dogs of any free relevance would also descend upon the village. We love riotous hoards. We love frantic excitement and chaotic stimulus. We also love the fresh reek of the village as the rotted edibles dampen the dog food aroma. The tension in the air was very high which might explain how, on that night, we hung out around each other as kinda' our own gang. We were off the outskirts of the skirmish in the area of the library. We just didn't know how to stick our noses into the middle of the fray. Teenage boys can be mean and you never knew when they would turn on you and pelt you just for fun. And it wasn't always the "splat" kind but the "thud" kind as well.

When one of us would wander close to the hoard the others would stop sniffin' in the bushes or lickin' themselves and ease on over as well. Feeling safe in a group but wanting so desperately to be a part of the riotous energy- negative as it may be. Something would scare us back and we'd retreat to watching and wandering at our own safe distance. It was definitely uncharacteristic of us to be so timid. As much as we loved the chaos it was uncomfortable to feel it turn ugly.

Even Laddie was uncomfortable to go it alone. He'd been a bit timid as of late. The hip that Master George injured had become very arthritic and age was catching up to him. This had made him a bit more amicable, at least when I'd confronted him. He was concerned about Scamp's safety as our free village was becoming more dangerous due to General's vicious nature. The great protector could still escort the average children's choir to church with the best of the doggie do-gooders but it was Scamp who had shed his father's shadow in the world of animal survival and was leading the charges. His independence was evidenced by his absence from the Halloween village mayhem. He preferred to take on some personal business- hubba, hubba!

Laddie, by his regressed presence, was making allies- understanding that he was no longer strong enough to be that balance between the dogs of promotion and the dog of violence. Though uncomfortable having to make a choice, his instincts and intuition were pure enough to know that safety can best be achieved in packs. He knew that Scamp was too eager for his own good. Laddie was just as impulsive as a youth but learned his lessons from being a stray and roaming in an environment that was less probable to imminent harm. The children of Laddie's Master Family were very young when he was taken in to their home and the return appreciation of protecting such a large young group of kids was his primary consumption. Scamp learned much from Laddie but learned it from the comfort of his shadow and without the subtleties of responsibility. Scamp was becoming a dog of self-promotion in an effort to define himself beyond his father and Laddie recognized the flaw. Sugar and myself had mastered chaos in order to promote our agendas. Ours was a purpose of fun and freedom. We fought because we were free to do so and because it promoted us well. We didn't fight to protect our domain; we just made a lot of noise about it.

Scamp was trained in discipline and responsibility. He wanted to carry that on from his father but had taken the mindset that aggressively attacking any threat would preserve what he was responsible for. A flawed mindset because he didn't have a definitive purpose to defend anythng, except his own promotion. Compound all that by the fact of his need to step out of big daddy's shadow and you have a dog that alienates himself from those that are no real threat. The father and son were a formidable balance but the son rarely took a crap without the father kicking his shit off the sidewalks. On his own Scamp might just leave his shit stinkin' up the wrong sidewalk.

So, Laddie was carousing the same space with all us hooligans. Imagine him following stumpy ole' Scooter into the crowd and back, mothering him with protective caution that his three good legs didn't get stepped on. There we were at the evolutionary peak of amicability, seemingly possessed by Halloween spirits intent on doing the ole' outta' body switcheroo. Our doggie spirits were imposed on the human bodies as they reveled in the chaos and the human spirits were imposed on us as we sat around amused yet scared to get in the middle of the fracas.

A loud siren spun piercing vibrations through the air and we howled in chorus. There was a momentary truce as one of those annoying medical vehicles jumped the curb and headed in our direction on the grass between the library and Congregational church. Most of us continued howlin' until the metal beast came to a stop and turned off its siren. The rotating flashing lights continued and I started up again solo only to get a "splat" on my face. Dang bone-it, apparently the audience didn't like my singing and pelted my head with an egg. Do you know the frustration of having smelly edibles on your face but no ability to get the goods to your mouth? It oozed a bit down the side of my snout and my tongue could get a taste but not enough to calm my salivating glands as most of the goodies were stuck out of my reach. Consider someone sewing your mouth shut then sticking your salivating face in ice cream or spaghetti. Both of which were often mixed in my doggie dish so I can vouch for the combination. I tried rubbing my face on my paws but every time I bent my head down Scooter would lick my face. I let him do this a few times without rebuttal, which speaks to the oddity of the evening. Finally I headbutted him and felt a little bit of my normal self float back to reality.

I guess the continued rotating lights stayed on to keep the peace while a "thud" struck combatant was attended to and escorted away. The bloodshed was now official and adults stepped in to scatter the crowd. Obviously the "thud" struck side was pissed over non "splat" objects being thrown and more "thuds" were thrown on both sides but the human adults with uniforms quickly got control and the war was finally disassembled. This usually meant that many of the kids would continue on in their inner groups with some type of side street pranks and minor skirmishes about the village.

My salivating glands got my intestines juiced and I squatted a fresh pile only to have three kids giggling around the steamy contents then scoop it up in a brown paper bag. Laddie happened to be witness to this as well and we were so taken with the bizarre incident we decided to follow these shit lovin' kids down the street. Nowadays, a dog is used to his Master's hand practically up his rectum to be sure no doo-doo litters the pristine walkways of the modern day village. The leash sucks for us all doesn't it. We're trapped to your pace and your interests and your only interest is to be sure we don't crap unknowingly along the way. In my day, when a human walked down the street with a paper bag, it usually had lunch in it. These days guessing what's in the bag is a crapshoot. Witticism intended.

The boys headed all the way up towards Laddie's home but took the final right turn on to East Street South. A few houses down one of them pulled out a lighter and started the bag on fire. They tiptoed up to the nearest door and rang the doorbell, dropped the burning bag on the stoop and dove into some bushes down the street. Laddie and I were utterly confused. More so than normal for dogs and we wandered up to the stoop only to get a charred wreak of my waste bellowing from the smoking bag. The door opened with some senior citizen holding a tray of goodies immediately spewing profanities as smoking burned dog shit blew into her home.

Why get mad at this? It's TRICK or treat and you got the trick. That's the chance you take for opening your door on Halloween. So we're standing there looking up at her and she spews on at us about God damning us dogs. I'm thinkin, "stop chewin' me a bone lady, like I'm clever enough to crap in a bag, then pull a match from my ass, light it and toss it up on her porch"- I wish! She doesn't even kick the bag off her stoop. Smoke is spewing on her tray and so she just chucks the whole tray of goodies at us and slams the door shut. This turned out to be a very fortunate incident because it was full of cookies. I guess she wasn't comfortable giving out shit steamed cookies to the village kids. Laddie and I had no misgivings; we ate the whole bag of shit steamed cookies.

Did I mention we were fortunate? I did, but this was the last meal we would get for a while so it bears repeating. After dining together without incident we wandered up Chapel Street towards the pool and saw some kids run into the brush across the street. We were practically startled out of our skin by a storm door falling off its hinges. Another trick in the works? The homes mother was responding to the ring of the doorbell expecting treat seekers only to have the door completely fall off the stoop. She was mortified and confused and apparently not handy with tools because she just left it and closed the door. The crash scared us to the other side of the road near the creek and we heard voices in the bushes. I was pleasantly surprised to find Master Tom and a few unfamiliar friends trying to contain their laughter. They were the tricksters and had quietly unscrewed the door hinges then rang the doorbell as it set unsecured for the unsuspecting.

The boys then headed down the bike trail in the brush in fear of getting caught. We followed them a short distance along side the brush on the grass but caught a strange scent behind us and heard some ruffling. A deer jumped out of the brush and headed towards the road and off towards the pool. Doggie chase big time, puppy! We went in fervent pursuit howlin' in glory.

The deer was so startled being in the open it allowed us to keep within a reasonable chase distance. The pool's chain link fence really freaked the deer as it banged up against it a few times trying to find an outlet. Eventually it made its way past the fencing and rounded the changing rooms towards the creek. It ran through the brush and crossed the creek to the steep incline on the opposite side and headed up towards the heights. There were enough obstacles so we could keep pace with the shifty creature. Adrenaline must have kept Laddie going because bad hip and all he was right there with me. He sensed the possibility that a co-kill on this beast could go along way in smoothing things over with me, for Scamp's sake.

Whatever. I'd never killed anything like this before nor considered it a possibility. It was a chase of senses and instinct. If we had dragged the deer down I could see my instincts clamping the jugular to lifelessness but I doubt I would have sat around and chowed down on a couple yards of intestines. I was already stuffed full of shit steamed cookies. I try to limit myself to one grotesque meal a day- and that's hard for a dog. Laddie had been hunting often with his boy Masters so he knew the bonding of the hunt and kill. He'd even killed a deer once though it had been shot and wounded first.

We were pretty juiced up on sugar so we managed a good chase up to the heights and beyond the residential yards towards Hunts Mountain. Once we reached forest and the deer was in a familiar setting our chase ended. We stopped about a quarter mile into the woods and just about died in a panting frenzy. We were freakin' tired. We rested in near pitch black and the chill was starting to catch up with us. The leaves and pine needles were as thick as snow, a comfortable natural mattress. About fifteen minutes had passed of sheer quiet and then Laddie gingerly rose to his feet. He was an adequate scent dog and had picked up a huntable smell. I'm wondering how I even got in the damn woods in the first place. We couldn't see but a few feet ahead so sound and smell were all we had. That's what Laddie was going to respond to. He headed in whatever direction his senses led and I had no choice but to follow

We roamed for another 15 or 20 minutes in utter darkness and an impression started to overcome us. We're stuck in this damp, cold forest for the night. Slap me back ten thousand years, I never though I'd be lickin' water off leaves and huddlin' in crevasses under fallen logs. The egg on my face was crusted stiff and itching but that was obviously the least of my discomforts. Still, it all compounds itself into one miserable existence. I'd spent half my life forging ahead the evolution of our species and here I am now playing wolf-dog.

It was completely spooky, a true Halloween misadventure. Laddie had the good sense to huddle up close and we sucked up each other's warmth 'til we were just plain cold. You'd think with our ears we'd be up all night homing in on the strange sounds of the forest but it was dead silent. The only good thing about this is that I was a dog and we have some ability to adapt to inclement situations. We're not as far removed as humans are from our "call of the wild" days. What I mean to say is we can manage to get some sleep anyplace, no bed required. The constance of my sleep was the issue. I was basically a dog taking a few dozen catnaps. The cold, isolation and Laddie's snoring made long periods of slumber impossible.

Gunshots finally interrupted the only extended sleep we had achieved. Our fur was wet with dew and chills ran through our skin. Light was bleakly piercing a dense fog as morning ascended. More rounds were expelled and I rose to my feet in concern. Laddie attempted to get up but his hip was stiff and he dragged himself forward a few paws to stretch out beyond the log cover that encased us. He finally got to all fours but was seriously limp. We didn't realize the danger we were in as it was not the best time of year to be an animal in the forest. It didn't take more than five minutes to spot the orange clad attire of the modern day hunter. It was supposed to only be bow season but those few abusers of the law were awfully dangerous. We were tempted to approach the first ones we saw for food but they began blasting away at some distant target and that scared the crap out of us. We wandered off, much more slowly than we had entered the previous night.

We didn't know where we were or where to go. We walked to keep warm but the distance between Laddie and myself was growin' with each paw step. Not just because he was limp but because of the doggie equivalent of blame and anxiety. It was tension on both our parts that grew as the monotony of the forest disorients your senses. Every ten minutes or so another shot would ring through the forest and we'd find our distance between each other a little closer for the next few minutes. After the long side of an hour, I stopped to rest only to notice Laddie outta' sight. I tracked back a short distance to find him nibblin' through some discarded tinfoil that had bread scraps and mayonnaise. At close range the smell of human food was obvious and I

T o m   M o d y

quickly charged in to get a portion. Our frustrations vented out and Laddie defended his keep by turning vicious on me. I held ground intent on getting my share and was able to snag a corner of the tinfoil and attempt to drag it away. Laddie pounced his paws on the goods and we butted snouts and took a few claw digs.

It didn't take twenty-four hours and we had almost fully regressed to dogs of the wild. Not that this fight wouldn't have taken place in the village, it often did. Those were just the petulant greedy rantings of our evolved social etiquette. In the depth of the forest we began to feel as if our survival depended on a dominant posture- and it was still early in the going. I shudder to think of what extremes we'd take if we'd been shut in there alone for days and beyond. In some way we were lucky we weren't alone. The hunters-city-beer-guzzlin', hobb-nobbin', no experience, wannabe Davie Crockett's were eager to take a crack at any ruffling in the woods. Before our spat over the tinfoil escalated we were deterred by the human shout of "over there". We perked up at first to try and figure out where these lifesavers might be. No sooner did our heads appear above some brush than a spray of bullets blasted the bark above our perky ears. Did I mention dumb and blind in reference to those hunters? Can't they tell a deer from a dog- or do they even care?

We got the expletive-laced adjectives out of there and kinda' figured out we'd better keep a little closer distance to each other. Laddie now had enough adrenaline to charge those sore joints and I made sure I didn't get too far ahead. Amidst a series of rests every so often we continued on for endless hours. The sun managed some rays of light and heat but the dampness on our fur still made any slight movement of air bone chilling. We nibbled on anything that may have resembled food and both our stomachs were beginning to grumble heavily from the array of leaves, plants and wood we tried to ingest. We hacked up often which lent itself to near dehydration. We lapped up the occasional dime size puddles of water cupped in leaves or in fallen branch indentations and dragged on slower and slower. The leash never seemed so appealing. Laddie was having flash backs from his days as a stray. He didn't have the constitution as a mature dog to be in that situation again and this was creating much anxiety. I think we both could have handled the extended lack of food and even the chilly discomfort but the inability to see beyond the next cluster of trees mentally inhibits your ability to reason and focus. Top that with having no bearings as to where you are or if you'll ever get out and you can understand we may have been in the early stages of a nervous dementia. As long as we kept our noses down and led with some sense of aromatic purpose, we could muddle through.

Late in the afternoon Laddie was dragging along pretty bad. I was panting so hard I felt like my tongue lost five pounds. The extended ranges in our canine ears can pick up the movements of your common rodents and small game and I was desperately hungry enough to actually kill and eat one. The problem was between our panting and the consistency of gunshots throughout the day, pinpoint tracking of that type was nearly impossible. However, as far as being poor lost souls in the dense dangerous woods, we were not alone. We were able to pick up some human verbalizations a ways ahead and though cautious that they could be armed and stupid, we had to move towards them. You can imagine how startled and overjoyed we were to find two young teenage boys, unarmed, sitting on a stump. They extended a welcome to us as well.

Seems we shared the same predicament. We extended the normal doggie-human pleasantries and allowed them to pet us as we lapped up the salt from their palms. One boy took out a baggie of assorted cereal and peanut mix and littered it on the ground for us to sample. The other boy also took out a baggie... and some rolling paper and a lighter. An interesting aromatic smoke, a smell I had also sampled on some of Master Tom's friends, now eased through the breeze. The boys caught up and began to walk and toke and we followed in the pleasant, calming air flowing behind them. They were nice enough to walk at a pace Laddie could manage and the journey continued.

About an hour before dusk we could hear voices again in the distance. One of the boys ran ahead while the other stayed with Laddie and myself due to his hip problem. The other boy seemed to be walking erratically anyway. I doubt he was in any condition to pick up his pace. He mumbled some slurred verbiage at us then laughed exaggeratedly at our quizzical expressions. He then carried on a conversation with us. I'm wondering if he actually thought we were talking back to him.

Let's be honest here. If I had opposable thumbs and a ball of string I coulda' tied it to him and we coulda' floated outta' the damn woods. In retrospect I wonder if smoking would be an activity we dogs might enjoy. I know I knocked it earlier in your post sex routines and was thankful we had nothing to do with it but I may rethink it. Granted, this kid's weed was a little wackier than the law allows but the activity as a whole could have doggie merit. In human calendar years our life spans are so much shorter so I doubt we'd suffer the long-term effects many of you humans seem to ignore on the labels. You engage in the activity as if you have nothing better to do. Well, as dogs, we definitely have nothing better to do. We chew on rawhide and chase our tails. Smoking's got to be more appealing than rectal grooming to waste time? And we've always got watery snot running down our nose into our mouth. I'm thinking cigarette smoke drifting up our snouts would help dry that right up. It would do wonders for doggie breath. If we could manage the mechanics of it you'd just need to add another "dish" and we're set, food bowl, water bowl, butt bowl.

Honestly, I'm not mocking you. We tolerate the second hand smoke of our masters and PETA or some of these other wacky animal rights activists have never claimed a dog death due to it. I say we could handle it and even share in the experience with our Masters if only God gave us the appendages needed. However, I doubt Master would be comfortable with us playing with matches. Hmmm, what about chewing tobacco? Nah, we've got enough saliva drippin' outta' our mouths.

So, this kid has stopped and decided to carry on a conversation with us. He didn't even talk to us like Master Mother and Father talk to their toddler Nat, which is how most people talk to us dogs. He's carrying on matter-of-factly then laughing apparently at something we said- which we didn't. All of a sudden he just keels over and starts dry heavin'. He's on his knees and we're sniffin' around his mouth waiting for the payload. We just love puke, don't ask me why. A couple more violent chucks yield little more than some warm saliva and he falls face first on the ground, just moanin' and holdin' his stomach.

It was like a switch was turned, you could see it plain as day. Laddie in all his pain and suffering of this hopeless predicament now has a purpose. He's hovering over this poor kid lickin' his face, and not to get a tingling of vomit on his tongue either. He's worried about this kid and is now the guardian of him. Laddie is camped out next to him and I start forging ahead but he's not following me. I get out of his view but he's staying right with the kid. After about ten minutes I decided I was going to move on without him and as I got about fifty yards out of view the other kid came running back so I followed him back to Laddie and his friend. Apparently this boy found a clearing and could spot his Father with the group of men he came hunting with. As I understand it now, these boys were along with them but had no interest in hunting so they hung out in their father's truck with strict orders to not go in the woods. But that weed was just waitin' to get toked and they needed the privacy so they headed into the woods and got lost. When the boy came running back he wanted to inform his friend that he found the clearing and that they needed to get back to the truck without being spotted. Now that he found his friend face down there was a panic and a little clarity that he may need some help. Fortunately his freaked out friend was coming around and able to walk with some assistance.

We walked on for another fifteen minutes and got to the edge of the clearing but the boys were scared to appear fearing the wrath for their disobedience. The one boy tried to physically sober up his stoned friend but failed as he fell again rustling the bushes. Within seconds a flurry of bullets rang through the woods and I ran the expletive-laced doggie hell outta' there back in to the woods. Laddie burst from the clearing and started barking in a moment as desperate as it was brave. The men were cocked and waiting for anything to jump from the brush and one guy even took a shot at Laddie but they soon realized it was a dog (duh!) and not a deer. The not so stoned boy appeared from the clearing and called to his father. I kept my distance a ways back in the woods. The father came running the few hundred yards to his son and discovered the other boy bumbling on the ground. The lacing those boys took was brutal and the father turned abusive on the son. It was a heated and physical confrontation that kept me at bay in hiding.

Laddie however was not appreciative of the abuse his newfound protectives were taking. He emerged from the woods and began a verbal assault of his own on the father. It didn't accomplish much. The father smacked him on the head with the butt of his rifle and Laddie painfully snarled in defiance. However, this time it was the barrel of the gun starring down at Laddie waiting for him to make the next aggressive posture. The son quickly begged his father not to shoot Laddie and pleaded obedience to save Laddie's hide. I could hear the confrontation from my safe distance and Laddie still would not relent in making his feelings known. Then the shot rang out. There was dead silence.

While this took place one of the other hunters retrieved their truck and drove it through the clearing to our location. It arrived seconds after the father had fired his gun. I could hear the ruffling of the brush as footsteps headed for the clearing. I carefully approached and investigated. At the location of the incident I found no Laddie and no blood. I snuck up and took a peak through the brush into the clearing. The boys and Laddie were loaded into the back of the truck bed and off it went before I knew what to do. Laddie was alive, the father's tactic was no different than the Wild West sheriff walkin' into a saloon and getting order by lettin' off a few rounds in the ceiling. If I was an overnight guest in the Wild West I think I'd never request a room on the second floor. Anyway, I was cold, abandoned, hungry, tired and seriously boned.

Right about then I'd kingdom to be the low pup on the pole of a pack of wolves. All my touting of evolved canine superiority was useless. I needed to regress- fast! I walked the few hundred yards through the clearing. There was a small embankment at the end of the clearing and a creek ran along its border. I stopped for a minute to take a drink and when I lapped up my final slurps the sun had completely fallen behind the mountains. I was already cold and damp and loathe to cross the water so I followed the creek border. It was overcast and little moonlight was coming through. Because of the recent daylight savings time change it was still rather early. I would be lost in the frosty darkness hours before midnight would even round to morning.

After a good hour the chill became intolerable. I decided to move away from the creek to locate any type of shelter but as I approached some brush I would hear rustling and steps. The wheels were spinnin' in my head- hunter, danger, predator, danger, person, savior, small game, food, dog reaper?

As the indecision continued to spin, a doe staggered to the creek. I perked up immediately. She grimaced as she bent down to take a drink. She was there only seconds and turned back towards the bordered woods. I was prepared to make a move of some type. I didn't know how to jump these things. I could feel it inside of me, the juices, the chemicals, all gearin' me up but I was too domestically evolved. It seemed like messy business but deep inside me I was still animal, it could take over. Moot point, the doe just collapsed before it reached the woods. It had been carrying a slug for the better part of the day and its blood had run too low.

I approached the curiously dormant animal and was drawn in by the body heat still present. It may have been barely alive but in shock or just on the verge of an exhaustive death. As hungry as I was, the body heat was drawing my full attention. I dug in next to the animal with my back as tight as possible to its extinguishing heat and I curled the rest of me fetal to keep in as much warmth as possible. I awoke some time later bone chilled. All life and external heat had vanished from the animal. Now I had to address my hunger and possibly my failing health.

I understood this was my meal ticket and had I procured my own personal butcher on this mission I'da had no trouble chompin' on some hacked leg of the creature. Unfortunately, I needed to burrow my own jaws through the fat and the cartilage and the bone of the creature that was twice the mass of me. I decided to start where many predators are drawn, to the scent of blood. There was a streak of red down it's left side which began just before the back hip. I eased my tongue across its fur to expose the wound and was taken aback momentarily by the chalky burnt taste that was apparently gun powder. I muddled through and wiped that taste as clean off the wound as possible then started to tear at the small hole of exposed flesh. I was tepid at first but the meat was fresh and still warm from the inside. That got the old ancestral blood percolating and I began to feel a surge of energy in anticipation of the meal to come. Within a minute I had ripped the fur and skin aside and was able to take my first jawful of relatively fresh kill. It seemed to tingle my taste buds like a hidden hope chest. The sensations had laid dormant in the vestige of my ancestry and now much of my past was becoming clear to me.

I suppose in your Heaven you get to have revealed the experiences your ancestors endured. Imagine Master Tom experiencing the awe and wonder of his thirteen-year-old grandfather leaving the old country and his mother behind. Arriving at Ellis Island he's overwhelmed with no English speaking skills and little money. It was a harsh, yet exhilarating, reality that nothing in Master Tom's current life could simulate or have any basis for recall. Even if the comparative regression was generations and thousands of years back in human ancestry, the stimulants of a primal man are not something the modern human can relive in full context. But here I was, consciously appreciating that very situation. I doubt the sensation of the kill meat was solely responsible. It was the reality of the entire situation- cold, hunger, fear, darkness, desperation, timelessness and the smell of death surrounding such a relatively massive beast. The modern human could face all these things and revel in his "manly" man survival mode but your true animal instinct has long since dissipated. Without it you can't understand my moment.

That's all it was, a moment. For I too was endeavoring in that feeding with the hope of returning to the world of dog lovin' chaos. Every rip, every bite and every enjoyable morsel would help me return to my evolved life. There was an even bigger picture to be appreciated later. Toss a silver spooned brat into the real world, recruit some skinny geek into the military, impregnate a reckless and petulant party girl, and often what comes out the other side is an inner strength only adversity can shape. I can assure you this experience would not eradicate the reckless and petulant creature I worked so hard to promote but would I still be intimidated by General? I know dogs of the wild sure wouldn't.

After I had filled my belly I took on a new resolve. I didn't ingest a particularly large amount considering the supply was more than I could consume in a days time. I understand our ancestral brethren could devour pounds upon pounds at one sitting but they needed to go days without and they expend much more daily energy. It was a new experience for me and I ate enough to where I felt a full days journey was consumed. Blood stained my snout and it's smell touched off the wild beast inside me. I howled at the moon but that set off a flock of foul into the air and their ruffling startled the crap outta' me. I didn't seemed to be as cold or as tired either. I pretended I could adapt and stuck my nose in the air to find a scent which would lead my evening journey. I picked up something kinda' sweet smellin' and headed along the river's edge.

After a time I finally reached a semblance of civilization. The river flowed through an underpass and I walked up the embankment to a roadway. I walked along side the road for well over an hour and never saw one car. The air was getting sweeter and it wasn't long before the scent led up a dirt driveway. A small farmhouse with a barn and outbuilding were barely visible as the moonlight sifted through the overcast sky. I followed the scent to the outbuilding and could almost taste the sugar in the dampness. It was a small shed for making maple syrup. I pried around the door but it was locked. I headed over towards the barn and discovered it had no doors. At last, some real shelter. I bumbled around in the darkness for another naturally sweet smell, this time of hay. I found a clump in the corner and nestled in for a slumber of the gods.

It was the first chance I really had to think about home and the family. The places and people I'd shared every night of life with. I felt an uncomfortable displacement and even concern that should I ever return I'd be in big trouble. But, I'd chew that bone when it presents itself. For now I needed sleep. The simple priorities of being dog, no need stressin' 'til it's absolutely necessary.

I stayed snug in the hay well past dawn. The sun's placement moved its rays through a broken window onto my damp hide and I exposed my belly to the warmth. I finally heard voices around mid morning and tried to reason the best action. Make a friendly appearance or sneak out with no plan and no known means of survival. Hmmm, I could be friendly!

I stuck my head out of the barn to notice a young boy and girl splashing wet leaves around. They stopped and eyed me down with a concerned stare. Ooops, they couldn't see my tail. I moved my entire body out of the barn and wagged my tail vigorously. Their demeanor immediately changed and they approached me unconcerned. They brought me to their door and called for their mother's attention. She approached and mildly admonished them for not being more careful around a stray. I guess that's what I had become. She tested my attitude and friendliness. Once she was comfortable she allowed me to continue playing with her children. As I had spent most of the day there she made a few calls to neighbors in reference to my potential home. No one knew of me. She then came outside with some leftover chicken scraps and tossed them too me but not before checking my collar for any identification. I just happened to have a dog tag dangling from my neck. It registered back to the veterinarians who then informed her of my actual home. It was quite far away. Seems I'd traveled over ten miles to the countryside of Norwich on Whaupanauca Road. Later that evening when the father returned from hunting she informed him of their days guest. A call was placed to my ecstatic family and I was loaded in a car and driven back to Sherburne.

Every house smells, you know. And that's not a bad thing. Some are dank, some perfumey, some smell pristine, some smell of cooking and some smell just plain lived in. It was nice to bury my nose into the shag which holds in the years of familiarity that makes my residence home. The whole family greeted me at the front doors as I was brought in. I was happy to see them of course, but I just needed to absorb into the shag. For once I didn't care about my balcony or the goings on in the village. I just needed to curl up behind the recliners and bury my nose in the aroma of home.

In the subsequent weeks, I carried a renewed confidence with me about the village but it was unshared. I was disheartened not to see Laddie at all. I was curious if he too felt renewed and tested. I was curious what an encounter with him would be like now that we'd made it back. But we hadn't made it back, only I had. The few instances I saw Scamp he was without confrontation. He was just stationed among the grounds of Laddie's home- waiting.

I remember close to a month had passed but I finally saw Scamp about the village. I was chasing some rabbits around the shrubs of the library. I looked up and there was Scamp on the sidewalk barking at me. Nothing overt, just normal doggie procedure. I didn't feel threatened and continued on with the hunt. He barked for a short time longer and carried on his way. It was enough of a change in him to peak my curiosity so I decided to head up East State Street towards Laddie's house. To my surprise, when I reached the front sidewalk I could see Laddie laying in the back driveway as the family raked leaves. He lifted his nose and looked up at me. It was a strange and distant stare, more

T o m   M o d y

that he smelled something familiar than he actually saw me. He achingly rose to his feet but began trembling as he attempted to take steps. One of the boys ran over to him to make sure he laid back down. The boy turned towards the street and saw me.

"Dallas get out of here" he yelled!

Another one of the boys and the youngest daughter all started yelling at me so I ran across the street. They didn't want me getting Laddie all worked up and one of the boys came all the way out to the sidewalk to make sure I didn't come back. I took one last stare in Laddie's direction and fled. It was the last time I ever saw him.

That day in the woods he had been taken along with the stoned boys to their home in the town of Columbus, a few miles outside of Sherburne. They lived in a trailer deep into a country road. Immediately upon exiting the truck his neck was tied with bailing twine and he was tied up outside unsheltered. The son was severely dealt with and Laddie wanted so bad to run in and help but he was too stiff to even resist being tied up. Over the next few days the boy had taken to Laddie and they both consoled each other in their plights. The father with a slight feeling of guilt at his abuse decided to let his son keep Laddie rather than send him off to the woods or worse, shoot him. They did turn a makeshift truck cab into a rudimentary shelter, stuffed it with hay and occasional water. He never was let off the bailing twine and ate only evening table scraps and any minor treats the boy could sneak to him. He barely left the confines of the truck cab. The singular boot kick from Master George the year earlier exacerbated the quick onset of arthritis to that joint. Coupled with the chill of his environment and lack of activity he could barely muster the desire to do anything but dream of home.

After a few weeks, it was becoming clear to the father that the dog was good for nothin' and he wasn't about to expend the time and money to a vet call. He informed the son a decision had been made. The dog would be shot when he returned home from school. An argument ensued in which the father subdued the anger of the son by insisting he shut up or the dog would be shot immediately. Shortly after the father went off to work the boy left the house at his usual time, normally throwing a strip of bacon to Laddie while waiting for the school bus. Except, that particular morning he dug as much food as possible from the garbage and refrigerator and let Laddie take in his apparent last supper. But that wasn't the intent. The school bus came and the boy convinced the bus driver he was taking the dog in for a school project. Columbus kids are part of the Sherburne school district and when he arrived at school he pleaded with any of his friends to adopt this stray dog he had found. One of his friends recognized Laddie as a village dog. He was desperate to find out who the owner was but the kid didn't know. He just knew he was common around town and convinced the boy to simply let him loose and he'd find his way back home. As class was minutes from beginning he cut the bailing twine leash close to Laddie's neck and left Laddie at the bridge entrance of the high school.

The boy's friend was correct, Laddie knew exactly where he was and his morning meal was just sufficient enough for him to walk that mile down Classic Street to East State Street. It was definitely the longest mile of his life. Weak and trembling it took every protein and carbohydrate in his system to reach the corner of the Catholic Church. It was a frosty late November morning and his hip was no better than Scooter's stump. He was only countable yards away from home but even the slight incline up East State Street took the same traveling time as that whole mile on Classic Street. Climbing the front steps of his home was unthinkable so he panted and moaned to the back door and pushed a few attempts of dead air before he could muster a bark. He was dehydrated and his tongue kept sticking to the roof of his mouth preventing feeble sounds to emanate. He looked for his old water bowl and found it filled with rainwater and leaves. After a couple slurps, audible sounds could now be produced and his Master Mother cried at his return.

The subsequent few days he'd been home he suffered convulsions, incontinence and surprisingly no appetite. He was full though, of love and appreciation. A lifetime's worth showered on him in a few short days. When I last saw him the family had carried him outside so they could spend as much time with him as possible. He had been to the vet and given a course of antibiotics and pain medications in hopes he'd improve. Days after I last saw Laddie he began suffering kidney failure and was put to sleep by months end. I'm sure he was guarding the angels his entire way up to Doggie Heaven.

Revelation II

Those that are the slowest
get to Heaven the fastest

Why I even bothered coming home during the months of March and April is beyond me. Well, most things were beyond me but here in revelation this question is still beyond me. I'd welcome some rubber paw goulashes. It's so damn dirty with the snow melting and the rains puddling mud everyplace. Now I didn't have a problem personally with all the mud but I got treated like some bum dog that had shown up at Master's doorstep every time I came home. They wouldn't let me in. What's that going to solve- it was outside where I got all dirty in the first place. It woulda' been different if the temperature was eighty-five and breezy but try stepping outta' your shower and drying off with a minus five wind chill. Then I'm sequestered in the kitchen or worse, the tiny washroom. Everyone's pushing brushes and brooms in my face and blaming me for every track of mud. Being the only dog in the house, it's hard to deny I'm the owner of the mud prints across the linoleum.

The beginning of spring gets us dogs very antsy. It's so damn cumbersome runnin' in the winter that when the snow melts you just want to go- anyplace. It's like walkin' around with weights around your legs for four months then taking them off- you just float with amazing speed and strength. I hadn't been notching any new tail all winter so sloppin' around without testicle icicles was welcome all winter as it did serve as a human proverbial cold shower. Most of us male village dogs had spent the winter getting our tongues stuck to our frozen 'nads and now that the thaw had come with our bags bulgin' the tension was high from the first day the temperature cracked forty.

The seeds of dissension were already blooming about the village concerning the reckless freedoms we'd achieved. Though none of the old guard Masters were about to start caging their pets, I was getting leash locked more and more. Particularly when Master did not desire my following and pestering. In the old days the ever favorite "open car door" routine would work to corral me so Master could leave in peace. Less effective yet more embarrassing was the fake stick toss and ditch. It's just a lack of brain size, you know. Master would toss a couple sticks. I'd go fetch and the next ones would be thrown further and further away. Ultimately Master would cock back that arm and put forth an exaggerated heave. I'd go bookin' in search of the stick that never was. It never left Master's hand but I'd be stupidly preoccupied looking for it while Master slipped away around a corner. He had to be pretty quick to get outta' my sensory range so it just became easier to leash me up. As Master Tom got older he felt less guilty about it, which is why it started happening more. Master Mother and Father didn't even think twice about binding me to shackles.

For the new local pet owners, they decided to get a jump on the lawyers and lawmakers and practice a more disciplined breed of Master. There's an interesting quote about how you humans accept drastic and seemingly unthinkable changes to life and law.

"First it's scorned. Then it's violently opposed. Then it becomes accepted as self-evident."

Kinda' like your taxes, huh. Your current burden would have been unthinkable and prone to violent acts a mere fifty or sixty years ago. Nowadays you not only accept the burden, you accept it knowing a good portion of it is pissed away. The same way in my day it woulda' been hard to imagine a local swimming pool without a diving board or a Fourth of July celebration without fireworks. But so it would become. I bring up these points with not even a whimper in my heart for your burdens because when you started to leash us you opened the floodgates of a tight ass society. Be honest, nowadays you're about as free as the very dogs you chain to submission. You think you're all happy now that your villages run like nice tidy little ships free of unfined dog shit piles. And why are you getting fined for dog shit piles? Because you accept your fines like your taxes as self-evident.

Stand up for yourselves, will ya! Fight back. Sugar did. His loins were achin' badly come the spring of '81. His years of yard hoppin' were becoming less appreciated by local lass owners. Even if they were spayed, Sugar crashin' your patio cocktail party, stealin' your chow and mountin' your dog was becoming less accepted behavior. Some Masters are just prudes I guess.

As the winter grew colder and Sugar went yard hoppin' for some warmth, he was finding that a few of the new ladies of the neighborhood were guarded and confined. He'd jump on a stoop and stare into the home of his intended mount and ache for the season to change. The season may have eventually changed but available tail hadn't. The leash was causing problems in many areas of our normal lives and we all were beginning to crack.

The more I got sick of being leashed, the more I lashed out when I saw one. An elderly lady was walking her little white poodle one evening past my domain. I was barking at the front door to be let in after another night of inaction in the groin department. The little rat of a dog muttered something in my direction. I turned and saw a poodle and a leash and I just lost it. I flew off the stoop skipping every step, airborne. I laid out a lung lashing that practically blew his cotton' pickin' lookin' head right off. You can imagine the elderly lady's reaction, totally feeble. In my mind I'm layin' it out to this poodle.

"You're a pathetic species of wannabe dog! How dare you test me by thinkin' you can just walk past me without getting your cotton ball head ripped off! And to mock me with your leash! No dog brings a leash to my property without it getting wrung around their necks- Mutant!"

I didn't know what I was sayin', I was just rantin' out of frustration- it was glorious. Did wonders for me. Master

Mother and Master Tom had to separate me from the situation before the old lady keeled over. Nowadays if this incident had happened attorneys would be bubbling out the sidewalk cracks despite the fact that no one was really hurt in any noticeable capacity.

But back to Sugar. He was basically being locked out of the local humpin' department by this new breed of fine fearing protective Master. One day when he was about at wits end he decided to look up an old address, a pure bred beagle he'd sired an offspring with. (You can imagine how well that mutt went over.) He bided his patience until he heard some back porch activity. After it was apparent the Master had gone back inside he approached the yard in hopes of this lass being outside. To his ire, the king of patience himself, Sam, already was liftin' her tail. Having been camped out at the opposite end of the yard he had a better view of when the Master went in thus the quicker approach. Sugar was livid. Physically interrupting Sam would be a prescription for pain and he knew it. In spite, he started howlin' at the top of his lungs forcing the Master to come runnin' out of his house and do Sugar's vengeance for him. Sam was forced to stand down and Sugar ran off to safety.

Now Sugar's situation was worse than before. He was still achin' and ever increasingly mad. Desperate and determined also could assess his mood. As he distanced himself from Sam through adjoining lots he caught a glimpse of seduction. A shepherd of wholesome purity and flowing golden locks? Nah, he didn't notice that, he just saw some tail in the doorway of the patio.

Sound the siren, crank the engine, lead the charge, it was time for action. Headfirst mind you- head first he plunged through the thin plate glass to cure his achin' loins. Doggie hell, he coulda' neutered himself right then and there. Amazingly though he was unfazed and unscathed and was locked on her in seconds. The Master Mother dropped her fresh outta' the oven roast right there on the floor and ran to the patio. It was a short ride with little satisfaction before Sugar was accosted with a meat baster. He scampered around the patio until the Master Father approached with a more blunt weapon chasing Sugar back from where he came.

A call was made to Sugar's Master Father detailing the uproarious incident but the best defense the Master Father could produce was that "he's not really our dog." I find that line of defense odd, considering that when Sugar's Master Father got his mitts on him, Sugar was leashed to a tree and scolded. Tied and unsatisfied he was practically unapproachable. Master Mark tried to console him but Sugar even lashed out ferociously at his beloved Master, nipping at his pants. Master Mark was stunned at Sugar's behavior but swatted him back and untied him. The Master Father did not appreciate Sugar being untied so he ordered him back on the leash. Master Mark tried to corral Sugar only to be nipped at again. Infuriated, Master Mark grabbed a baseball bat and took two legitimate swings at Sugar forcing him into a cornered submission. As he reached, Sugar nipped at his hands and this time the bat swing, though tempered, connected to Sugar's side and Master Mark regained control of the situation and tied Sugar back up to the tree. Punishingly, he was left there overnight.

When I happen to pass by there the next day Sugar was a rage. He barked at me in rabid fashion but I just looked him down from the sidewalk. "Tell it to the paw sad-sack, I'm not your Master" is probably what I woulda' said to him. I basically paid him no attention and went on my free dog lovin' way.

Did I say things were tense around town? Well, as best I can describe, he was doggie dissed and didn't like it. It's not the same thing as that close to comprehending humor incident I had with Sam- that was a reaction closer to human. Rage and respect are rudimentary reactions dogs can act out. It's part of how social orders are formed. In this instance, Sugar was in a bad mood and I was a free dog waggin' my tail away from him. My disrespect towards his leashing stewed a rage with him all day until Master Mark was allowed to let him free. Unfortunately, Master Mark's destination was to my house and an evening of Atari video games with Master Tom. It wasn't unusual for Sugar or any of us to follow our Masters clear across town. But to sit on a stoop waiting with a chip on your shoulder, now that's one pissed dog.

The two Boy Masters were engaged in brain dead digital battle as myself and Nat hung out with them in the den. They played their games for a while that evening and upon completion Master Mark decided to leave. He opened the den door to go home when Sugar just barreled into my house. That's twice in as many days this sex starved, slave tied, grudge holder of a mutt crashed someone's home.

His head was barely through the door when his vicious lung lashing began and he steamed right for me. I immediately clicked on my fightin' mode and defended myself as best I could for the moment. The boys and Nat just freaked. The preschool aged Nat clung to the top of the couch screamin'. The boys made a pathetic futile attempt to break us up that lasted mere seconds then fled the room closing the door behind them hoping to keep us confined. It worked as we carried on a particularly violent release of pent up anger upon each other in the den. The only problem was that they left Nat defenseless in the room with us.

We smacked up against the couch more than once disrupting her balance almost causing her to tumble into our hellish pit. As they ran into the living room Grandpa asked them what the "gosh damn hell" was going on". As they explained he then happen to bring up the question of where's Nat? Both boys then realized she was still in the den, or more appropriately, the lion's den. Still, due to our savage outburst I'm proud to declare they were very hesitant to play the hero but did so with much more fear than bravery. They cautiously opened the den door and didn't exactly jump right in to save her. They more or less motioned her to make her way down the couch and let her leap to escape. It may have only been a minute or two but really, that's a long time to have two dogs ravaging your home. Master Mark ran through the living room and out the front door, jumped through the side brush and opened the den door. Master Tom snagged an antique tennis racquet and tried to smack us to separation. Master Mark kicked in with his foot and they somehow got Sugar out the door.

I hate to admit it but Sugar kinda' beat the crap outta' me that night. Nothing blood gushin' or flesh tearin', it was just a good ambush resulting in some nips, aches and pains. His bag may still have been bulgin' but he definitely left there feelin' like a dominant male. He needed to get it outta' his system. He hadn't jumped something that successfully in a long time.

The first few weeks of that summer were a difficult adjustment to be in the house. Usually if I wanted to slumber during the day I was unbothered as a busy growing family went about their business. If I wanted to slumber during the evening the family usually settled in about their routine. A TV show was chosen and everyone chilled to the tube's steady glow. I could relax to that. There might be one or two flickers over the course of the evening as viewing options were tested but nothing to continually disturb me.

That summer, it all changed like a demon had infested the house. I was laying on my cool slab of fireplace slate and the TV kept flickerin'. Different glows constantly seeping into my eyelids like some type of Chinese torture method. Sounds in continuous disruption. Sharp clicks of static then clarity only to be altered again. There might be a few minutes of consistency but then my perception would quickly shift, then back to some brief familiarity from minutes earlier. Morning, noon and night, there was always someone in the living room possessed with indecision. They were drugged, drawn to the light like a mindless moth. When more than one of them was in the room there was screamin' fights and minor acts of violence. Oh, the joys of human's first family experiences with cable television!

In the centuries of human existence never had there been fingertip options like this. Maybe, just maybe, some lucky Monarch was presented with thirty or so daily options of mistresses to his frolickin' delight but for the rest of you peasants, cable TV was the next best thing. I often escaped Master Tom's room because the blaring distorted assault on my ears he called music was intolerable. Now it was in my

T o m   M o d y

main living space every minute Master Father wasn't thanks to something dubbed the "VJ". Then when Master Father was home, there'd be a constant crowd roar and some type of loud ball impact I only previously had to endure on Sunday afternoons and Monday nights- now every night. I adjusted eventually but at first it strung me pretty tight.

I'd get out of the house and head downtown some evenings only to find Hobie in the same frustrated mood. Bar business was boomin' at the inn now that sports could be viewed at all hours and as much as he enjoyed his sense of family from their business, many patrons would leave drunk and pissed at the game's outcome. For a dog with his intuitive vibe that created some very tense nights and a few mean customers.

I guess a lot of things were pissin' us off. It wasn't just the leashes or MTV or our growin' Master's disinterest. Optimism seemed down amongst us. A new decade was here and it started to feel different. You humans were actually turning a corner of prosperity. The end of the 70's was so fiscally tight that your release was in your disco and your braless statements. You appreciated the diversion of dog lovin' chaos on a certain level of entertainment. Now things were getting better and our act, though appreciated nostalgia, was a little too unchecked in the new rising conservative climate.

I don't know, maybe it was just a disruption in the familiar continuity we'd known. I found myself often looking up East State Street to see if Laddie was around. Pondering the potential encounter as amicable or adversarial. Of course, he never came. Scamp was hardly present, often walking the back streets and odd spots of the village for any scent of his father. Sugar was still grudgin' me. Most of the females were leashed and guarded. Maybe I was just promotionally dry. Maybe I was suffering a bout of human maturity. A mid life crisis. Oh, God forbid, that's an evolution of dogs in this new century, not mine. In fact, what we needed was about to come. Something festive, something uproarious, something congregative.

The Sherburne Pageant of Bands!

For decades it's been the preeminent event of the year. Our tiny village infused with thirty thousand street lined spectators cheering the sounds and marching of high school bands from across the state. Themed floats, candy spewing trains and even Mr. Peanut make the long trek clear across town from the primary school to the high school. Every church had bake sales. General stores couldn't stock enough squirt guns and balloons. Ice cream flowed like Niagara Falls. If we were feeling uncomfortable with the changing and dull social climate, this steadfast embodiment of a less complicated simple American life was just the remedy. As dogs of a self-proclaimed evolved state, if we couldn't create dog lovin' chaos during the Pageant then indeed a mid-life crisis was at hand.

I must admit, as I ponder now our obliviance and limited self-awareness of aging, I much prefer that naiveté to being so in crisis with the impending approach of unstoppable time. Every little gray hair sends human males off to another airplane jump or bungee leap or to spend your kid's college funds on a Harley. I excuse you human women because it is a biological change in body and mind but I don't envy your anticipation of it. Nope, we dogs just bide our time in a state of blissful oblivion. I suppose I've expressed concern when there was a current lack of promotion or humpin' but not because my days were numbered due to aging. My instincts told me there's some type of end but my expectations are that the next day I'll function as well as I did the previous day and even though that may not be true, it's what I lived by. I didn't go into crisis when I got arthritic and could no longer easily climb stairs or chase squirrels. I didn't consider myself as any less than I was the day before or in my youth. I got angry, obviously, but not because I used to be able to do things but only because I currently couldn't do them.

Too much knowledge is just a bad thing. Comprehending your future inevitability is suppressing. If you're stressed because you're currently pent up in some capacity of life and you can't get around your obstacles then that's reason for anxiety- today. But if you think that clump of hair in the sink means you can't go bag some tail that weekend then my advice to you is to squirt soap in your eye every morning before you comb your hair. There's a great quote in The Bible, "If your eye causes you to sin then tear it out. It is better to be blind than to have it lead you to damnation"- or somethin' dreadful like that. But the point is valid for sin as well as your pursuit of sin. If your eyes cause you to stop chasing tail, then rip out your eyes! I guess my interpretation of that biblical quote doesn't exactly help me earn brownie points up here. But now that I'm here do I need brownie points?

You'd think I could relax a little more but heavenly anxiety and uncertainty is just part of the eternal ascension process for us dogs. But you unascended people of today really need to back off your preconceived fears. Remember, humans in my day didn't have Viagra and yet, your species survived. Of course, a lot of you Viagra takers are going to Hell but just forget you heard that here and try to see your midlives as half full instead of almost empty.

The first Saturday in June is Pageant of Bands. It's another one of those mornings where the bustle of activity drifts through every open door and window. I doesn't disrupt your rest because the air is filled with such energy and celebration. You just want to get up and go. By 10:00 AM I was out the door for good. The parade and marching band competitions didn't start until 1:00 PM but lawn chairs were already being positioned along the main streets. I headed up to the center of the village, pissed on a crate of peaches outside Quinn's Market doorway and sniffed around for anything. I stopped to lick up the remnants of a slush puppy that was spilled on the sidewalk by Bigelow's Pharmacy when sharp snappy detonations disrupted my progress at turning my tongue blue.

Whipper Snappers they were called. They came in small playing card type boxes and looked like oversize sperm packed in sawdust. Maybe there were a dozen or two per box. You simply chucked them on the ground and they made little cap type explosions. Bigelow's Pharmacy would always stock up on those type of quick sale gimmick products for the Pageant. These were by far the favorite of kids because unlike a cap gun where the detonation was in the gun mechanism, you could actually hit someone with a Whipper Snapper and it would detonate on impact with at worst a minor prick type pain. As you can imagine, dogs and little brothers were the optimum targets.

So, off I went meddling around the Congregational Church grounds looking for baked goods crumbs with one eye out for any opportunities to promote myself. Meanwhile, clear across town, Sam had followed Master Jimmer down South Street towards the primary school parking lots. This was home base for all the bands and floats. Master Jimmer was regarded as one of the best artists in the area and he was lending his talents to the high school float. Sugar and Scooter were already roaming the lot when Sam arrived. Over the years their definitive pecking order had been established so that allowed them to peacefully coexist, otherwise Sam woulda' chomped 'em to bits.

Sam usually dismissed Sugar's antics but more and more he found himself drawn in to the little dramas of Sugar's promotion. As stately a dog as Sam was, if you're a closet juvenile in private it can come out in public if you let your guard down. The three of them had spent a good portion of their time near the varsity football team float as Master Jimmer livened up the drab design. Activity all over the lots proved to be too provocative so Sugar and Scooter ventured off to other points of interest. Sam was inclined to stay behind but Master Jimmer was indifferent to his presence and it was good to have some like companions around so he followed Sugar and Scooter.

The SPCA, which was located in the rival city of Norwich, was also preparing a float for display in the parade. The obvious animal theme didn't escape Sugar's eye and he was spellbound with the large mock cats and dogs. Also not escaping the eye were prank interests of some of the Norwich varsity football players volunteering assistance with the float. They noticed the dogs were likely pets of the Sherbune float workers and were considering some type of practical joke. Sugar was going to make their cause much easier. The big mock cats just fascinated him and he hopped up on the float and hoped to find a sniff of life in these large felines. Some of the kids petted him and even tossed him a few treats. Sam appreciated the way Sugar just stuck his nose right into the situation and noted the rewards he received so he then hopped the float as well. Scooter was too small to make the leap and he looked sadly on from below, intimidated to yelp by the large mock animals.

It was approaching time for the float to make its way down Chapel Street to the Main Street intersection and begin their march across town. Problem was, the float was to incorporate live cats in a small pen. The cats had yet to arrive from the facility in Norwich and people were getting anxious. They couldn't float on down the parade incomplete so the option was clear. A rival varsity football player opened the pen gate and threw some treats in for Sam and Sugar to retrieve. When they did the gate was closed and the problem solved. When one of the adults asked where the dogs came from the boy claimed they were owned by some players on the team. The float was then hitched to the truck and off it went down the parking lot. Scooter was not about to be abandon and desperately tried to keep up with the float. Eventually an amused float chaperone picked him up and placed him along with Sam and Sugar in the pen.

Actually, to them this was pretty cool. It's really a better version of a car ride, and there's food and no visual encumbrances. It was going too slow for the anticipated gush of oxygen rush up your snout but very enjoyable nonetheless.

Moments after the float turned down Chapel Street the SPCA truck showed up with a small cage containing about six cats. There was no way the truck could catch up to the float because it was surrounded by marching bands and the streets were closed to traffic. Eventually they procured a large pull wagon and placed the cage of cats on the wagon. One person pulled the wagon while the other walked along side and supported the cage from falling off the wagon. They made slow progress down the sidewalks towards the float.

When the float rounded Chapel on to Main Street the bands cranked up the volume pretty good. Quite deafening in fact to the dogs. It was just a short distance to the judges starting point at the center of town and by then our three stars of the stage were getting hyper and feeling pent up. The wagon with the cats was now making time along the roadside and eventually caught up to the float just past the North Main Street row of businesses. Needless to say, the SPCA workers were stunned to see three howlin' dogs penned up on their float. They didn't know what to do with the cats and they had a mere split second to decide. It would have been quite a haul to go back to the truck and they attempted to voice out to the kids on the float as to why there were dogs in the pen. The music was just too loud and before any explanations could be understood, two of the football players reached down and snagged the cage and placed it on the float. Helpless, the delivery workers just let it go... oh puppy!

At this point I was way ahead of them scavenging at one of my favorite locations, The Dairy Isle. Kids can't hold on to their ice cream cones. One in thirty will drop the whole thing. One in twenty will lose all or most of the top portion. If you don't mind lickin' up a few ants then any scrounge, bum or stray could almost survive there. As a side bar note, Lew's beloved poodle Tuffy use to lick the ants off the pavement without the ice cream. Just the dry crunchy ant itself. Maybe it was therapy like rock barking or some basic response action but either way you look at it, chasing ants and eating them is hardly worthy of canine stature. Again, my case is made, poodles are a whole other species all together.

For real dogs, cool chocolate ice cream is a great diversion on a hot summer day and it's a wonderful doggie experience. There's not a lot of foods we get to lick and take in a full reward. I get more full on tongue sensation from licking my balls or someone's palm than say a slab of beef or a bone. With general foods we usually do a teaser lick to get the saliva flowin' then chomp into our meal- kinda' like sniffin' your wine then swiggin' it. Ice cream is lickin' food and our tongues were made for it and it's one of those human foods that's perfectly sweet for our tastes. There's no blast of sugar or tart reaction. Just smooth lickin' from the tips of our tongue to the back of our throats- over and over again.

I really needed the diversion anyway. The pageant is so freakin' loud. One band after another. Those damn trumpets push so much air our ears get ringin' then- BAM, the cymbals just crash in without warning. At the moment, chocolate on my tongue was the stronger sensation to the monotonous music and I was finding calm in the rhythmic licking of my fallen delight. Back on the float, Sugar, Scooter and Sam couldn't have been more over stimulated. Music blasting in front and behind them. Massive crowds to their right and to their left in a continuous stream. Trapped, in motion and now encumbered paw steps away from a cage of cats.

Sugar and Scooter went howlin' right away at the felines. It was a bit of an over reaction because they both live with cats, but in general, dogs are only comfortable with other species they learn to cohabitate with. They are trained and expected to suppress instinct and accept them relatively peacefully as family. Any non-family cats are fair game in doggie natural law.

The pen that was holding the dogs was originally designed for the cats; just a couple feet high and made of thin coop wire. The dogs were amicable at first because the ride was fun and they were getting treats. As I stated however, moods had changed. Sugar in particular was over hyped at everything. He was in a full on rage at these cats. Despite being surrounded by boisterous marching bands his bark was carrying weight. The conductor of the band following their float was clearly becoming distracted and almost tripped over himself as he kept looking back at the disruption.

Sam was just a bit confused wondering how a simple walk with his Master had now turned into bizarro world. Confusion in dogs tends to lead to an angry reaction and since the only release was to bark at the cats, he again was pulled into Sugar's world of dog lovin' chaos. All three of 'em are at it now and these cats are practically doing back flips in their cage. Totally stressed out being within breathing distance of angry dogs. The kids were basically helpless. Some of the football players in true doggie heart enjoyed the chaos. It, however, was determined that they were now a spectacle and a detraction so one end of the coop wire was cut in hopes the dogs would exit the float... oh puppy!

Sugar and Sam charged out of their confinement and bore down on the cat cage. They both raised up on their hind legs to enlarge their appearance and pounce on the cage but their impact slid the cage clear off the side of the float. The cage fell the modest distance to the ground and the impact busted the cage door open and the half dozen cats fled into the public. Sugar and Sam jumped off the float in cat chasin' pursuit.

The crowd was in a gasp as Sam charged through the marching bands interrupting timing and forcing some baton twirlers to miss their catches. Sam snagged one baton off a single hop and fled with his fetch in pursuit of a particular cat but his chase was over in seconds as the cat escaped into the crowd. He headed back towards the float as a chaperone and the parents of the batonist attempted to regain the baton. Sam weaved through the band with baton in mouth smacking the legs of various band members along the way, totally disrupting their performance. I must admit, that woulda' been music to my ears.

Sugar had locked in on one particular stray and chased him off the road through the crowd and to my surprise, clear past me up the Dairy Isle parking lot. I decided to forgo my final licks and stick my nose into this fiasco barking in chase as well. We circled around the back of the Dairy Isle in route with the "U" shaped driveway and back towards the street.

Scooter was stuck on the float. Three legs and a stocky body were not about to make any flying leaps off a moving bed. He peered over the edge of the float in contemplation but one of the kids nudged him back. Their float along with the adjoining section of the parade was in some disarray and trying desperately to regain some composure.

Our cat chase, which circled the Dairy Isle, sent us back through the crowd and into the street. We had no possibility of catching that cat but we almost got it by default. The cat ran under the float and missed getting treaded by a hair. It escaped safely to the other side of the street and we halted our chase. Scooter moved to our side of the float and barked in our direction. Sam also had arrived with baton in mouth and angry humans in tow. Sam wanted nothing of a confrontation and just dropped the baton which was collected and returned to the despondent twirler. I hope they had the good sense to towel it off.

The kids on the float realizing their misfit group of dogs had returned were going to now place Scooter off the float into our possession but chaos ruled our course. Mr. Peanut came skippin' down the street wavin' his big white hand and tossin' peanuts to all the crowd. Another tradition on this bizarro day.

Mr. Peanut for those who need a refresher is the "mascot" of a major peanut seller. Basically, he's got these skinny black legs and arms and a huge peanut shell for a head and body. He carries a cane and a top hat and to be honest looks like a big bloated stick to us dogs. He's intimidating yet he forces us to pursue him because we just don't like him. He skips by us and like a pack of rapid wolves we're on the case. Scooter is ditched again and left to be the sole animal representative of the SPCA as he floats on down the parade.

The young kids came runnin' from the sidewalks to get some peanuts and see this interesting character and their visit would last about two seconds as we just start howlin' at him. Parents ran to the street and pulled their youngsters from the scene as we continue to inspect this odd and grotesque stick thing. He tries to calmly skip away but we pursue, now disrupting the bands ahead of the SPCA float. I guess we were kinda' mean but Sam, Sugar and I don't eat people. Not that we knew this was a person but he was way too large for us to consider as a kill, though we had to inspect his edibleness. We just gotta' chase him, ya' know.

We gotta' bark at his intimidation and investigate his being. We gotta' promote our thoughts on this subject.

I doubt he could run very fast without tippin' over and though we kinda' calmed our barkin' and were just having a playful chase, he starts to beat us with his cane. Sam doesn't take well to this and gets a bit aggressive at which point this backward fast-steppin, bobble-headed, no-air-conditioned-sweatin', parody of a peanut, kinda' looses balance and backs into the middle of a marching band that had yet to be affected by the dog lovin' chaos. You can imagine the sequence of events. The trombone player stumbles into the tuba player who stumbles into the drum corps who drop their sticks and trip all over each other. Fortunately, no one hit the ground but it's total disruption- music to my ears.

Despite the attempts to dam the proceedings the flow of the pageant moved steadily on but by now a more formal investigation was in progress as to the disturbances in the parade up the middle of North Main Street. A couple of police officers and parade officials were making their way in our direction getting detailed updates from spectators along the way. A few of them handing cats to the investigators which they scooped up in the chaos. One parade official made the mistake of carrying an already spooked cat with him as they reached our location. They probably coulda' snagged one or all three of us with some assistance but the cat was outta' the bag- literally. Once that cat spotted us he exploded from a ball of fur to a fully extended circus acrobat and tore away from his holder. The chase was again on and we fled potential incarceration in pursuit of this cat.

Interestingly, we chased this cat right through my formative years parking lot at the old apartment and into the cornfields but lost it from that point. I must admit, I prefer losing the chase all together than having it run up some tree and taunt me. Outta' sight, outta' mind let's me move right along with my day. Barking up a tree is a complete waste of time and not even therapeutic. I'm just compelled to do it and sustain it until some other form of stimulation breaks my intensity. I mean, has a cat ever fallen out of a tree by sheer force of barking?

Tom Mody

Hmmm, I wonder if there's some kind of archives & data facility up here in Doggie Heaven. I assume I'm suppose to be able to just think of a question and the answer will pop into my head but it doesn't always work like that as I've previously explained. I hate to think us dogs get some second-rate version of Heaven where God assigns some trainee to manage our afterlife affairs. Don't get me wrong; this has been really cool up here. I kinda' hang out and mingle with some other dogs and enjoy the free human chow. It's just that all these revelations and thoughts and suppositions come to me in a stream of consciousness. It's not like I can make an appointment with God and shoot the shit about it. I suppose I need to first learn and comprehend all these grand revelations that pop into my head but beyond that I'm willing to do some legwork for the small insignificant stuff. Just show me where the filing cabinets are, or where the microfilm is, or how to get on-line up here. Isn't there some "dot GOD" web site I can access? Really, I wanna' know if a dog ever barked a cat out of a tree.

The internet is killin' earthly dogs these days you know. They're getting fat and lonely and their brains are twisting from the constant hum of CPU's and weird unseen signal waves from your monitors. Everyone's on-line tryin' to meet a mate and chat about their interests and have cyber sex. Dogs these days are just a ten-minute break from your cyber lives and then it's back to your zombie land. Don't you know that dogs are the ultimate pickup tools? Just put on some nice clothes to make you look hip or some workout clothes to make you look fit and drag us along in the world where there's air and substance and warm-blooded creatures. It doesn't matter if you have the face of my tail side. My lovableness will make up for your butt ugly faces- just dress properly!

Eventually the jig will be up on-line and your first computer written impressions of intelligence and compassion and humor won't cut it when the other person finally meets you face to ass face. First impressions have to be visual and having a cute dog there with you softens your offensive looks plus projects your compassionate nature in a way words can't.

Once you get to Heaven then the internet in some form should be available to you. Need to find the status of dead relative, go to "HEAVENORHELL.GOD". Need to find the weather forecast for the next millennia, go to "FOREVER72.GOD". Need to figure out the protocol for determining which one of your deceased wives you're expected to spend eternity with, go to "CATFIGHT.GOD". And remember to always use upper case letters when typing your addresses. Unlike Doggie Heaven, I'm sure you're Heaven has a terminal on every cloud tapped right into God's brain. So for now, will ya' just spend time with your dog? I've resigned the fact that you've got 'em leashed but I can't ignore the neglect you're digital society has caused. Sooner than you realize you'll have eternity and the ultimate search engine at your disposal.

Back to that warm June afternoon, despite our efforts, that "tour de force" known as the Pageant of Bands continued merrily on. For the good part of that day, Sugar and I got just what we needed. Dog lovin' chaos was back in motion and the opportunity to promote our freedom was witnessed by many an outsider to our little doggie village. Even Sam was a bit stimulated at being so open about his inner evolved dog. Maybe when we were younger we might have let our enthusiasm and aggressive tendencies turn on each other once the excitement waned. Now that we've associated through the years, it was more common to let some camaraderie rekindle our ancestral pack like prowling. So the three of us paced along the borders of the cornfield until we reached the back road of Classic Street. Our minds were refreshed, our purpose renewed, our mission accomplished. Sure, we had strayed a few cats at our expense but really, they're just cats.

And speaking of animals going astray, Scooter was slowly being escorted further and further out of his zone of familiarity. He, on occasion, might have explored as far as the convenient store just past the town center and on his wildest adventures made it all the way to the Dairy Isle but that was it. He was too small and too handicapped to be exposed outside his comfort zone and safety net of his little quarter. As the lone remaining animal representative of the SPCA for the day, the duties beyond his control were taking him all the way up to the high school parking lots. That's as far across town as you can get before all other company is cows and sheep.

The kids on the float took good care of him but he was caged and drowning in anxiety- and quite possibly going deaf. When the float did make its stop at the top hill section of the high school by the band room doors, Scooter was given a few courtesy pats on the head and set down to stable ground.

He looked up with uncertainty at his escorts but these were kids without attachments to him. Their thoughts of his well-being were quite detached and any modest concern was quickly trumped by the inquisition of SPCA adult personnel curious as to the whereabouts of a half dozen cats. Dog, I'd love to have been a fly on the float wall at that conversation. "Gosh Miss Cat-do-gooder, these terrorist dogs hijacked our float and practically held us as ransom with their savage ways before tossin' the cats overboard. We were lucky to have escaped with our lives."

Whatever their excuse, the adults weren't buyin' it. Scooter never did respond well to human tones much beyond a single sharp command. Any extended berating by Master to dog or even human father to son sent him off to a more comfortable corner. The tone around the float was elevating in intensity so Scooter waddled off around it and into the road. Damn Beagles, I swear they are like magnets to rubber.

Tires screeched and a horn blasted inches from his head but his ears were already ringing with confusion and disorientation. Instead of jumpin' outta' his skin he froze in a cowering ball and forced the car to go around him rather than dart further into the road. This turned attention on him from the SPCA adults and more inquisitions as to where this dog came from escalated their ire. Scooter wanted as much separation from that scene as possible and went back to the sidewalk and headed down the school hill. At the bottom parking lot there was a mass of people crowded around food and flea market vendors awaiting the end of the parade and the beginning of the band field competition on the football field.

He muddled through the crowds and was recognized by a few surprised villagers but none of them considered he may have been out of his element. There were plenty of food scraps available and he made a late lunch from discarded hotdog bun ends and dropped french fries. His hodge-podge meal may have perked him up a bit but the sensitive bones in his ears were still rockin' from the piercing and the pounding and the crashing of his surroundings. The crowd's legs were similar to the constant forests Laddie and myself had to navigate and its endlessness can make you crazy. Fortunately he only had three paws that could be stepped on as he made progress across the parking lot to a large stretch of grass bordering the school drive way and the football field. Clear vision ahead helped him gather his bearings and he followed the grass down to the main road. Maybe if he had a thumb he could have given the international sign for "I'm a long way from my dog house", but unfortunately as a dog we only have two clear-cut, non-verbal signals- waggin' the tail (your hand may touch me) and exposin' the fang (if your hand touches me I'll dismember it).

He walked along the roadside snooping around tents set up by medical personnel for any emergency needs of participants and spectators. His homing instincts were correct in wanting to cross the road to get home but the flow of bands kept him at bay for another hour. He found a shaded spot behind a tent and buried his head under his paws to drown out the constant barrage of contemporary marching band standards. He even slumbered off for a while probably dreamin' of a world without cymbals.

The silence woke him. Not a pin drop silence but the intermission of music was noted subconsciously and he arose to try and figure out how to get home. A large influx of cars and people were making use of the road but at least he was adept at navigating around this type of cluster and he managed to get across the street. Being a village dog he was use to following along sidewalks and that left him only one route to follow, the Classic Street mile, which Laddie had taken as his final stroll of the village. It was as simple as "follow the yellow brick road" to get to a place of familiarity but his handicap made this type of hike exaggeratingly difficult.

In fact, as the three of us dogs exited the cornfields an hour earlier we walked the same path to the village. It was a venture that helped to expand my appreciation of pack companionship. Once Scooter crossed the road and turned up Classic Street, he was only a few paw steps from that very cornfield border. I'm not sure he would have taken that long walk alone and may have opted to try and camp out on some porch or worse, beg for help at the side of the road to be picked up by any deranged stranger.

As he considered his options, a rustling came out of the cornfield. Even further from home, the SPCA stray cat we chased earlier had reared its mangy head from the stalks of monotony. Both creatures were startled of course, but it's amazing what being out of your element does to your normal instincts. One is much less likely to react in a normal aggressive manor. Anything that doesn't come at you with razor claws and two-inch fangs is better than being alone. And let's be honest, Scooter with his dopey face and stump could probably have shared the roadway with a mouse and been the more uneasy one. However, he lives with cats so the company wasn't all too foreign.

I for one hate to see necessity bring out this type of pseudo-evolved coexistence. Gettin' chummy with a stray freakin' cat might seem like a higher state of acceptance practiced by dogs in this new century but moving forward doesn't make you evolutionarily higher. You may be literally further ahead but it's on the down slope of the peak. However, God works in mysterious ways and Scooter was damn fortunate to have this mangy stray to trot down Classic Street- not as a companion but as bait.

By the time these two lost misfits reached Hilsinger's Bar, a little more than half way down their journey, Scooter's three legs were functioning like two- he was pooped. If trouble came, there wouldn't be much he could do to avoid it.

Who are we kidding here...? "If trouble came"? What do you humans call it, Murphy's Law? Scooter would have done well to just stay put and hang out by the bar door. Eventually, someone local would have recognized him and hitched him where he needed to be. But that stupid cat procured a discarded cotton candy handle and continued on to actually get ahead of Scooter for some lone licks.

Having made many trips to the village pool, Scooter was well aware of the sweet delights still obtainable from the sugar-soaked handle. For years, one village girl had a soda and cotton candy enterprise out in front of her house near the pool and it always seemed she was making enough money to buy the damn pool. If I was tired from the long walk from the village center to the pool I could count on finding some type of sugar uppers discarded by her stand. It was usually enough to fuel my incessant barking fix for a good hour. Scooter had experienced the same sugar jolts from his travels and understood some licks of that cat's stick is just what he needed. Scooter expended whatever final energy he had left to catch up with this cat. When he finally did there was an amicable sharing of the stick.

For doggie freakin' sake, they can't even fight over that? It's natural law you know- highly acceptable behavior. A snarl here, a scratch of the eye there. Even if the end result is mutual sharing there has to be some type of standoff to predicate it. Oh what ever, it was in Scooter's best interest anyway. They settled on a spot at the intersection of Classic Street and Park Street across from the Episcopal Church and began swappin' inter-species spit along the cone shaped paper stick.

Maybe it was interspecies sin. Maybe that explains the events that occurred next better than Murphy's Law. In fact, those poor displaced innocents were being stalked. Primed and eyed if you will. Evil was lurking in the Summit Street cemetery and moving from behind the stones of the dead. Quietly yet swiftly it followed the border of the church brush to the roadside. The evil was momentarily delayed by a pickup truck, which happened to stop at the curb. It was the SPCA workers truck and they were delighted to recognize the unique black patches on this gray coated stray. The driver side door opened and the woman called out to her friend named Ratty. The worker did not want to approach Ratty unsure of the friendliness of Scooter so she continued to try and lure the cat with advanced human facial muscle skills- whistles, lip smacking, compressed breathing hisses.

I refuse to refer to the damn cat by some name so I'll continue to call her the stray. The stray recognized the voice of her caretaker (jailer, medicater, euthenizer, etc.) but was having difficulty separating herself from her treat. In time the stray would have responded and likely returned to the woman but this was a rare opportunity to enjoy a candy stick. The woman continued with her impressive vocabulary of cat calling and this standoff was testing the boundaries of patience... for the evil in waiting. It would wait no more.

General raced across the street under the cover of the parked truck. He pounced on the first warm-blooded prey in his path. Scooter was fortunately second in line at the candy stick. The strike was precise, directly to the Stray's neck. The cat's body curled up in a ball with all four paws flailing at General's head but its nails had been pulled, a suppressive procedure for captivity. What could have been skin slicin', blood spewin' stabs of defense were mere taps on the head to help gauge the preys eventual submission.

The woman driver screamed at this horrific and blatant ambush. A man on the passenger side jump out of the vehicle in a useless response action and ran around the truck but General came towards him with the stray still flailin' in his jaws. Even in a cat muted snarl it was clear who was the baddest dog and the man retreated to his truck to find something for leverage. It was too late, General ran off to the cemetery to add to the dead.

This kill was a lot easier than the fowl that littered a farm outside the city. General would often venture the mile west of the village to Rogers Conservation Center, commonly called the "Game Farm." There, an assortment of non-exotic creatures were caged for human viewing. Mostly wild winged game like peacocks, pheasants and turkeys. Humans also enjoyed the picnic grounds, nature trails and information centers which made up a full day of family fun. Before being chased off the grounds, he would work himself up into latherous rages over such delectable sights being a mere paw steps away yet safely contained behind wire. As he fled the premises he would find himself in the open fields of an area farmer with a genetically induced appetite for grounded bird. If undetected, he could have a choice of rooster or hen and unlike the cat, he found them savory meats. They just happened to be a bit more capable of harm with their pecking beaks and dagger claws. The bigger concern was that one particular farmer had caught him red handed and with shotgun in hand almost made our lives a lot easier.

General did manage to escape unscathed but the shotgun was loaded and placed near the coop for future encounters. The close call put some fear into him but if you venture west much past the river, the smell will draw any hunting canine towards the Game Farm. For any dog to step on those grounds is asking for temporary insanity. You just want to crap bird that night and you can't because the damn kill is caged. Without hesitation, any reasonably aggressive carnivore is going to continue on to the next property until they are appeased. Once you get all worked up that even means risking having a hole shot through your colon.

But back to the cat killing at hand. It all happened so fast really. Scooter was still lickin' sugar off his nose by the time General departed. Once the sweet sensation had dissipated from his tongue the shock finally set in. He began whimperin' and withdrew towards the bushes off the sidewalk. In our drive to consume anything other than dog food he reappeared again to retain his sugar stick and brought it under the bushes. The SPCA workers considered taking Scooter with them for his own safety but there was no protocol for it. The debate soon ended as the woman driver became nauseous and puked on the roadway, sickened by the grotesque attack. The man assisted her to the passenger side and he took over the vehicle and drove off. Oddly, puke trumps sugar and Scooter came out to sniff around the puddle of barf. He wasn't too fond of the beer remnanced puke steamin' off the vomit so he left it alone and began walking towards the intersection of East State Street.

From my back stoop I can look across the neighbor's yard over the short iron spiked fence to see anything approaching the East State Street intersection from Classic Street. And to my interest, there was Scooter waddlin' down the sidewalk. I leaped off the stoop, ran through the yard and jumped over that iron fence which borders the neighbor's yard. I always enjoyed doing that. It's a doggie version of a minor athletic accomplishment. The fence had dull spikes so it presented a certain risk yet a quick high upon landing safely. Scooter had moved further up the street out of my view, blocked by the neighbor's house. I was going to chase him down, maybe give him an earful when half way through the neighbor's yard I stopped in my tracks.

General was on Scooters trail and stalked right past my view. At his pace he was only about thirty paw strides behind the oblivious beagle and I let it be known. I snarled at General and he stopped on a dime. Remember now, I'd torn the flesh off a deer and lived in the wild (for a night). I was just stupid enough to think I could engage this killer. I approached another paw step or two and set as mean a tone as I knew how. The iron fence I had just leaped wrapped around the yard so though I had leaped one side, the opposite side was a barrier between us. It's strange though, as I went to leap the opposite side fence, it appeared much higher than normal. But it couldn't be, I'd leaped it many times before. I moved forward again but my paws felt like they had lead weights around them. Also my hind legs seemed to be developing the early stages of arthritis, they just locked stiff. And beyond all belief, the gravitational pull of the Earth's center was grounding me to my location and the dirt below my feet was turning to tar pits. Yes, the whole molecular make up of universal matter was changing around me, keeping me from advancing on General.

I wish that was the case but sadly, the only real odd occurrence was that the fur on belly was turnin' yellow. And changes in the universe wasn't the cause, the prospect of engaging resident evil was.

I'd hoped when the time came I'd have courage enough to take on General. Had we gone a few years back I probably would have fought him on youthful ignorance alone but since he had me in his clutches once, he held the intimidation factor over me. I thought I could summon the wolf ancestry in me that got me through my ordeal in the woods but maybe that needs a situation of dire straights. The truth here is that we were separated by a fence and until one of us crossed that line, no imminent harm was at hand. I just couldn't do it. Doggie hell, I probably wouldn't have even made the jump successfully let alone had a chance at defeating him.

I wish I could act with the human factor in considering the fate of Scooter. That charge of bravery that does bring you humans to protect and overcome even when the odds are against you- it could have pushed me forward, or got me killed. Either way I was feeling a sense of desperation for the poor beagle and a doggie type of disappointment in myself. The difference between our species being that I turned and went back to my yard and basically forgot about the whole incident. I just resumed barkin' at rocks or sniffin' around for a good place to crap. A setback like that for you humans carries a lifetime of regrets, guilt and expensive therapy.

But all dogs must die sometime. It's not like Scooter could have gone on to save the world or even that generations from now his offspring could make a blip in the outcome of life on earth. He's an animal and this is how things end for us. Even at our most evolved states it often comes down to survival of the fittest. That's the luxury I had in tuckin' tale and puttin' him outta' my mind. At least I thought I had put him outta' my mind.

Anyway, maybe Master Mark would shed a tear and Sugar would have to make a routine adjustment in the familiarity of life, but fortunately, there's a Doggie Heaven and Scooter would ascend. We just didn't know it then.

General probably could have jumped the fence but he'd never attempted it before so the barrier was sufficient to keep him from chasin' me. Besides, Scooter would offer much less resistance and he was the initial target. In earthly context it's easy to hate General- vicious, cold-blooded killer. But up here in Doggie Heaven my disdain of him goes beyond the obvious. As I suppose in your Heaven as well, you get to understand the motivations, the history, the programming and the genetics of each soul and situation. It's not so black and white. Especially for animals that eat meat.

I don't absolve General (nor can I) of his actions because they aren't sins. They are just old archaic animal laws collecting dust on our proverbial books. Given all the factors of understanding, he did what he does. What it says animals can do. My disdain for him is in the protection of my place in time. As a collective, we Dogs of Sherburne aspired and attained a state of notoriety in an evolutionary peak. At that point in time we had greater opportunity of promotion than was ever possible, past or future, and we seized it. General continued to jeopardize that. Most frustrating is that because of the old laws of our wild ancestry, General reaped the rewards of freedom by those bygone standards. He wasn't free on a daily basis but when he was, the old laws of achievement by being stronger, faster and meaner were unnecessarily in play. We didn't need those laws anymore- we had new rules of chaos and promotion now.

But back to the facts, General, through all the genetics and environmental conditions, was an animal, a carnivore, a killer. If you sat him on a doggie bean bag and let Sigmutt Freud take a crack at him, he at best could be diagnosed as aggressively confused. Calling him confused is not making excuses- he was confused. He wasn't stalking Scooter to eat him and he didn't eat that cat he carried to the cemetery. He wasn't stalking Scooter because he was a threat- obviously! German Shepherds need to be raised a certain way. They can be a violently aggressive breed if they aren't given purpose, structure and freedom. A non-aggressive breed of dog in the same environment would be all bark and no bite but because of General's breed the brain chemicals churn full force and his physical attributes empower his desires. He's confused into being aggressive but is under no duress to do so. In fact, if he was raised without human environmental conditions, he may have been more clear as to when the necessity for that type of aggression is appropriate. But being a "bad" dog was reinforced at home to mirror his Master and that programming was now in charge of his actions.

So, because the odor of a friendly dopey beagle activated the salivating glands and chemical instincts of this resident evil, the fabric of our freedom was about to suffer another tear. The moment I leaped back over into my yard I would never have given it another thought except that General's vicious growls could be heard across the back yards of the area. He didn't swoon in from nowhere as he did to that cat- he didn't have to. Scooter was at the corner, too slow to make any attempt to hastily cross a street and too in touch with his own liabilities to know that he couldn't get away even if he attempted. General basically made sure Scooter knew his hopeless fate by lung lashing him into submission. I sat yards away trying to mind my own business but my eyes were envisioning what my ears were hearing- inevitability.

It was cruel really, General's taunting. Almost beyond savage behavior but that's what happens when programming gets corrupted and manipulated. When you take inherent evil and inject confidence, mere killing isn't enough. It in fact becomes the evil alter ego of what us village dogs had evolved to. General was us, a promoter of his doggie agenda. Kill Scooter straight up and he borders the line of old school vicious canine acceptability. But to taunt and impose fear upon the helpless and unassuming without survival cause, that's flat out personal promotion. A twisted version of what the rest of us evolved dogs were all about. It saddens me to now understand that General "got it" just like we did but messin' with his breed's programming twisted it to evil.

Scooter just cowered with General promoting himself so violently that his own barks were drawing blood from his tongue and cheeks. It littered on Scooter's mane with saliva. "Kill him already" is what was going through my mind. Yards away the promotion of General's evil was building up a strange emotional type reaction in me. I was supposed to be able to let this go but at the risk of making you think we dogs had emotions, I was ashamed. I have to describe it some way and I'll be damned, I was ashamed. Again, if he'd just shut up and done it, killed him, I coulda' put it outta' my mind and enjoyed the detachment we dogs are accustomed to. But just like many of your action type movies, the bad guy just won't kill the hero. He's gotta' tell him his twisted motivations and taunt his superior intellect and laugh and see if the hero will crack and show fear. You probably have seen it so many times in your entertainment story lines you probably think that's how it really happens. Then that extra posturing buys the hero or the cavalry the requisite time for assistance. Totally fiction, right?

Hmmm, I heard screechin' tires, slammin' of car doors, humans screamin' and yellin'- possibly man on dog violence. It was better than the cavalry- it was the SPCA! Animal lovers with guilt and concern- cool people! The very two workers that left Scooter to his own survival a short time ago rejected protocol and found a higher conscious. As they were heading out of town they decided to turn back and take responsibility for the dog. Armed with a tire iron, the male driver braved General's potential to cause him harm and beat him off Scooter before any physical damage was done. The passenger-side woman, refreshed with a couple minty Tic-Tacs, snagged the bewildered beagle and secured his safety within the truck cab.

Scooter was taken to the SPCA in Norwich where dog tags helped to identify the owners and he was returned home the next day- but not without consequence. Scooter's Masters wondered how he got himself into that mess to begin with. They could only deduce that he was chasing some tail so in order to keep his "supposed" libido in check- he was neutered! Since he was down at the SPCA anyway what the heck, right? It's no different than asking the gas station attendant, "since you're fillin' me up do ya' mind checkin' the oil too!" Can you hear them down there, "we'll wash and rinse the mutt for ya' and well we're at it, sure, we'll be glad to crack his scrotum open so he'll have no reason to ever leave your porch again.

I at the time didn't know what had happened to poor Scooter. I heard the incident but for all I knew Scooter was dead. When the ruckus was over I barked to be let inside. I didn't see Scooter for a while but mostly the incident was out of mind. It's odd though as I think back on it now. I stayed pretty close to home for a few weeks. We don't know why at the time we shelter ourselves like that but with revelation I know why- fear and guilt.

Revelation 12

Meat eaters puke
63% more that vegetarians

Seven years was a long time to be livin' on a bar terrace. I assumed that's where Hobie lived but it doesn't make sense really. The owners of the Sherburne Inn must have let him inside during the winter nights? I guess that leads to an interesting question for earthly dogs- do we actually assume? Are we capable of it? Can we take things for granted? And what level of intelligence is required to achieve such evolved brain growth?

I would say that if we can walk around in our environment with a warm and calm feeling about us, then we are capable of the core basis of assumption. Otherwise we'd be all freaked out by the world around us like most animals of the wild. It's not so much that assumption requires intelligence. It's more a response to conditioning over time. A repetitive familiarity of which we grow accustom. I think what separates us domestic animals, and dogs in particular, is that familiarity makes us warm inside- emotionally. Most animals can probably generate the same basic comfort from their mother or a safe familiar nest but domestic animals seem to connect with their whole environment. For us dogs of Sherburne at this peak of evolution, assumptions and expectations drive the bulk of our daily activities. We get a warm chemical reaction in our brains when the noon time whistle sounds and when we catch the scent of new leather from an open doorway at Hodge's Department Store. We get a high when the things we assume to happen about the village do in fact happen.

You'd think the same anticipated high would work in anticipating actions of the other dogs but it doesn't. I'm never calm when I'm south of the village and Scooter jumps out of a bush. I'm always surprised to see Scamp sittin' right on his front porch. It can get tiresome freakin' out every time we cross paths. It suppresses that anticipation high. The exception, of course, was Hobie.

Even without his weirdo-karma-voodoo-sixth sense shit, his place upon the Inn patio in the center of the village was anticipated. You didn't go out on adventures with him and you didn't engage him in any manner other than looking to him as a grounding point to what ever was affecting you that day. If things in your existence seemed off or you were simply too static charged with doggie enthusiasm, you might head his way.

I remember one time a rather obnoxious metal beast was coming down the hill as I was out on our front stoop barking to be let in. This things was loud and caught my attention right away. I leaped off the stoop to begin chase but it quickly turned down Classic Street before I could reach the corner. I got some kinda' gut feeling, instead of chasing it down Classic Street I turned and ran towards the center of town. I put my doggie ears to good use and was surprised at how well I could make out its directional movements. Just the tonal shifts alone guided me to cut through the Sherburne News parking lot and around some brush to the Qwick Stop convenient mart. Sure enough, that metal beast pulled in the lot to grab a carton of cigarettes.

It kept its motor running and I howled at it the entire time it was parked. The owner came out minutes later and spewed some profanities at me. When the car tried to back up I attempted to block the path but he revved the engine, hit the horn for a warning and then basically tried to run me down. I jumped outta' the way and chased him to the end of the lot then ran in front of him as he turned on to North Main Street. He paid me no attention and gassed it quickly- his forward burst caught me off guard. The bumper actually smacked upside my head as he sped off.

Damn, that hurt, and I kinda' stumbled to the roadside yelpin'. There was a bench nearby and I laid up beside it while an elderly gentleman patted my back. I had a mild concussion of sorts, whoppin' headache and slight disorientation, but after a few minutes I got up. We are animals- we can tough it out. The physical effects didn't bother me beyond the obvious discomfort. However, I was a little hesitant to cross the street.

I had such a wonderful high in tracking that car using my hearing and now to have the incident end up with a little phobia was distressing. Physically and mentally I'd been shaken and was at a small little crossroads in trying to cross the road. Traffic would pass and clear but I just couldn't take that step. Partly because my vision was blurry but mostly it was the fear of getting bumper thumped. I turned to head for home in defeat when a bark came at me from across the street. My vision may not have been too clear at the time but it was indeed a familiar sound. Hobie had watched the whole incident from the Inn patio.

An extended break in traffic was at hand and he continued to bark for my attention. I was disrupted in every capacity but that sense of familiarity brought a warmth and calm inside. In some "Hobie-weird" way I trusted in that familiarity and crossed the road (twice actually) to reach him and regain the bit of nerves I had lost.

I spent an extended amount of time at the Inn that day, mostly just recovering from my headache and appreciating having a familiar grounding point outside of home. That day Hobie was right where I would anticipate him to be at the very moment I needed him to be. You humans often turn to others in reference of them being a "moral compass." Hobie was kinda' like that to us. Maybe more of a point of trust in the free outside world where it's hard to trust in anything. Which is why the night we found his lifeless body at the bottom of a stair well outside the inn certainly jolted us to the core.

For a good portion of that summer I thought Scooter was dead as he sheltered himself for a time. Being a dog it wasn't an overly conscious realization but Laddie was dead,

Scamp was still sequestered in mourning and I was feeling a bit exposed in my free roaming. After a number of days it was important to my familiarity of life to see them out and free at some point. As days turn to weeks, the anticipation grows and it brings a certain stress. You humans understand and rationalize changes in your life- we dogs don't. We can deal with witnessing great, one-time traumas but losing our sense of warm familiarity is a tough adjustment.

General had trotted by my window a number of times sending me off on a saliva spat at each pass. He was loose much more frequently and a sense of concern was affecting me. I was not going to be able to fully frolic in the day without keeping a portion of my senses at watch. Still, I could venture downtown and trust that Quinn's Market would have some fruit to piss on and that Hobie would be setupon the Inn steps.

The subtle glory of being a free dog, though, is losing yourself in the mundane little pleasures we come across each day. When we find them, our minds and senses tend to forget any heightened concerns in our consciousness. Even if a dumb beagle seemingly rises from the dead to disrupt you, our focus on a current pleasure is paramount. At that moment that I finally saw Scooter alive, I coulda' cared less.

Of great interest to the villagers was the local men's softball league. The past few summers it had attracted quite a gathering of spectators enjoying their own last years of open container freedom. For now they could pull up a lawn chair, pull off a beer can tab and litter it along the roadside while the village males played Russian roulette with their skulls, knees and testicles. There was much dog folly at these events as well. If you let us run free it's likely we'll disrupt a game every once in a while for promotion's sake. You'd expect us to steal a ball or batting glove or some unattended necessity to the game. Sugar was so regular at the Paddleford Park games that when I often ran into him he smelled like stale beer and sweaty jockstraps.

I too would find my way to the ball fields and take a quick dip in the creek, which bordered the fields. One day as I was refreshing myself in a spot that wasn't too shallow from the August heat, I uncovered quite a prize. A severed deer leg was trapped against a rock in the slow current. It was far from hunting season but even in that season where deer blood and guts are splattered about our area, I never came across any random intact flesh.

I took possession immediately carrying the deer leg up the embankment and attempted to put my concerns aside and delve into the doggie moment. The pungent leg had a salty, soggy, slightly cool taste that would send you humans hurling on your shoes. To me it was a curious delight. My glands had barely begun salivating its enzymes when a secondary scent crossed my snout. Seconds later there was sniffing in my ear. Scooter was on the case and apparently hoping to share. Let him go lick sticks along side a cat again- I wasn't sharing this find. Had I been less consumed I mighta' given his apparent resurrection a second thought but the casualness in doggie nature let it have no relevance. For I was with meat and in meat I do pledge sole attention.

I didn't even give him the doggie equivalent of "nice to see ya', Scooter." I just lashed out at him as if it were any other day and he moped off. I was however, able to conclude that where Scooter roams, Sugar is not far behind. The last thing I wanted was to have to fuss with that relentless scrounge happy bastard. I just decided to head home with my find and chomp in peace. Getting through the street lined spectators wasn't a problem. No one seemed intent on impeding the path of a soaking wet dog with a severed animal appendage in tow. Moses never had a path so clear.

By the time my ten minute trot to home was over you coulda' parted my saliva like the red sea. It was flowing in pools at the anticipation of finally settling down for a good leg munch. I sat at the side of the driveway under the kitchen window and let the rest of the world's problems fade- briefly. Moments later Master Tom and Lew came out from the house to shoot baskets in the driveway. Master Tom was kinda' disgusted with my treat and banished me inside. He was too squeamish to actually handle the severed leg so he kicked it down the driveway into the front shrubs.

The next morning I happen to be at the side stoop barking to be let in when the breeze was just right to pick up a familiar scent. You might say the smell had a little more bite too it after a night of bacteria growth and fly spit but that made the deer leg even more intriguing. It was practically right under my nose and I fetched it from the shrubs. This time I hoped to find some chompin' peace in the park. I sat at the side of a large tree and let the rest of the world's problems fade- briefly.

Well, yank my tail- into the park came Scamp. He'd been around a bit over the summer, finally coming out of our type of grief. This was the first time I'd encountered him downtown, though. He mostly was seen up the street or accompanying his Masters near the basketball courts at the old school grounds. It was almost a year since we had even been snout to snout. He looked bigger now being in his prime. Was he more amicable now without Laddie's presence or was he just gonna' be pissy? I didn't care really. I had my deer leg and just wanted to be left in peace as I had only gotten my teeth into a few bites of fur and skin.

Scamp approached me but as with Scooter, I coulda' cared less about their long awaited reappearance to our free village. I picked up my find and trotter further into the park. Scamp followed me. I paused and snarled at him to stop tailgating me but he growled back. I concluded he's gonna' be pissy. I wasn't going to be able to just walk away. We were just gonna' have to fight over this deer leg that was suppose to bring me a moments peace. I turned even more menacing and began to snarl as best I could with a severed leg in my mouth.

You figure, I gotta' look mean, right? Imagine if you were walkin' down some alley and you encountered a guy comin' at you with a severed leg in his mouth. You'd crap your pants right there, right? It's almost like I was packin' a "piece." For you humans, when a guy flashes a gun or knife you know he's seriously dangerous. We'll, I was packin' the doggie equivalent- a severed deer leg which should leave the impression that this was fresh from my recent kill so don't mess with me.

I musta' set a pretty good stance because Scamp acted a bit spooked at my crazy severed leg in the mouth look. And I was feelin' mighty crazed because I just wanted a little peace with my find and I kept gettin' bothered. For the moment though, this was really cool being the crazed killer dog that hunts down game and tears its limbs off. Scamp was feelin' trepidation at any further advances towards me and I was about to turn and walk confidently to a new spot, secure that Scamp wouldn't jump me.

Then my stomach got queasy.

You humans sweat but we dogs pant and drool at intestinal distress. This uncontrollable reflex was thumpin' in my stomach as drool poured out the sides of my mouth. The stomach convulsions grew stronger in intensity almost liftin' my hind legs off the ground. Bile backed up in my esophagus getting the previously digested fur stuck in my throat. I now started hacking causing the deer leg to shoot from my clutches. I was trying to heave whatever was in my stomach but the fur balls were stuck causing my throat to contract and sending the stomach contents back. My hacks became more exaggerated. You know how us dogs can make the most ungodly sounds when we get stuff caught in our throats. Scamp stepped back even further but not because of my earlier intimidation, but because my sounds and gyrations were hideous to his sensitive ears. I was practically epileptic at this point trying to get this nasty meat out of my system while still attempting to get my throat to stop contracting.

Scamp couldn't stand it any more and just ran off- but not before he procured the deer leg, of course. I obviously let him go. I doubt I had any sensory perception of anything at the time. All my bodily resources were being expended to my very sick stomach and its expellment of rotten deer meat. I heaved and I contracted and I heaved and I contracted and ultimately released the steamy contents to the ground. When my senses finally cleared the world was spinning and my ears were ringing. I took a few steps then collapsed in a shaded spot. Things calmed within a short time later but I had blown a great opportunity to hold some intimidation over Scamp. He didn't think I was crazed anymore, he just thought I was a freak! I headed home in desperate need of my water bowl and a Milkbone brand dog biscuit.

It was just a stupid deer leg anyway- nothin' but trouble since I got it. That's why as enlightened dogs at an evolutionary peak we should aspire to more self-promotion and not go in hiding with regressive savage gains of our ancestry. But such is the power of temptation. It's comforting to know that God has bestowed temptation upon us as he does his precious man. It affirms our place at man's side above all the other stupid insignificant species.

The deer leg is as alluring to us canines as money or drugs are to man. I would also consider some warm tail as well but I think that's a temptation we both share. We can avoid temptation or it can avoid us (as it violently did in the park) but until it's disposed of, it will continue to draw trouble. You might think that's a bad thing, and it usually is, but on occasion temptation has a destiny. Not to draw destruction from its possessor but to set in motion a higher plan. The fruition of that plan would certainly not be without dire consequence but at a decisive moment one can be revealed of the intended destiny- if they are willing to accept it. And so Scamp headed into the village with the rotten spoiled stench of temptation in his jaw. That he would carry it into the village instead of a secluded spot for personal pleasure tells me that decision was a destined decision not of his own doing. It's too bad- I really wanted him to puke on it.

After a time I freshened up and was ready to pester Master Tom and Beaner across town. They were headed to Abby's for an annual chow & chug fest known as the South Main Street Clambake. It's an invite only party for south side of town residents but the kids can bring their friends so Master Tom and Beaner attend every year. No mention of dogs was included but Sugar, Scooter and Sam are all Southside dogs, it's only fair that they bring a friend- if that's what you'd call me.

Despite all the freedom we free dogs forged for ourselves, I look back now and am amazed at how many village dogs there were chained and shackled along the back streets. Master Tom and Beaner headed to the party by way of Union Street then up South Street. So often along these streets and others in the area, barks and yelps could be heard from the back yards and windows as I passed by. It was like an echo was following me as I trotted along the sidewalks. I don't know if they were cursin' me or cheerin' me but it had grown to such bizarre proportions I would dare call it a phenomena. Such is the celebrity of being a free dog in a world where the leash was becoming more prevalent.

I loved it. In my own way I reveled in it. I didn't have to engage in any outrageous behavior or risky theatrics. I could now just trot down the street to create a stir. Way too cool. It was double cool when humans would be startled from their chairs and daily routines and verbally scold their dogs for acting up. Yes, yes, I feel for the dogs now but am I not allowed to revel in what limited doggie vanities were allotted me? This street walking hysteria would continue for the rest of my years but it was on that walk with Master Tom and Beaner that the previous repetitions made an impression on me as a phenomena.

When we arrived at the clambake late midday, it was already in high gear. I guess another way to put it is that the kegs had been tapped. This pleased the teenagers because the sooner the adults got smashed, the easier it was for them to sneak beer. Though, in those days, teenage drinking at a private party carried the adult reprimand equal to having too many sweets before dinner. The adults didn't want you to do it but..., it was okay this one time. Still, the teenagers couldn't just comfortably go up to the tap and talk politics with the village trustees as they filled their mugs. As long as they snuck a cup here or there, no one really seemed to care.

Gambling, nickel and dime stuff, was also acceptable for all ages and Master Tom was just the right kind of pigeon you wanted at your disposal. Like any small town, Sherburne has its generational lore. Among the teenagers of Master Tom's generation, one of the great legendary places of recollection was Master Father's change drawer. It was the Fort Knox of the village- without the fort. For years this seemingly inexhaustible well of nickels, dimes and quarters supplied pizza, ice cream and video game plays to the less fortunate youths of the village. Sometimes at the generosity of Master Tom and many times at the creative theft of plotting boys. The top layer of black dress socks was the only sentry. Now if they were dirty socks then maybe stench alone could have kept some paws outta' the kitty but it was his clean socks drawer and a quick pushing aside of them revealed a depth of coin that could be measured in inches.

Us dogs had spent the early part of the afternoon looking for something useful to do but it really was rather boring. Someone would toss us a raw clam or a piece of hot dog and we were fine with that. That's a successful day in the life of a dog. I can't speak for the other mutts in the place but I just wasn't myself. Pukin' up that deer leg took a lot outta' me and I mostly just laid in the shade.

Scooter was enjoying an unexpected windfall of attention. Under the gambling table he was receiving all the pats on the head and free chow you could ever want as a mutt. Sadly, he was a pawn in a devious scam to get the bag full of money Master Tom possessed. As Scooter eagerly met the waving hands under the table he received a pat, a treat and a slip of an ace in his collar. Once his immediate gains were met, another accomplice in need of the ace just happened to be waving a piece of meat under the table. Scooter trotted to get his treat unknowingly delivering a scam in the process. It was nice to be needed for something and he played the pawn for a while. Eventually Scooter's interest waned and he wandered off with an ace in his collar- no one noticed.

I managed to get off my butt and chase the frisbee around for a while. It is a neat little thing this floating disc. You get the full landing anticipation during the chase. With a stick it's in the air, then just as quickly it lands and the retrieval part is kinda' lame. I mean, it's just layin' there. Half the time we come back with a different stick than the one that was tossed so what was the point of even throwin' it. At least with a ball you get the roll so there's the potential to snatch it while it's still in motion. And that's the whole fun of it. How many times did I chase a squirrel and then have it just stop dead waiting for me to pounce on it- never! Look, the stick fetch was fine when humans only had wood and rocks at their disposal but evolved dogs, like evolved man, need the challenges and advantages of rubber and plastic.

The frisbee disc floats like the birds, an ultimate prize in the eyes of dogs. At its peak it just hangs there seemingly still in the air. Then it does a B-line right back at us testing the quickness of our reflexes to react suddenly and swiftly yet with full concentration. We almost always get an opportunity to leap and snatch it right from out the air. It's never quite the same chase so it doesn't lose its interest among repetition. Despite my sub-par health, I must admit to being the better of us dogs there. Sugar doesn't have the discipline. He was always overrunning the disc or not anticipating its curve directions. Sam was too casual. He'd kinda' watched it in the air to a point, wait for it to land and then go fetch it. A few times there were some scuffles over possession of the disc but in relative terms, we played nice.

I tried not to be too friendly with these other mutts but it's this freakin' maturity thing- and the General thing. I'm not going to let them come up and steal a bone from me without having somethin' to say about it but unless there was some type of promotional gain to be made, I could do without the bickerin' and nippin'. I guess the constant fighting was becoming old. I know this now because it's been getting old reminiscing about it.

As I patiently awaited my opportunities to snag the frisbee, I watched the others carefully. Over the past year I had been developing a more advanced comfort with these free dogs of the village. Seems as of late we had done more together than we had in conflict. I had grown accustom to not being on the aggressive defensive when they were around. But for the first time I really watched them and tried with my limited abilities to read into them.

It's funny, when I would get all worked up in their presence I never used the intuitive skills that helped us canines advance so far for anything other than reading aggression. I used intuitive skills with humans for all facets of contact. Tone of voice, posture, eye intensity, palm height, finger erectness, muscle tension, lip position, scent of sweat, vibration of step, speed of approach, and about twenty other subtle nuances of complex human motion. I could tell not only that Master wanted to play but at what intensity. I could tell when Master needed attention from me and when I better stay the doggie hell outta' his way. Even when I was gettin' in trouble I knew what Master's reaction was likely to be-though being a dog I had no mechanism in my brain to prevent me from continuing with my naughty behavior.

Dogs really only had a couple of standard reads that I learned to pay notice to. The growl, fang exposure, neck hair stance, head low to the ground, tail position or motion. All tell tale signs I looked for in determining how much blood I may potentially be donating that day. I never looked for the good, the playfulness, the need for kinship. It was just a pleasant surprise when we all got along.

So, I watched Sugar to find more than I knew. The mutt I use to envy running loose by my window and the scrounge that use to always want a piece of my misbegotten goods had a charm you find in most pranksters. It was only evident in his interactions with humans but they really seemed to be taken with his outgoing personality. We both could annoy humans with our barkin' and pesterin' but unlike myself, he never came off as a delinquent. I noticed Sugar getting' in Sam's face over the frisbee and though Sam was more than calm in keeping Sugar at bay, it was viewed as nothing more than a bit of hyperness in the eyes of the humans. If I did that, they'd chastise me as a troublemaker.

Everyone there knew Sugar was a troublemaker but he made his promotions seem so playful. I had been the stronger of us for quite some time but I always had a nervous feeling around him. I wasn't comfortable with his jovial demeanor and I always felt he was going to turn vicious when I least expected it. As I watched him charm people and act so innocent, even when he was causing trouble, I felt any lingering apprehension about him melt away. He may be annoying at times, like a bone spur in the roof of your mouth, but I could never see him as a threat again. Although, since our fight in the house was to be our last, I'm not happy sittin' up here knowin' he got the best of me. But that's what personalities like him do, they getcha' and still make you appreciate and even forgive them.

Sam was wise to Sugar all along, that's why he's so calm even in the face of his devilish demeanor. I watched Sam deal with Sugar and never before noticed the patience he possessed. Most creatures with Sam's stature would be vicious and posturing, knowing they had the physical advantage. Sam had a level of cool that could only have been inborn because it's not our instinctive way.

Sam's cool was evident to all present. In public he was the polar opposite to Sugar's whimsy yet human appreciation of him was of equal caliber. I usually never had too much trouble with Sam, but now, I was becoming totally disarmed as these fresh observations came upon me. I guess the cause of my ease was Sam's subtle uncomfortableness in promoting himself around humans- a trait I excelled at. The cool he portrayed on the outside was actually a bit of shyness from within. He didn't want to go leapin' around for the frisbee but he also didn't want to pass on the attention so he just calmly fetched it at his convenience. Understand, he was a dog- frisbee fetchin' cannot be subdued by inner shyness. I, of course, didn't harbor any of Sam's reservations in being socially playful.

This leaves me to ponder why I had such trouble being beloved village wide to that point. I had fame of the highest order. I was the most notable and quotable of my generation and as well rounded as any of the others. I also had those classic Black Lab features which makes us so desirable. But as I enthusiastically ran across Abby's yard, leaped with skill and grace for the floating disc and properly returned it to the humans, their subtle expressions I had learned to read so well didn't have the same warmth accorded to the others. Not that they were acting any different than I was accustom but in watching reactions to Sugar and Sam, the difference was evident. That realization at whatever level of doggie comprehension actually helped strengthen my personal resolve, which in turn aided in my newfound comfort around my brethren.

You can't teach an old dog new tricks, so you humans say. It is true. Even as I understood the other dogs more I was never going to be like them. We all were so vastly different, the whole lot of us. And you humans lack such skill of observation, being that your senses are so dull from too much use of intellect. I could never be more than a creature of chaos in most of your eyes. But that's okay, I aspired to that. A champion of dog lovin' chaos, runnin' free and promoting our evolution.

My success of that achievement was never more evident than it was that day. Despite our differences as doggie personalities, we all aspired to the same thing. I understood the need for our collective purpose, which dropped my defenses towards them another notch. Freeing me even more to the pursuit of fun and frolic. The humans viewed me as the embodiment of us dogs as a whole and that stature is more enduring than being beloved. I mean, I wasn't hated. I was just a little more public in dry humpin' little girls and chasin' metal beasts across town. Those things tend to interfere with the calm daily activities of you humans so it's understandable to want to keep me at arms length in your affections. I was, and still am, first in your recollections. Humans lack the intuitive sensory skills to be at complete ease around me but because of my observations that day, Sugar and Sam should have been able to detect I was now less adversarial. I had renewed security within and was now comfortable with them as well.

On that moment of clear understanding it was evident what needed to be done. I charged across Abby's yard with purpose. Sam and Sugar were bound by curiosity to follow. They wondered, why was my charge so sudden and what curious thing could have my attention? I ran past the large carriage barn in the back fields- the others eager in anticipation. I leaped from the dry brush and floated (a half second) in homage to the frisbee, eventually belly flopping in the smelly swampy marsh. I submerged for a second and came up with slop coating my top fur. Sugar vaulted behind me in more of a headfirst dive. Sam just stopped at the waters edge. He'd taken too many dips in the dank muck to want the inconvenience and scorn.

Sugar and I treaded a few paddles to soak up the full rank effects of the swamp and quickly hoisted to shore. Sam walked up to Sugar and gave him a quick sniff-over but ended up getting half the swamp on him anyway as Sugar shook out the excess muck from his fur. Green flakes of algae stuck to us and we looked like a doggie version of your "Swamp Thing".

How come we dogs never get to be those great movie mutations you humans are accorded? Swamp Thing, Creature From The Black Lagoon, all your macabre zombies and mummies, and your "scientifically challenged" Frankenstein- which I'm assuming is this new century's preferred "PC" term for him. Poor "Frankie', you made the guy a bride and she was such a bitch. What Frankenstein needed was a dog.

I appeal to your Spielbergs and your Polanskis and your Camerons. And how about you Stephen King, you made us mean and rabid and you made kids scared of us. Playin' a rabid dog is of such little stretch for us. I know most of our actor dogs are classically trained in the on-cue fetch, roll, and bark standards but we can do more. Do you make Meryl Streep play the mother-balancing actress in all her roles? Do you make Jack Nicholson play the zealous basketball fan in every movie! How about it, you writers, producers and directors. Surely some dog is talented enough for the lead role in "Dog of Frankenstein."

In my day, Master Tom and Beaner in particular had an affection for the classic monsters; both in magazines and the Saturday TV monster movie show EIVOM. They would thrill to see a "Curse Of The Mummy Dog". Remember we were not only beloved in ancient times but mummified with our Masters. Or how about Man Wolf. This is the same concept as Wolf Man except a savage wild canine loses all his hair and fangs while increasing his brain size. He falls in love with a local dog warden and is scorned as they try to raise a family together. Eventually, he's shot by the jealous police chief as the Man Wolf attempts to set free all the caged strays in the pound. I like this one. A dog trying to act human is Oscar worthy stuff.

And finally, Doctor Beagle and Mister Doberman. I see a certain studly charismatic Black Lab mesmerizing audiences in an unprecedented dual role. Like the great human actors of his time, this leading dog is an enigma, seemingly aloof, misunderstood by society yet captivating in the role of a lifetime that will ultimately make him a beloved and enduring icon of his generation. Sounds like a great doggie fantasy but in reality the end result is more biography than fiction. But if you had to compare a movie to my life, how 'bout "Brave Heart", minus the neutering scene, of course. Leading the leashed on a battle for freedom and the pursuit of dog lovin' chaos. And so my eventual biographical movie will be titled "Dog Of Brave Heart."

Despite the noble fantasies of having A-List directors lined up to employ my services, I was currently caught up in a B-Movie plot line of "Dogs of Swamp Thing". Cool and refreshed, I sprinted back through Abby's yard. Sugar was side tracked a bit trying to pry a leach from his ass, but he soon followed. We ran around the yard looking for someone to throw us a frisbee but no one cared to even get near us with one of your ten-foot poles. They started naggin' on Master Tom to do something about his dog. As usual, I was the issue. No one there complained to Master Mark about Sugar. He was just being hyper. I was the problem. I was the menace. So be it- it's me they'd remember most when Sherburne's tall tales (or tails) are told. Anyway, Master Tom had been down this road many a day. This time he just went through the motions, listlessly calling me to stand down and heed with monotone enthusiasm. His words came out defeated. He tried a nonchalant brisk walk in my direction but if he got in three steps that was progress. I playfully proceeded with Sugar through the yard tent looking for discarded chow. If wet swampy dog can out stench garbage bags of shellfish on a humid summer evening, then you know we overstayed our welcome. The humans were offended.

Scooter had been camped out all afternoon in there with them, stuffed with butter soaked gems of the sea. He wasn't feeling too well- gut wise. Our presence peaked him enough to get up and greet us. Poor dog, our stench was just too much for him and he heaved whatever was ailing him right in front of the chowder pot. All the adults got in an uproar and chased us from the premises. Sugar and I snuck around the nearby yards until dusk- sniffin' each other. It was kinda' fresh to us.

When darkness came the party was in its last hours. Most everyone was inebriated and paid us little attention. Sam and Scooter were still there looking just as deadbeat as everyone else. When Scooter saw us he just got up and left. We weren't so pungent any more but I assume he was still of ill intestines. Moments later there was a loud tire screeching from out front. I had heard it and seen it before, someone had gotten treaded and it didn't sound good for Scooter. We three dogs ran out front only to practically get trampled by some of the boys charging back to the house. Those heartless fiends, just leaving the poor mutt pancacked in the road. Expecting the worst we continued out front only to see Scooter sittin' quietly on the sidewalk. We hung out there a few minutes. When the boys came back they paid us no attention. There were about seven or eight of 'em and they split into two groups on opposite sides of the street. When they spotted headlights they all inexplicably ran into the middle of the road. Were they playin' chicken'? Was it a mass suicide? Where they just too drunk?

As they became visible to the car they all reached down to the middle of the road and grabbed at something. They split up again to opposite sides and waited for the car to approach. Once the car was just a few feet down the street they reached up and grabbed what looked to me like thin air and pulled back like they had a rope. The car was a split second away when it slammed on the brakes skidding past them. They again ran back to the house in hysterical laughter. It seems they were giving the illusion of grabbing a rope in the street then pulling it taught when the car approached. It was dark enough to fool the driver into slammin' on his brakes. Why he felt the need to fall for this juvenile prank is even beyond Heavenly doggie comprehension. Wouldn't you just plow right through the supposed encumberance and give them the rope burn of a thousand suns?

It was a pretty lame stunt all around but who knows, I guess it was a case of teenage lovin' chaos. It seemed to work for them. The mild excitement kinda' charged us up a bit and we decided to follow Master Tom and his friends up town. All of us except Scooter who hung back and rested his ailing gut. Besides, he lacked the proper number of legs to keep up with us.

I guess it's just me being sentimental but it was a surreal kinda' walk. Us dogs and the Masters, just hangin' out in inter-species camaraderie. Usually were fightin' amongst ourselves or scattered about tryin' to keep up with them on their bikes. This was just a group of God's creatures on a slow pace reveling in the unusually warm summer evening. Musta' been the full moon or the alignment of the planets or the simple contentment of fully satisfied bellies from sharing in the food, fun and frolic at the South Main Street Clambake. Life seemed so harmonious on that walk. It's hard to imagine all-important creatures of God weren't feeling the same way. But dogs can't comprehend what goes on beyond their range of senses. We can't anticipate, extrapolate, encapsulate, theorize, realize, memorize, compartmentalize or any other "ate" and "ize". Particularly when we are so content. And indeed there were a few creatures right here in our close knit village that were not in step with our walk's bliss

We'd realize that soon enough, but for its fifteen-minute span it was a walk that was a lifetime in the making-the peak of the peak of doggie evolution. It unfortunately was Everest-like in its climax. You know, Mount Everest! Braving the cold and oxygen depravation and all the life threatening perils to reach a very brief moment of awe and calm you hope will stay with you even beyond the grave. Some people reach their life's peak then slowly ascend, relaxed and content. The Everest-like peak is an all too fleeting moment in time with a descent as equally dangerous as the effort up. True, it was the middle of summer and our ground was quite level but the comparison works for me. When the walk was over our time would be done basking in that peak and it was going to be a difficult path to safe and comfortable ground.

Once we reached the village center our Masters left us for their newest hang out, The New York Pizzeria. In those days it was all the pizza, video games, billiards and foosball a pocket full of change could buy. With a change drawer like Master Father's, Master Tom developed pretty deep pockets. I'd already spent many hours that spring and summer parked in a shaded stairwell next to the Pizzeria entrance. It was right across the street from the Inn and yet Hobie never came over. We just stared at each other as the traffic and time went by. I was stubborn too, I always thought Master Tom would be out any second and faithfully waited in that stairwell. Sometimes there are places your Master goes and you accept that he's gone and move on with your day. If it's an establishment that's of heavy traffic we dogs can get all weird about it. At first it's a stubborn curiosity as to why the place is so happenin' and there's the hope that we might get let in. Eventually, it's just a practiced habit to sit out there like a lump and wait. It was downtown and stuff happens for us to watch so it's a time of relaxation while still keeping a pulse on things. It's just part of the choices we had as free dogs- to watch, wait and do nothing.

With a little initiative I coulda' crossed the street and furthered some quality brethren time with Hobie but there was always another day. Like I said, we don't generally think that far ahead but for all the years I'd been alive, I always assumed there was going to be another day. Maybe Hobie thought the same thing.

Actually, now that I remember it, a strange thing did occur the day prior to the clambake. This woulda' been before the softball game and the whole deer leg incident. Around midday I followed Master Tom to the Pizzeria and sat in my usual spot. I saw Hobie making his way down the Inn steps but Master Tom came right out. For once he didn't stay in there, he just grabbed a slice of pizza and I followed him home. I didn't think much of it as we walked to the center of town red light. His brevity caught me off guard but I did look back to the Inn to see Hobie standing at the curbside just watching me walk away. From what I know now he was actually going to the Pizzeria's side of the street. What a curious day to make such a gesture. Another instance of Hobie's crazy-karma shit. This though was just spooky! He may have had a gut feeling about circumstances yet unrevealed but for all his intuitions, he couldn't anticipate Master Tom was only interested in taking out a quick slice that day.

I guess it could also be thought of as odd that the very next night, after our harmonious inter-species walk, I did cross the street to the Inn. However, I was in the company of Sugar and Sam so it was more of a "go with the crowd" kinda' thing. It certainly wasn't by the power of my intuition. I thought the world was just peachy, harmonious and indisruptably in sync. Even as we were peaked by the scent of blood that was staining the sidewalk in paw marks right under noses, the potential at finding some insignificant kill to amuse our evening was to hopefully be a nice added bonus. It was a short trail to the back of the inn and we approached a stairwell that leads down to a basement and garbage area. Sugar seemed eager to make his way down the well when out from the shadows Scamp emerged. Strange to see him just lurking in darkness, it wasn't his scene. He didn't pose any aggressive stance towards Sugar but to use a Master phrase, he seemed a bit whacked.

Sugar was spooked, we all were. For the moment none of us moved any further towards the stair well. We kinda' just watched Scamp waiting for him to move, snarl, wag, juggle sticks in paws... anything! Finally he just kinda' lowered his head and nodded in the direction of the stairwell. Sam and I approached Sugar- Scamp didn't show any signs of disapproval. My stomach was taken with a sudden onset of mild nausea. It wasn't nerves, it was more an aromatic flash back. It had gotten a little breezy and a smell was causin' a slow creep from my stomach into my throat. Damn, it was that rotten deer meat I thought was so feakin' wonderful earlier in the day. I didn't see the deer leg, it was just a vestige in the air but it was a fresh enough experience to put an uneasiness to my bowels.

Still, I moved forward with the others. The streetlight illuminated clearly to the bottom of the stairwell. Clear enough to see Hobie's body, lifeless and propped up on the last few steps. His head laid flat on the floor base. Dried blood trailed all the way up to us at the top. We didn't know how to react. We were just dogs, there was no panic or howlin' in the night. Certainly we were shocked but I think what struck us more than anything is that those weird feelings we were so use to in Hobie's presence didn't surface. We all looked at each other tryin' to get a read on the situation but all was normal- and that wasn't normal around Hobie.

Our curiosity continued and we walked down the well just to absorb all the sensory input of the experience. The picture wasn't too gory. We didn't quite get the eyes open thing but we knew death when we saw it. Hobie's fur was mostly matted with saliva. No gash or tears were evident but blood tainted his dirty brown color in a number of areas, most notably the neck. What stood out to us all in a harsh reality was the smell of General. There was a brief panic in us thinking he was around but it was quickly evident that the odor was on Hobie.

The day had already brought so much bonding between us dogs; our connection was now getting even tighter. It was clear we weren't going to get down from Everest without a helping paw from each other. Doggie hell, we could barely get ourselves outta' the stairwell with all the confusion in our brains at that moment. We didn't know if we were suppose to just leave him there or what was awaiting us if we left that place. I'd had no experiences of witnessing death to a doggie peer- or a Master family member. Just empty feelings of their prolonged absence and the strange gut instinct I may never see them again. Sure, I'd inflicted death upon birds or rabbits or deer. They are things to me- meaty vegetables. I'm animal enough to kill out of instinct and yet be unaffected if it was in the natural order of my code. I, however, understood this wasn't a peer death brought about by the need for self defense or meaty vegetable sustenance.

All intelligent creatures have a code. Something internally that helps our brains properly react to the just and the ghastly. This was the ghastly and the sight of Hobie's dead body was a first for us all. I am proud to say it affected us in a manner that went against our newly enlightened internal codes. I don't need to see violent acts on TV or video games or any other preprogrammed method to understand what happened here. I just need a little sensory stimulus to know that Hobie had been killed.

One creature who did need to see it was Scamp. His father was hopeful that his acceptance of us chaos lovin' dogs would provide Scamp with an example of strength in numbers. Laddie, unfortunately, was ill and died before he could make that happen. Scamp now knows this very well coulda' been him in the stair well and his humility was immediately evident. As I understand it now, there was another dog of the village who knew the importance of us free dogs gettin' along for our own good. That was Hobie. He managed to make Scamp realize something that night his crazy, whacky, weirdo-karma-shit couldn't quite do before. Sadly, he was forced to do it in the only "earthly" way Scamp would understand.

Scamp had easily taken the deer leg into his possession earlier that day. I was too intestinally epileptic to put up a fight. I mentioned though, it was odd that he took his gain up town rather than find a secluded spot to chow. I guess the garbage bin area behind the Inn could be considered secluded but it wasn't like him to hang around in town. Still, that's where he went and he tried to settle in with some peace. Where that deer leg was concerned, there would be no peace. On the earthly surface you would call it a magnet for trouble, in heavenly revelation it was an instrument of God-though I doubt the deer who donated it would agree. Ah, screw him- Bambi doesn't have a Heaven.

Master George was playin' the Marlboro Man in the Pizzeria game room so General was on the hunt for like entertainment. That dog's got a pinpoint nose and it wasn't long before the rotted deer meat breezed across his snout laying a path to it's location like a travel club's "trip tic". With the deer leg's wreak and the strong smell of garbage, Scamp had little chance of detecting General's presence. In fact, it was General's forceful steps rather than his odor that caused Scamp to look up from his digs. A leer that was about ten seconds too late. General was already breathin' germs on Scamps neck.

Don't believe everything you read about our mouths. Our breath stinks and we carry more than enough bacteria where you humans shouldn't be letting us lick your mugs as often as you do. Scamp could only wish it were friendly licks and some harmless wet nose rubbing General was interested in. His only good fortune at the moment is that General wanted the deer leg. Otherwise, the arteries in his neck would already have been gushin' like a Texas oil strike.

I'm sure Laddie was up in his cloud lookin' down sayin', "boy give that mugger your money." Scamp wasn't about to be held up without a fight. He'd already robbed me of the leg, he felt he'd earned it. He raised his head slowly at General. Everything was deliberate from the lifting of his quivering lips to the steely eye contact. There were no sudden movements to give General any indication as to his intentions. Scamp was reasonably confident inside and it showed in how cool he was handling the situation. General let Scamp adjust to the situation and gather himself, just as long as he was going to calmly move away from the deer leg. To Scamp's credit, his body language indicated he was going to do just that.

At this point, the outside world is but a faded background. No sounds other than their breathing and no sights other than eye locked on eye can penetrate them. It's an old fashioned western dual I remember well from my very first encounter with Sugar. The dynamic of this face-off is that General is expecting Scamp to move away and Scamp is hoping to slowly move into a strike position without first provoking General. The miscalculation here is that Scamp underestimates General's willingness to simply plow right through him to get to the deer leg. One can act calm, cool and collected to a point but seconds before the moment of truth, subtleties can creep in.

In a great western duel, the extended paces between the combatants allows for some of those subtleties to be masked. At this standoff, General's breath was close enough to bead moisture on Scamps tuft. Scamp continued to slowly lift his head but was still looking up to make eye contact. His head was up enough, though, to make a legitimate strike at the underside of General's neck. And so the moment of truth was seconds away. A duelist with his sweaty palms and shaky thumbs could safely conceal his tension by distance alone. Scamp's paws don't sweat but if he wants a shot at General's neck, he'll need to open his jaw upon attack. That requires the facial muscles to have impulses ready to hit the brain. A seemingly instantaneous transaction of neurological electricity if one is a hundred percent calm and committed to the attack. Even at eighty percent committed the attack will take place but there will be flaws. Most notably nervous tension or tics.

A mere second before the moment of truth that twenty percent snag kicked in and Scamp's lip quivered enough to expose a fang. General was on top of him before the sun even hit a glimmer of that tooth. Scamp had no idea what hit him and was defeated in confidence before General even found an artery to pop. It was so fast and so crushing he was expecting a deathblow to come immediately but reflexes helped keep General's fangs off any flesh for the moment. How quickly ones confidence can get shattered, particularly without the sure and steady backup of your respected father.

The attack was only a mere five seconds in progress but it's amazing all the realizations that can flash at hyper speeds through your mind. Realizations of your under estimations, your limitations, your lost expectations. We dogs have 'em, I've been very dogmatic in trying to justify these assertions throughout this revelation. You gotta' know by now that we've got a life and it can flash before us. The lessons compound over a lifetime but the ultimate enlightenment can come in an instant. Sadly for many it's when the grim fanged and fury reaper is pressed upon you. How in a moment of desperate confusion can great clarity of our lessons overcome us is a wondrous mystery left for human pseudo intellectuals to ponder. But if you learn the lesson well in the mere seconds you are allotted, your chances of getting to lick your balls and drop flatulence bombs in the dining room might not be bygone just yet. Maybe God will give you a pardon so you can learn to express "pardon me" for stenching up your Master's dinner party. Or maybe you can learn that being a pious loner is not what your father was about and that a life coexisting with the dogs of chaos is a better choice over being crow meat.

Have you ever dropped yourself on a bomb? Most likely not or you wouldn't be here reading this. But if you by chance have thrown yourself on a bomb and are still suckin' up air on this planet, you know it's an awfully painful and prolonged experience. The bomb of course is a metaphor but it could be a grenade or bullet or some other knowingly painful object that required your immediate attention to prevent something dear to you from being lost. We dogs have been sniffin' out land mines and runnin' in burning buildings for years now. All in the protection of your loved ones and for the greater good- your freedom. As a species of those sacrificed in human servitude, I'm both proud and dismayed. You know, that fine line between honor and stupidity. The blurred definition between a loyal pet and sacrificial lamb.

You need not be a dog of heavenly enlightenment to understand my deep admiration and respect for Hobie. For once, a dog's sacrifice was of choice and for the preservation of freedoms our species had achieved. When Hobie picked up that deer leg he was the Boston Tea Party and Pearl Harbor for us village dogs. That bone of contention had been dragged and passed around the village for two days as we swapped and blended sloppy spit among us. And now, here it was, a severed deer leg as the catalyst for unification.

Hobie didn't just snag it and run off, he shook it at General- who as you can imagine, was incensed. It was General who mocks and struts and postures at the weak and feeble that he bullies. Not only did this gangly mutt dare bate him, he confiscated his intended possession.

Well, General just discarded Scamp aside like he was a rawhide appetizer he could chew on later. General must have been charitable that day because he glared at Hobie as if to give him the opportunity to drop the fleshy bone and tuck tail. In retrospect, it was kinda' General's style to work intimidation into his routine. He was intimidatingly calm in stalking me clear 'cross town at our first encounter. He taunted Scooter as he pressed himself upon the defenseless beagle and today he was perfecting his death stare when he simply coulda' struck cleanly and got it over with.

Scamp was still on his back looking up in disbelief. First at the fact he was still breathing, and secondly, the fact that Hobie was still breathing. Hobie was a few paw paces from General, growlin' and shakin' the deer leg in his direction. General's mood seemed to go from incensed to amused at the audacity of this mutt and stretched his head to a whiskers length from Hobie's snout- with fang now exposed. Hobie had strategized to get General's curiosity and was hoping to play on his love of intimidation. Once their eyes were fully locked, Hobie slowly walked backwards, almost trance like towing General along at the calm pace. The plan was working and about a half a minute later General has curiously followed Hobie around the garbage dumpsters and outta' Scamps sight. Confusion and bewilderment had kept Scamp unsettled and he laid still trying to clear his senses to get a hint at what may be transpiring out of view. Heavy panting and racing heartbeats within him were deterring any internal auditory receptions but momentarily the internal pulsing would be drowned out by outside aggression.

He heard it and understood it clearly. A vicious snarl that slightly changed pitch during its two seconds on the wind indicating a lunge type motion. A screeching yelp immediately followed by the twang of some tin cans hitting the cement. A low-pitched rumble emanated from deep in the bowels as if one was using all his internal muscles to compress something into submission. Scratching and clawing like nails on a blackboard gave Scamp a queasy sensation and in a matter of moments their frantic rhythms slowed to a sputter. Eventually there a was thud, like a large sack of grain being dropped. Echoed sounds of tin cans falling down stairs into a hole completed the audio broadcast.

A few seconds passed and all was quite except that heartbeat that had accelerated wildly. You didn't need to have the street intelligence of a K-9 unit dog to figure this out. Our ears have quite a pallet to paint pictures very clearly. Hobie was dead or dying. Discarded from Generals clutches in a textbook attack. Scamp's heart rate now had his whole chest lifting off the ground. If General was done with Hobie, was he coming back for his appetizer? Tense and wide eyed, that possibility had him too scared to even get off the ground and run. He just sat there as still as can be, hoping to not make any sounds that might remind the beast of his location. Suddenly, his eyes caught a motion. Fortunately it was far in the distance. Clear across the street it was General heading into the alley which borders the Pizzeria- deer leg in tow. Moments later he rounded a corner and was gone from sight- but not mind.

Scamp managed to get to his feet but was unsteady and walked a few steps to a grassy area and set himself back down. He had yet to look down the stairwell but he needed no confirmation as to Hobie's condition. He sat there all evening waiting to hear something from around those disposal bins. Any hint of life that could spring optimism into his heart and will him to try and contact some of the inn patrons as to Hobie's situation.

Even though he didn't inspect the situation, it was part of his instinct to stay there and wait it out. He was so far out of his comfort zone that the only comfortable place he knew was right where he was planted. His screwed up brain rationalized that was the only place he could be sure wasn't in harms way since he already survived a near death situation. So he rested and calmed himself and thought about the events of his day. Not like you humans in deductive sequences and permutations as to what coulda' been different. Simply the raw gut impressions of instinct versus learned responses. He now could do the doggie math of one plus none equals none. On his own he was in a no win situation. He understood that runnin' around lookin' over your shoulder was not the dog free life of choice. Scamp never had to consider it when his ego fooled him to believing he could defeat any challengers. The fact was, the over confidence he attained was never supported on his own. He always had his father to be his backbone and never understood that his father preferred to be his conscience. Fortunately, the confidence he had with his dad he can have again, it's just going to be in chorus with a few restless dogs of chaos.

And so we showed up to this Hobie induced moment of unification. Maybe Scamp's wait there had more to do with fate than fatality but he was relieved to finally be able to shed some of this weight on us. To be able to communicate with a head nod and glassy stare the burden on his shoulders.

We didn't sit around drawing battle plans in the dirt and yelping out recruitment calls to any other free dogs of the village. We all went home eventually and shed this off in whatever moments brought a head rub or a chewable treat. It would be safe to say that our dreams often brought forth some of this disturbing imagery but we wake up and continue on with our lives fully in the moment. We might run around the village subconsciously uneasy and we might continue to be strangely amicable to each other- we don't consider why. A time will come when circumstances will jar this bitter incident to the forefront and what we've seen and what we've learned will call us to protect what we desire and what could be lost.

Oh, and General puked rotted deer meat all over his Master's carpet. A beating soon followed.

Revelation 13

The barking of orders invites insurrection

I had to be perfectly skilled- no sudden movements and no jerky reactions. Slowly I could move my head inching closer and closer. My age was starting to be revealed because my spine was creaking a bit more these days. I was still limber enough to twist and curl it ever so carefully, easing to the still lying prize. I was so close now but my body was stretched too tight and my lungs were compressed. I wouldn't be able to hold my breathe much longer but I all...most...got it.

I made a desperation nip but it eluded me by a whisker. I jumped to my paws and the chase was on. Around and around and around went the pursuit but my damn friggin' tail stayed that whisker ahead of me- or was it a whisker behind me? Anyway, I chased it until my front paws began trippin' over my back paws and my momentum was broken.

I envy those huntin' dogs where they just whack the thing off to a boney stub. They never have to lay bored in the living room tempted by their own body's chaseable anatomy. We dogs just lounge around so much curled in that balled position. Our tails setting there, right in front of our noses. Eventually our laziness passes and we need a quick jolt of doggie playfulness. We don't require much, you know. We don't always need to chase a metal beast or winged fowl. We just want to be able to bend and twist an inch or two further for the moment of self-satisfaction that comes with a simple catch. Be it a fluke of evolution or God's little joke, the damn friggin' thing is never friggin' long enough.

Hmmm, that's three "friggins" in as many paragraphs. I wish my revelation vocabulary would allow me some "R" rated expletives but being in Doggie Heaven and all I'm only allowed a "PG" rating off my tongue. No "F" words can burst forth. But let's see if there's a loophole or substitute. It's all based on a vulgar sex act reference. We dogs hump, we mount, we thrust- nothing too vulgar there. How about "bone." It's a four-letter word that's tossed about in other places of vernacular like your human "F" word. I've used lines like "toss me a bone," fetch my bone," etc. Let's try it out on my last "friggin'" laced sentence.

"Be it a fluke of evolution or God's little joke, the damn bone'n thing is never bone'n long enough."

Works for me! But is it as universal as the "F" word? "Bone You!" "Bone Off!" "What the bone is your problem!"- Yes it is- sweet!

The only issue is that the human "F" word is rarely used for its original crude meaning- except in adult films. You can't publicly use it in any sentence without getting slapped, fined, return gestured- or if you're lucky, laid. You can ask someone if they'd like a bone and as long as you keep a straight face your actual intent is not clearly implied. You might be expected to give away an actual bone. Of course, unless you're a cannibal, there isn't often the giving of bones between humans.

I guess the exchange of "bone" for "frig" isn't perfect but hopefully you humans are smart enough to understand in which context it's being used. In these last few chapters I get the feeling I'll be using it a lot. So, why don't I cut the chatter and get on with the bone'n story.

By the fall of 1981 I rarely ventured uptown alone. Over a few months I had spotted General about half a dozen times carousing the village center and was fortunate to stay outta' his senses. Previously I mentioned the instinctive leers over my shoulder because I had General in my brain setting off false alarms but now my trepidation had turned to phobia. A black period was setting in for the fun lovin', free roamin' Dogs of Sherburne. Maybe Hobie had a pull on us we took for granted. Him sittin' up on those steps day after day was a type of anchor that drew us back to shore.

You humans always have one guy that everybody likes. The jocks, the potheads, the computer geeks- they all kinda' interact when this guy throws a party. Then he goes off to college and everyone is lost for a while. Smaller parties pop up between the clicks but without the melting pot diversity the taste is rather bland. Maybe that was Hobie? I don't know, maybe I'm looking to make excuses and reasons for my yellow streak. Maybe it's a little of both, but once again, the continuity of our lives and our free roaming has been disrupted and this time it's a bone'n doozie.

I wasn't necessarily at full health either. I developed worms and I wouldn't be surprised if it was from that bone'n deer leg. I guess worm and parasite issues can be present but dormant until some onset of stress triggers their infestation. Tapeworm larva coulda' come from fleas on the deer leg fur. Those white flea collars use to work well for me so I never had too big an issue with bugs on me, thus ingesting fleas would seem a reasonable cause. Never mind that those white collars were like dangling a poison soaked rope around your neck. How many times did Master snag me by the collar and eventually stick his fingers in his mouth or grab some food. If a human had lice would they dangle a pesticide-spewing agent around his neck for a week?

As I said, it worked great for me so I was cool with it but I only had a life span of 14 human years. By the time some freak illness hits me, I'm ready to cash in my bones. We dogs don't stress over stuff like this anyway. We're suppose to have worms in our crap and we carry on with faulty organs and conspicuous lumps. We don't have jobs and ambitions and responsibilities to stress us out. You humans would handle your health crisis better if you'd digress to medieval times. Accept pain and suffering as a part of life. You get a little cut nowadays and you just apply some topical ointment to heal it fast. Back in the dark ages that little cut got infected and all pussed up. Eventually you got maggots growin' in there and they'd hack off your arm and torch it to stop the bleeding. After an experience like that a little cancer and a slow death is one of the more tolerable experiences in life. Then again, there wasn't as much cancer back then because their animals weren't walking around with pesticide laced collars.

I guess I am being a bit unfair because I did have ambitions creating stress in my life. It was my own ambition to continue with my free dog evolution that created stress- in turn creating a proper environment for worms in my bowels. My point is that the stress wasn't over worms in my crap. It was a stress of my own fear repressing me. If it wasn't for that bone'n deer leg I wouldn't have gotten worms, Hobie might be alive and Scamp would still have a full tank of confidence. As it stood, we were all the lesser because of that bone'n bone.

Lookin' back, it's kinda' funny how the fear and tension bonded us in ways that otherwise would have been unthinkable. In the spring of '82, Master Mark and Rett (Brandi's Master) walked the creek from the base point at Paddleford Park up to Rexford Falls. They had a few things in tow with them- a couple of fishing poles and Sugar. As they approached Paddleford Park, they happen to run into Scamp meandering the fields. Now normally, depending on Scamps mood, he'd either pay them no attention or show some type of confrontational demeanor. Since the Hobie killing, things haven't been normal and Scamp choose the more amicable third option of following them up the creek.

This was one of those days where you just got the impression that spring might be here for good. I understand you humans can "smell it in the air" as you say. A semblance of environmental changes start to tickle your nose about mid February. From an animal that can really "smell it in the air," I give you humans credit for developing that sensory use over time. By March you expect Spring to just start bloomin' right before your eyes. I know this because we dogs do the same thing. We let our noses run away with us in anticipation then another cold spell or snow storm blows through and we muddle around in confusion as if our noses betrayed us, only to start the cycle again a few days later.

But on this day things really seemed as though they were finally going to thaw. The creek water was still too cold for even booted human feet but Scamp and Sugar splashed in and out of the water allowing the chill to adrenalize their play. The human term is roughin' it and us dogs enjoy the throw back when our ancestors had constitutions of grit and guile.

After a short time there was some rufflin' in the brush up the embankment behind us. The breeze that periodically blew through the channel confirmed a warm-blooded creature of some kind. That aromatic confirmation was needed because the thawing of ice on the embankments was creating a series of loud constant drips that added to the already high ambient levels from the crisp rushing water. Thus their ears wouldn't have picked up the creature. The dogs immediately rushed at the embankment howlin' and startled a doe hoping to finally find some decent chow after a sparse winter. The doe easily ran to the roadway, which followed the creek, but the dogs were detained a bit by the icy conditions. Eventually their paws gripped in and they managed to reach the roadway. The doe was long gone but they followed the scent up the road a short distance eventually giving up and wanting to return to the boys.

Sugar and Scamp ran back into the now wooded area that bordered the creek and immediately came across a problem. Their chase of the doe was an uphill run. Meaning the embankment had become much more steep and the parks department had fenced off the embankment border for safety. As they jumped up with front paws to the fence they could see the boys continuing their walk up the creek but that lack of doggie troubleshooting held them back from determining they need to follow the fence back to where they began chase. Instead they followed the fence in the direction of the boy's walk. The dog's walk continued at an incline and it became harder to see the boys as the embankments turned to cliffs and the boys were deep below them. The dogs turned on their super sensitive hearing and continued to follow along the fence. It wasn't long before the boys reached the deep pool at the base of Rexford Falls, their intended fishing hole.

As the boys set cast, Sugar and Scamp were stumped, annoyed, and getting more pissy by the minute. They wanted to be down there but even if they could traverse the fence, it would pretty much be a straight drop down the modest cliff to an imminent death. Now I've heard of deer and cows and some other dumb excuses of brained creatures that might unwittingly test the laws of gravity for some fear response purpose, but dogs usually know the potential for death when it presents itself. So they sniffed around hoping for a scent based solution or a scent-based distraction- either would suffice. They followed scents along the fence to of all things, the Rexford Falls bridge which spans across the cliffs and over the falls.

At the entrance of the bridge on either side are turnstile type revolving gates. Now, creatures the size of Sugar and Scamp didn't need to bump their snouts along the gate to get it to rotate. They actually could jump under and through the gate without having it turn at all. But it's still a puzzle of sorts and either way they didn't quite understand how it worked. Even if they could get passed the gate somehow, they may get too spooked to even get on to the bridge. Scamp is pretty no-nonsense so he had little interest in fooling with the gate. Sugar saw it as any mischievous soul would. Since he seemed to be locked out from getting past the gate, it was his duty to not let anyone or anything keep him from any area he deemed of interest. So he stayed at the gate, sniffing around the perimeter and bumping his nose against the hard steel, often jumping back as the gate slightly moved and "creaked" upon touch.

Scamp wandered around the nearby trees finding a treat of thawed edible garbage to lick and becoming bored by the minute. Sugar wasn't his buddy or anything and the boys weren't his Master so he saw no reason to hang around. Scamp actually made a doggie attempt to say goodbye by placing himself in potential view of Sugar before he headed off. Sugar, hearing his approach, made a halfhearted leer in Scamp's direction but continued on investigating the gate. He'd stick a paw through as if he were going to try and walk under it but he kept bumping it and the slight movement and "creak" scared him every time. Scamp seemed almost jilted like he'd come over to some kids to play and the kid ends up ignoring him the whole time. He just tucked his head down and headed for the road when the grinding of rubber on dirt made him take notice. A pick up truck was speeding up the hill making quite a racket. It was enough to make Scamp uncomfortable and he walked back a bit closer to Sugar who was oblivious.

The truck eventually pulled into a dirt parking area that lead to a pathway for the bridge. For the moment the dogs were secluded by the dense trees of the area. Two human males jumped out of the truck, both had rifles and headed to the forest on the opposite side of the road. One of the males was recognizable to Scamp- it was Master George. As he slammed his car door shut he called out to the truck cab, "General, let's go".

Scamp found himself hugging the nearest tree a little more intimately than he'd prefer. He'd followed Sugar and the boys a seemingly safe distance outside of town only to end up at General's eventual location. He didn't dare make a peep to Sugar, he just stood there and leered around his tree friend. General jumped out from the truck cab and seemed to follow his Master into the brush across the road. Once out of view, Scamp approached Sugar and attempted some type of whiney yet forceful communication. Sugar's just a dog and not too familiar with Scamp. He didn't know what his bone'n problem was but nonetheless, Sugar was going to find a way on that damn bridge. From there he could at least see what the boy's were doin' down in that ravine. A dogs' just gotta' know what his Master is doing- he's just gotta'. He heard the laughin' and ribbin' from deep in the small canyon. Being separated from that was almost torturesome. Scamp tried more communication at Sugar, eventually working himself into a bark. Unfortunately, he was just a little too loud a little too soon- and the fact that he smelled like a wet dog didn't help either.

General had picked up the scent once he got settled across the road. He then turned from his Master who was more intent on his small game hunting than keeping tabs on his dog. As he crossed the road back to the parking area General heard the elevated yelps of Scamp. Eye's wide, ears open, tail erect, fangs exposed and drippin', General stalked eagerly down the pathway. In view about seventy-five paw steps away he made eye contact with Scamp. Sugar was still testing the mechanics of the revolving gate like it was a rubix cube. He was clueless.

A smile almost came across General's face as he increased his fang exposure. At the absolute peak of his lip's muscle motion he began to charge towards the two dogs. Scamp had a split second of instinct to respond and did so in the only plausible option. He thrust forward into the metal gate, smacking his head like a battering ram in painful desperation. The gate revolved and he shot his full body onto the bridge. Sugar was dumbfounded but it happened so fast his only reaction was to follow suit and he dove under and through the gate just ahead of General's snapping jaws. General hit the gate flush knocking his head straight to the ground and welting a knot in his skull. The gate "creaked" and turned just enough at General's impact to make jumping through it seem awkward.

Sugar and Scamp were now on the bridge and about ready to crap. It was a modestly long and thin bridge to a dog and they felt so exposed. Both dogs had no idea how they even got there and as they stood paws away from General they were expecting the worst. After some momentary fog had cleared in his head, General began a verbal assault. Like Sugar and Scamp, he wasn't sure how to get past the gate and settled for the moment on barkin' at them in his vicious tones. The boys looked up from below at the commotion and realized the situation. They yelled at the dogs to run to the other side, waving and pointing in that direction. Whether they understood the hand signals or not, they were able to surmise that they needed to get off the bridge and headed for the other side. Once again, they were confounded at the same exact gate on the opposite side of the bridge. Scamp had already smacked his snout painfully on it and Sugar had no short-term recollection of himself even jumping through. So now, all three dogs were standing around trying to figure out how to work these revolving gates- each with different intents.

Tom Mody

I'd been up to Rexford Falls a number of times myself but I always went on the bridge with Master Tom. I wonder if I coulda' figured out the complexity of the revolving gates alone. Yeah, I'm sure I coulda'. I woulda' been off that bridge, pissed on the gate for good measure and been down the road before General's welt had even peaked. I understand their dilemma though. It's one thing to have to figure out the gate, it's another to be on that bridge suspended high up from the rushing waters and rocks and fighting the clock with your intelligence against a cold killer's will. Given the circumstances I may not have been down the road so fast but certainly I woulda' been at the gate pissin' stage of my exit.

It seemed futile to Sugar and Scamp. They didn't know what to do and actually came back towards the center of the bridge to get some guidance from the exuberant boys. The dogs looked down at them scared and tense as if they were danglin' off the side of the bridge, holding on by a few human fingers. The boys tried to direct them back to the far end of the bridge but the dogs just stared at them desperate for help and hoping the boys could find their way up to the bridge and rescue them.

General had sensed their fear and took a more proactive effort in trying to get on the bridge. Smacking the gate with his snout and testing the options of jumping past it. He had set his snout against one particular steel pipe on the gate and bumped it along ever so slightly. Like Sugar, he stopped at every "creak" of the rusty mechanism. It just grated a little too sharp on his ears. On occasion he'd continue his bark and sneer, letting Sugar and Scamp know he was inching closer to them. Sugar and Scamp definitely knew this and began howlin' for assistance. The boys got the feelin' that maybe they were needed above and decided to pull in their lines and find a quick path up.

The fact was that there was no quick way up to them. General had now pushed the gate far enough where his body was partially past the entrance. In less than a minute he would have gotten all the way through. In retrospect, it may have been a good confrontation. Scamp was at his physical peak and he had some back up in the wiley Sugar. It would have been a two on one fight. A great opportunity to finally regain some confidence, respect and a partial payback for the death of Hobie. Okay, who am I kidding, there was going to be a lot of pain inflicted, most of it by General. Even a potentially fatal outcome.

If the gate had been on solid ground, General would have been well through it by now. The prospect of going on the bridge was unsettling to him as well. It made his movements a bit more deliberate. But, he was a dog of stalking patience and he took careful steps to ensure his mental stability prior to his attack. His patience was about to pay off. He was almost through the gate. Sugar and Scamp yelped down to the boys in a futile last-ditch plea. The boys were going to help but as they pulled in their fishing lines, Master Mark's was snagged in the shallow outlet past the deep waters. The boys rushed into the chilly flow to try and quickly unsnag the line. Never would two fisherman be more grateful to have caught a log. A wall of ice that covered the entire embankment above them had absorbed enough sun to send it plunging to the basin. It was a loud rumbling of very low frequencies that disrupted the situation above. The dogs became greatly unnerved and reacted in irrational response. All three of them fled the bridge. General backed off from the progress he'd made. Scamp and Sugar fled in panic towards the opposite end with Scamp again plowing his way through the gate and Sugar in tow. They were now separated from General by a seemingly insurmountable two revolving gates and a canyon between them. Surely there was enough time to flee for home.

Two lives may definitely have been spared above but what of below? More fate I guess. The wall of ice had fallen to the very spot the boys had been standing seconds earlier. Master Mark's snagged fishing line and the dog's urgent need for assistance both contributed in the boys avoiding a demise of their own. Needless to say, all parties above and below were shaken to the core by their close brushes with potential death and they all headed immediately home on a day that started out with a fresh smell of spring promise in the air.

It was just another incident of us freedom lovin' dogs being pushed. Pushed in a corner, pushed together, pushed too far! Scamp in particular. His pride was busted the day Hobie was killed, his confidence shattered. Just the concept of him and Sugar even hangin' out together lends a kind of human Abbott and Costello feel to the whole Rexford Falls ordeal. After his father's death, he was next in order as the protector and now he'd become too mentally depleted to protect himself even when he had back-up help.

At least Sugar and myself had no paternal issues. We weren't living in anyone's shadow. We were the ones making our own legend but all us dogs shared a common need for freedom and we weren't feeling it at that moment in our lives. I cringe to think of Scamp and Sugar up on that bridge howlin' like a couple of scared girls tied to the railroad tracks by a dastardly evil villain. I'm not being unfair; I've noted my streaks of yellow as well. If something inside me didn't change soon, that streak may stain- permanently!

Over Easter the family went away for vacation. They'd done this before and I had been attended to by relatives who let me out for the day, filled up my food bowls and let me in for the evening. It's quite stressful to be home every night with an empty house. We don't know what's going on and assumptions run wild in our head that maybe this is how it's going to be for the rest of our lives. A sort of depression mounts every day and it actually keeps us in check from doin' anything too crazy while the family is gone. We tend to hang around the house a lot waiting for the routine to return and we're bone'n ecstatic when it finally does. However, this year there was to be a different routine- and no, it didn't involve the family even thinking of takin' me with them to some sunny southern beach.

It's weird now as I learn about things I didn't understand. My life was so confined. I never saw the ocean, a big city, spectacular mountains or other awesome landscapes of the world. I'm not resentful of this. I had reached all my aspirations during my life and exceeded those of most dogs-particularly dogs in this new century. There was something infinite about my Earth which you humans have lost. I didn't know what was beyond my sensory range. I explored as far as my comfort zone would allow and even further when a damn deer lead me astray. Our reliance on domesticated food and shelter kept us from being true explorers but that wasn't our drive- freedom in domestication was. Still, we looked beyond our borders with wonder yet our shallow doggie reasoning figured it was just more of the same. You humans know just about every inch of your rock and most will leave it with the knowledge that they may have missed some spectacular stuff. I just wonder now how I would have reacted with all the stimulus of a large metropolis or the soothing consistency of the ocean's flow. Both those scenarios seem boxed in to me. I ultimately just judge them on crapability. On the beach I can crap all over the place. In the metropolis there's barely any place to comfortably take a crap.

But, as I've said all along, I'm a dog of man and not of the wild or of places. I need to run free but it's a stable Master that defines my core and settles my place in time. So, you can imagine my dismay at being shipped off to a kennel while they soak up sun and surf. They get me in a car, get me all lathered up with excitement and anticipation then practically dump me off at some way-out, second-rate foster care facility. I knew it was trouble when I didn't even get accorded the sensation of the arrival high. I was leashed before we even got out of the car.

Imagine, me having a baby sitter. I dry humped every baby sitter that ever came to care for Baby and Nat. Now I've got one and I gotta' get tossed in with a bunch of other whiners whose Masters ran off on them. Well, that's what it felt like to us. They even had poodles in this God-forsaken slum. I'd rather hang out with cats at the SPCA for the week. I'm sure from human standards it was an adequate facility but for doggie bone'n sake, I was housed in a cage with straw and water. That's a slum to me- or worse, a prison.

The "warden" of the place tried to be understanding and spent a few minutes getting aquatinted with me hoping

I'd warm up to her. My head was just spinnin' though. My family was just dust in my vision. I'm leashed and disappointed. All kinds of strange dogs are howlin' at me from all directions and some stranger is acting like my long lost Master. I was escorted around the grounds for some quick familiarity and just bombarded with scents from all the dogs, their stale dog food and piles of excrement that had yet to be cleaned. I wasn't a farm dog, you know. I wasn't use to having the smells of thirty other animals tweakin' my nerves. It created the sensation I was being haunted by a mob of canine ghosts. What was worse was that I didn't know if I was going to be there for a week, a month or forever. One thing I did sense was that I was going to be spending an extended stay there. I could tell by the way the family was fawning over me the past few days that some type of change was imminent.

After a short-leashed romp around the grounds I was dragged, with my claws screechin' the whole way, into a cement walled room with a floor drain. My leash was latched to a wall hook and they began to hose me. I loved the garden hose when it was a balmy eighty-five degrees on a July day. I'd jump after the water stream and let it splatter in my mouth while a few weeks worth of doggie grease and grime dripped off my skin and fur. But this was a forty-five degree April morning and I was leashed and abandoned. I just cowered in the corner and let the onset of chills spew the excess water off my body. Then for my troubles I got a bucket of soapy warm water dumped on me and my warden began a scrub down and delousing. After that I was taken to another room and propped up on a table where I was held down while some guy with a sharp implement clipped my toenails. Let's just say it was a struggle for us all to complete that task. Then finally I was shoved into my cell where I sat for a few hours lickin' water out of a tin bowl. I'd always had a plastic bowl at home and found the water to be much purer tasting. Not that I was too discriminating having licked water from mud puddles, swamps and toilets but the tin bowl had a strange metallic tingle. Kinda' like when we lick scraps off discarded garbage in aluminum foil. What a bone'n day- and it wasn't even noon yet!

My cage was the last one in a row of about ten and next to me was this lazy white and black squatty Bull Dog called Joop. Jupiter was his real name because his head was so big compared to his body but the shortened nickname stuck. He was propped up against the bars bordering my cell and strangely trying very hard to mind his own business. In the cage next to him was a tan Great Dane named Snyde. That dog couldn't sit still. He constantly paced about his cage assumably making everyone uneasy because the dog to the other side of his cage was acting like Joop. That dog was a Greyhound named Nagle and he was propped up against the bars opposite Snyde's cage just minding his own business. All the cages were full, I guess due to the human holidays. All us full sized males were in an area of our own. The larger females had their own room and the Poodles and other gangly rodents had their own room.

Not that the warden and other staff weren't nice, but we definitely were second-class to the animals there for breeding, which were in another building. Even outdoors we were separated from them but you could tell by the attention and pampering they got where the priority was.

Some of it was familiarity with the dogs. Some of it was that their pups were the money train of the business. It didn't affect me, I just wanted out of the place. I mighta' been a little more prone to makin' the best of the situation had they tossed some dame into my cell for mountin' purposes, but I guess they just didn't see that kinda' potential in my genes. I was to sit down and shut up and thank you very much for the week's payment. Maybe they saw things that simply in their eyes but digress down to the animal world and you'll note a more complex social outcast situation happening.

It can take only a few hours for us dogs. When we sense abandonment or banishment to a strange and distant place, our learned social skills get damaged once we're tossed out the back of the station wagon. I can't speak for the other dogs. I don't know if they had the free roamin' and promotin' lifestyle I was accustom but that kind of confinement and daily structure certainly didn't bring out the best of my social graces. The initial few hours I'd been in my cell I paced some, rested some and began the buildup of my animosity towards the place. Most annoying was my neighbor, Joop, practically molded to the bars bordering my cage. He laid there with his head set on the ground between his paws and his eyes sheepishly fixed in my direction. After a while a smell interested me enough and I went over and gave him a sniff-over. He musta' dropped a gas bomb or somethin' but I made him nervous and he moved to the back of his cell. Joop set himself down and peeked over to Snyde's cage for about a minute. Snyde was still pacing and paid Joop no attention so Joop fixed himself back on me.

Eventually a few prison guards came in and took me and three other males out on leashes. They trotted us around together and after a time they brought those dogs back and brought out a few more dogs. I guess they wanted to give me a chance to sniff-over the other dogs and see if I could coexist with them for my stay. Had I been that young pup runnin' around Sherburne some years back I definitely would have set a more adversarial first encounter. For now I hadn't stewed enough over the situation to act up and the leash tends to keep you down anyway. Most of the dogs had the same curious demeanor about me as I had about them- except, of course, Snyde. He took a quick whiff of me, registered my scent on his brain, and then just stared me down as I investigated his privates.

The damn dog had no balls. Scooter didn't have any balls either but I thought it was just a fluke or a beagle thing. You could barely notice since he was so close to the ground. Of course, now I know he was neutered but all the other village dogs I encountered were kept unsterilized. It was freaky to sniff-over such a dominant male and have him missing such important packaging. On earth it really spooked me but up here it makes my balls ache. What's worse is that your human logic for doing it is so sound I can't take issue. I should be spending at least a couple pages rantin' over the atrocity, the de-masculation, the humiliation, the inhumanity and the insanity of snippin' our 'nads but in your new century it makes perfect sense. You don't like unleashed dogs so you control the population, keep wild strays under control, ensure no horny hounds will be knockin' up your lass with vet bills being so expensive and everything. It makes me almost curse this place for bestowing on me the intelligence to reason this out. Damn, my balls hurt right now.

After the parade of dogs came out we all went back to our cells and were tossed doggie treats. Pathetically stickin' our noses and tongues through the bars as the prison guards came down the cell row with our little "good doggie" rewards in hand. It was some multicolored bone shaped biscuits. You'd think with the money my masters paid I'd at least get a slab of beef. We scarfed up about a half dozen in under a minute and were left with our water and boredom for a few more hours. I had to take a crap and spent a good fifteen minutes just sniffin' around for that right location. I sniffed that cage over and over and over. There was no right area so I just held it.

I know you dog "experts" have your theories on why we sniff around so intently before we go "potty." Sure familiarity to a repetitive area is a conditioning of it, but you may not be aware of the "ding." When we gotta' go, we sometimes do what we did previously based on that conditioning but for the most part we just sniff around until we hear "ding" in our heads. That not only identifies the spot but it also signals the brain to empty the pipes. I don't know exactly what triggers the "ding." It's probably subtly different for each of us but as long as we're maintaining healthy adult bowels, we ain't goin' without the "ding." There are a few problems with this.

It's very frustrating to hear the ding and be constipated. Once we find the spot the "ding" goes off but the pipes are closed shut. We may reset ourselves and walk around a moment until the "ding" comes again. But after a few unsuccessful evacuations, the "ding" just keeps piercin' our brain tryin' to induce us along. When it eventually stops the brain has accepted the constipated state.

Diarrhea is another quirky situation. We'll just be lyin' there, not even sniffin' around or anything and the "ding" just goes off repeatedly. Kinda' like a school fire drill bell prompting us to get out of the building but in a not so orderly way. Sadly, as we get geriatric, the whole system just runs in a state of confusion. We arthritically work so hard just to get up that our pipes burst and we mess all over your carpet. About twenty seconds after the accident as we're tryin' find a place to hide, our brains go "ding" and we're thinkin', "thanks a bone'n lot for the warning."

That finally brings us to my situation. I feel like I gotta' go but there's nothin' around that's ringin' my bell. Same goes for us dogs who are stuck inside for long periods of time. We've got good bowel control so we hold it, maybe get some cramps but it's not that big a stress. The "ding" is a natural function in us adult dogs and it generally takes natural environments to set it off. Not cement or linoleum floors. Maybe when we're in a nervous situation we'll crap on a vet's floor or maybe we've got a bit of incontinence workin' against us. These things can supersede the "ding." The nerves in particular have precedence and when Master isn't home in a timely manner or we're trapped somewhere that isn't settin' off the "ding" then we get really nervous. Eventually the nerves will win out and we spend the rest of the time in a corner actually hoping you don't come home.

I tried to rest in my cell but I was getting cramps, there were dogs periodically howlin' and there was too much nose sensory overload. Mercifully, the warden and prison guards came and we were set loose about a modest sized confined area. They watched us intently for a short time to be sure all doggie hell wasn't going to break out but then they went about cleaning cages and attending to other things while keepin' an eye on us.

I wasn't too social at first. I sniffed around the grounds waiting for my "ding" to go off but it had been holding it a while and I may have disrupted the system. I continued sniffin' with a much more vigorous pace to no avail. There was a water troth that I eventually discovered and within a few minutes I got things lubricated enough to get the pipes working. The "ding" came shortly after.

Nagle, the Greyhound, came over and inspected my droppings. He was a wiry elusive dog. As I turned in his direction he gracefully ran off and continued to encircle the bordered area. Moments later he ran back and gave a little more interest to me personally than he did my pile of shit. We gave each other a sniff-over- it was cordial. Nagle seemed a bit more at ease after he had gotten a run about the place. We sniffed around the property together but we didn't have any other physical contact. He'd run off like a gazelle on occasion then come back to my area. The other dogs seemed oddly corralled to a particular half of the grounds. The half where Snyde wasn't.

After about a half an hour, the whole grounds began getting all worked up. There was yelpin' and howlin', tails waggin' vigorously- a group sense of anticipation. In a fenced off area that bordered our grounds, the breeding females were let out and us males on the "lower decks" were left to pant and prop up on our hind legs with our erections stickin' out like flags. All of us except Snyde, who increased his testosterone level by struttin' about as the buffer between the horny hounds and fertile femmes.

Who the doggie hell was he? A Laddie protector of the canine ladies? A General bully of the prison yards? I was soon to find out. I wandered over to the fence's far border to get a look at these dames. Oh, you better believe they looked nice and groomed and pure. Most importantly, they were primed to mate and that was just the daily diversion I coulda' used to get through this bummer of a confinement. I'd say I got about five full heavy pants outta' my tongue when Snyde just blew up like a firecracker. He came roarin' over at me like he owned the place.

All I kept feeling was that I didn't want to fight. I wanted to hump. Can't we all just knock this fence over and get it on with these willing vixens? I guess I was just gettin' tired of the same old fights. We're so damn limited in how we fight- it's all jaw and a little bit of claw. Same old vicious snarl, same old low gurgling. I didn't have a problem with

264   T o m   M o d y

the confrontation. The animal in me still gets me reacting as I should with all the necessary senses and stimuli on full alert. There was just something bored and fruitless about smackin' my jaw against another dog's jaw a dozen or so times. Don't you college wrestlers get tired of the same old routine? Grab a leg. Try to mount on top. Go for a headlock. Curl the guy up. Match after match after match you do this when you know full well there's a world of pile drivers and sleeper holds and a host of airborne maneuvers while you're limited by rules.

I wish my only limitation was rules because I'd break them. I unfortunately was limited by lack of knowledge and ability set forth by God. You know what I'd love to be able to do- martial arts. That's right, Dallas The Kung-Fu Dog. I'd get up on my hind legs from years of balance training with my tail. I'd motion forward with a few karate chops from my front paw, though, it would just be an intimidation maneuver with some mild defensive applications. I don't think we can generate enough power from our front paws to punch or slap like humans, apes and kangaroos.

I could dazzle my adversary with mystifying front paw chops and swirls. Then, while he's stunned in awe of my skills, I'd jump back down to my front paws and lunge kick him with my hind paws- kinda' horse style. The coolest part though would be to return balanced on one hind leg then use the other leg to repeatedly kick him in the muzzle. My adversary would savagely lunge at me and I'd skillfully dodge him using my aforementioned balancing skills and outstanding anticipation. For authentication purposes it wouldn't be complete without the stereotypical karate howlings. You know, a "hi-ya" at every chop. Also, an "oooowhaaaa!" that drags outta' my mouth in long form as I expertly assume the defensive position. The only problem I have determined is that I don't have my own closet to hang my robe and belt. I guess I could earn some money on TV or doing instruction to potentially buy my own house with a closet. Then again, if I was Dallas, the Kung-Fu Dog, Master would probably give me my own closet so he could continue to be the Master with the coolest dog ever.

But, back to the situation at paw. I was going through the only fightin' routine I knew. Makin' the sounds, showin' some fang, gettin' all serious. Problem was, I just couldn't help noticing how distracting a Great Dane's dingy black muzzle was. It's like someone threw a glob of mud on his saggy mug. Basically, it would be the same for you humans if some guy was tryin' to intimidate you after being flattened in the face with a blueberry pie.

We eventually got in each other's face but Snyde made no aggression on me. I finally had enough of it all and just went past him. I jumped up on the fence and peered over to the crop of tail parading on the other side. Snyde bore down on me again but it was only noise from his dirty mug. I got myself in a barkin' tizzy as well but it was to get the attention of the femmes. Snyde eventually ran to the middle of the yard and began calling out. Shortly there after some prison guards came and escorted me back away from the fence. When they set me loose again I ran back to the fence in defiance. Some of the other dogs had made subtle movements in that direction as well but nothing overt. The guards came and got me again, this time I was banished to my cell.

Those were the highlights of my first day in the captivity of the kennel. I pissed off the guards and the yardmaster. That's what Snyde was, he was the yardmaster trained by the warden to make sure all the dogs behaved. Snyde was trained for it well because he avoided a physical confrontation with me which is key to his job- intimidate but don't aggravate. I don't think it would be good business for the kennel if they returned dogs in their care with flesh missing from their bones. I gotta' admire Snyde for having cool control. Had I known it at the time I woulda' been even more defiant in his presence.

Still, the other dogs seemed to take his posturing as if it were law. Well, it was law but they acted as if the punishment wasn't worth the crime. I've discovered in my life that most crimes (of a doggie nature) bring a pleasure that greatly outweighs the consequences. Ducking the consequences even doubles the pleasure- how cool is that!

There was nothing cool about my current situation. As I laid on my straw bed that night my free roamin' world already seemed as if it existed years ago. Maybe I could have accepted my confinement better had I left Sherburne as I remember it from my unrestricted rompin' days in the 70's. I couldn't help feeling this situation wasn't much different than how life had been lately. I'd been leashed up quite often. I was being intimidated by another dog. Master Tom as a teenager was less and less available for my attention. I wasn't capable at the time of sorting out all the different reasons that shaped my mood and attitude. I could, however, recall what was and what is and let it stew internally.

That night I was visited by an old friend... well let's call him an old inspiration. There isn't much, even in a stressful day, that can keep a dog from getting some good slumber. I slept deeply. The sleep could even be described as natural. Barring a few minor details, consider that I was in a pack, out in the boonies, sleeping on straw. Keeping the fact that I was confined out of my subconscious, there was a sense of wild dog freedom in it all.

I dreamed I was on a hill barking at the moon. The moon was so close I could practically lick it. It made me feel so close to my desires. It was just a few paws away. Someone was calling to me from below. I wasn't sure if I wanted to leave the hill and the rays of the moon. The calling stopped then I heard a car. It was getting further in the distance. I ran down the hill but when I reached the bottom the iron spiked fence that bordered our yard was for some reason in this meadow and in the way. It was much taller and I tried to jump it but I couldn't. I looked beyond the fence and there were the cornfields, which ran behind the old apartment I lived in as a pup.

The corn stalks seemed to go for miles. I heard rustling in the stalks and a Scarecrow emerged. It tried to spook me away from the fence but I still heard the car in the distance and tried to leap the fence with no avail. The scarecrow came at me again but I paid him no attention. As if he had given up his chore he just went stiff, lifeless, fake. Once this happened a crow flew from the dark sky and landed on the scarecrow's shoulders. I started barking and jumping wildly on the fence. I kept this up for a short time and the bird just stared at me. Eventually I calmed down and gathered myself. I sat patiently with no real understanding of what to do next.

The crow finally lifted off, crossed over to my side of the fence and flew up the hill. I turned to pursue but my feet were wet below me. The sky was lit beautifully with the moon so close and I noticed I was standing in a small stream of red liquid. I continued up the hill only to be stopped by the source of the red liquid. It was blood and Hobie lay before me as lifeless as the scarecrow was now. I didn't know what to do. What killed Hobie could have been up there, on that hill. I couldn't go back either. I was very isolated and exposed. There were no trees or brush to hide me. Just a bright moon illuminating the truth of what was behind me, a spiked fence and what may have been Master's car motoring further and further away from me. I was in essence being locked out of my past. I couldn't go back. That moon was illuminating the truth of the moment. That death had created a barrier but it was only impenetrable because of fear.

But that fear was great and I laid at Hobie's side. He was the only available object to hide behind. I played dead, so to speak. I kept hearing the call of the crow in the night but I wouldn't move. I laid still and it was getting cold- Hobie was getting cold. I was so alone it was frightening me. Then a much more aggressive sound came from the cornfields below. A rumbling like there was a stampede through the stalks. Eventually it became motorized and definitively a metal beast- a station wagon. It plowed through the stalks and over the spiked fence. The car horn sounded and Master Tom called out to me. Finally, some help! The family came back for me.

It was then I realized they always did. Even when the night got late and the unfamiliarity of having them gone so long started messin' with my head, they eventually returned. When I was chained as a pup and the crow was mocking me they came for me and took me to a better place. But was the crow really mocking me. Maybe I had it wrong all those years. Maybe he was simply calling me, inciting me as he was in my dream. As much as I wanted to go back to my family at that moment, I knew they'd always be there, or at least be back for me.

The crow called some more and I ran up the hill, my head down because the moon was so bright. Maybe I wasn't suppose to see my path or what may be in it. I just needed to trust it. I was just a dog and couldn't reason myself to overcome fear so I had to be blind to it and face it when it comes with no preconditioned hesitation. At least that's what overcame me in my dream state and I wasn't scared anymore of what may be ahead of me even though I could see or smell nothing. I just kept going until I felt myself reach the top. Once there I looked up with all my effort to try and peer through the shimmering beams and when my eyes could adjust I saw the crow was on the moon, still calling. Well, toss me a bone- if the crow could do it I could too. I had already proven that once in my life by becoming free as a bird. I backed myself up about twenty big paw strides and raced back up leaping high with my ears flappin' in the wind...

A cool breeze burst up my snout followed by a startling slam. No, I didn't run head first into the moon. My cell was the closest to the door and as it opened I was startled and awoke by the rush of fresh air and the arrival of the prison guards for morning chores. They went to each cell and cleaned up any mess and filled our bowls with fresh water and the minimum daily requirement of breakfast kibbles.

Us dogs don't generally wake up too groggy. I can get from comatose to excited in 2.4 seconds. But that dream really had me under and I kinda' stumbled around a bit while my cell was being kept. To my extremely limited analytical mind it was just a sequence of bizarre images that settle around the perimeter of my awoken consciousness. But to my psyche and subconscious, there was a subtle change. This confinement and abandonment took on a more motivating challenge as opposed to a sullen dispirited beat down. I looked up at my prison guards, then through the cell bars and over to Snyde. It all was pissin' me off in a positive way. I was going to step over dead bodies if I had to. I was going to confront bullies and evil if I had to. Every moment I had that was of free roamin' I was going to dedicate to my pursuits and my promotion as I had before my naiveté was burst.

I started this rededication the moment we were out in the corralled yard. Particularly the times when the dames weren't out yet. Snyde and his overblown self-importance wasn't so uptight about where I roamed when he had nothing to protect so I spent my time investigating the borders and corners. Joop had taken a comfort to me being cell neighbors so he and Nagle often were in my area keeping Snyde from having his sole focus on me.

It was just a wood fence with posts and two by four barrier beams across to each post. Like most weathered cob jobs, it was sturdy in some areas and a little rickety in others. Things ran like clock work there so every day the dames came out at the same time and there'd be the usual dog howlin' and erections. It was crazy, there were dogs humpin' all kinds of stuff- trees, yard equipment, each other! Every day at that time Snyde hunted me down and we'd jaw a bit. Dog, he was a mental rock. I think he really, really wanted to take me on but he did his job and I made sure not to create too big a problem where the prison guards had to escort me away.

After a few days of seeing these dogs just going humpin' wild every time the dames came out, a cause of sorts started brewing in my consciousness. It wasn't just about me anymore- my repression and my horniness. A few things brought this upon me. First, I could share in what we all were going through. I have eyes and ears and sensibilities. The chaos and confusion does imprint upon me. Second, I was developing a bit of a following. More and more the dogs would congregate in my area, even if I was within a closer proximity to Snyde. Some even started jumping upon the fences as the dames came to pasture. Snyde's work and reputation was being undermined. He still had enough intimidation to force them all back but without the green light to kick some doggie ass on occasion, he was losing credibility now that his authority was being subtly challenged. Intuition can go a long way in any creature and for a dog, it can be useful as another sense. I had developed it well over the years and it was now guiding me in my actions.

Like me, these dogs had suffered great anxiety in their current displacement. That is easily sensed. They all needed a release and to not be held in by bars, fences or bullies. I guess I just had a bit more experience pushing buttons and shakin' things up. If you can believe it, I even longed for Sugar to be here and reprise some of our "magic". The two of us wavin' the flag for dog lovin' chaos.

As I recount the unfolding of events in my life, nothing amazes me more than how circumstances seemed to sway in the direction of necessity. Humans of a higher conscious say you create your own luck. I guess if you firmly believe with no doubts that something you lack is a necessity, you are more likely to react in a way, conscious or not, that gets you what you need. The great thing about dogs is that we don't harbor doubts- it's not a capability. We have trepidation based on experiences but once we set a conscious idea in motion that we need something, it's an ironclad necessity. Inevitably, opportunity would knock and from that point only physical barriers could prevent us from walkin' through.

One night there was a violent storm. Yes, it was a dark & stormy night. That's beside the point, though. It was a very tense situation for us all. Being trapped in a foreign place with the rain pounding on the tin roof, thunder just rippin' our ears to shreds and our nerves to a fray. All of us, even Snyde, were howlin' like frail little pups. There was no place to run. We just had to sit there and take it. The prison guards would check in on us and try to settle things but what could they really do?

The rain continued for almost the entire next day. Whatever tension we were able to release during our unleashed time was now just festering inside. Joop and I spent some bonding time playing tug between the bars with a two handled rubber toy that was tossed in my cage. Mostly, though, I caught up on some sleep after being up most of the night. More storms followed that night and what was a tense and hyper group of dogs the night before had now become a depressed defeated group cowering in fear in the corners of their cage. What little spirits they had left before the storms were now extinguished. However, that festering frustration was waiting to explode.

At some point during the night the storms moved out and a morning calm set in. The routine we had become accustom to over the past week was definitely blown away in the storm. As dawn broke many dogs in our building were already barking, expressing their need to get out of the damn cells. There were tree limbs and other debris scatter about the property all requiring the labor of the prison guards. The only way to attend to all the situations was to just let us out in our fenced area and fill a big troth of food and water for a community feast.

If ever there was a class system among us inmates, it had certainly become evident on that morning. Snyde, myself and a few other larger dogs bullied and snarled our way to first dibs. Joop didn't bother even trying to fight through the crowded food line. He wandered off to a far part of the pasture where a large muddy pool of water had collected. It was actually quite a large pool that had some floating nibbles of soggy chow which had been washed away from the troth in the storms. The pool of water was actually deep enough to tickle his torso and he waded in there to hunt down anything edible.

After I had filled my belly on dry crunchy kibbles with a processed chicken flavor, I wandered over to Joop's area. The pooled water was settled in the corner of the fenced area that borders the other pasture. In fact, the corner post was right in the center of the pool and the water was evenly distributed to the other side as well. Joop had splashed his way to the fence for some nibbles when he heard my paws slap along the borders of the water. He turned awkwardly bumping his ass against the post- and the post moved! This made Joop uncomfortable and he ran out of the water. He had a very good sense of what is trouble and he knew the post was there for a reason. I however had a different agenda.

I trampled through the water and inspected the post. I shoved up against it a few times and got it to lean quite a bit. It wasn't long before Snyde found my separation from the group curious. When he came to the puddle, he didn't exactly know what I was doing but he knew enough not to take his eyes off me. I held off drawing any more attention to my actions and played around in the water with Joop. Nagle and a few other dogs noticed the pool of water and came over to splash around in curiosity as well but Snyde was gettin' a gut feelin' there was more going on at that spot than water follies.

No sooner had things began to relax when the breeding dogs were let out in the adjacent pasture- males and females. There wasn't time for rotation. The dogs needed to get out and the prison guards were too occupied cleaning the grounds. Our side of the fence just erupted. Dogs were howlin' and gettin' all horny. Having been cooped up for the better part of two days there was a lot of tension to release. It really was madness and Snyde was overwhelmed. He went on a beat down that was as forceful as I'd seen from him. There was major intimidation and jawing to the point of physical contact. He was particularly excessive towards the smaller dogs forcing them off the fence and trapping them to submission. He was successful in squashing this insurrection but internally the dogs were just waiting to burst. You didn't need empathic powers or human emotions to get a sense of tension in the pasture. It resonated from every creature that was fenced in that lot. I had stood on the water border and watched Snyde intimidate the other dogs. It was now time to move away... to the corner... to the post.

That damn dog was amazing. His senses hadn't left me for a second. Maybe because I wasn't acting up with everyone else. Probably though, he just knows better than to let me outta' his sights. At this point I didn't care. I wasn't scared of him and I'd had enough of this whole bone'n week. I didn't care about the available tail on the other side of the fence anymore. I just cared about pure promotion and dog lovin' chaos. Freedom!

I trounced through the puddle to the fence post. Snyde didn't like my sudden movement and ran towards me jawin' all the way. The dogs were desperate for some excitement and they followed behind in anticipation of a confrontation. There was indeed going to be a confrontation but I had more than just fightin' to consider in my promotional agenda. I leaped up, almost in a dive onto the post and the whole fence was now compromised. There was no support under the corner post. It had been rotted for some time and now the water had washed away most of the earth holding it in place. All that was supporting the fence were loose rusty nails splintered in the side supports. The dogs behind Snyde began howlin' like a crazed mob hoping to storm the gates.

Snyde hadn't expected my kamikaze thrust on the fence and just freaked. He came rushin' at me with the other dogs in tow. The fall of the wall was inevitable and I slammed myself against the post one last time as the breeding dogs on the other side looked on in stunned silence. Let's be honest. Those dogs, males and females, were just a bunch of prisses-high society wimps. They weren't exactly breeding Doberman's over there. Every day they pranced around their pasture, noses up, while we uncomfortably tried to find anything to rub against our stiff bones. Thank God we don't have soap to drop!

My final thrust sent the whole corner supports crashing to the ground with me on top of 'em and Snyde on top of me. We rolled into the other pasture and rose to our feet. Snyde now realized the scope of the situation and immediately turned to the other dogs that had congregated to a now imaginary border. He had to keep them out despite his desire to engage me.

He lashed at them and they edged back. I, however, had my pick of any "upper class" dog to fight or hump. But this wasn't about me, it was about dog lovin' chaos and the more dogs runnin' free and wild then the better. My decision to sacrifice for the greater good was met without hesitation. Instead of looking for a snob to mount, I charged back at

Snyde and engaged him. We smacked jaws, battered our teeth against each other, clawed and scrapped. Nagle snuck up to the fallen fence. He watched intently to be sure Snyde was too occupied to notice and he made the leap across the imaginary line. Like a swarm the other dogs followed. I wish I coulda' enjoyed the moment but I was occupied.

By now, the prison guards had become aware of the break. Normally, this wouldn't have been able to get so far outta' control but they were scattered about the grounds cleaning up from the storms. They converged at great pace to witness their female breedin' dogs attempting to be mounted and their male breeding dogs being overrun. Thankfully, someone with a blunt object was able to separate Snyde and myself. It may have been a painful separation but it allowed me to see the rebirth of freedom. It's like what would someday happen in Berlin at the fall of the communist wall. Truth is, that freedom would be a little more lasting. It took a while but the prison guards restored order though not before some of us got our jollies and others got their aggressions out on the "upper class".

Even better, they didn't know who or how the fence was broke so no punishments were doled out. Back in our cells, Snyde was staring across Joop's cage at me so menacingly that Joop practically wedged that big planetary head through the bars bordering my cage. However, most of the other dogs had their fear bubble burst when it came to Snyde. Fortunately for him, many of the dogs there would soon be going home and there would be another batch abandoned there for him to intimidate. I just wonder how effectively he could have done his job from then on. If he were a brutal dictator like General, he'd probably go on a reign of terror, insanely enraged at the uprising. But fortunately, he was a well-trained and responsible dog that just happened to come across an antagonist desperately needing to get his mojo back. I'm sure in time Snyde would do the same.

I slept well that night and the dream came back. It was just a brief vision. I was on the hill gazing up at the crow on the moon. I guess my attempts to get there had failed but I was satisfied with just being atop the hill. I heard the car horn again from below and was pleased it came back. Once I heard Master Tom call my name it intrigued me to go but I wasn't quite ready. Moments later he uttered the magic words, "Dallas wanna' go for a ride"? It works every time and I ran down the hill and jumped in the car. A few hours after dawn, it would become a reality.

Revelation 14

Canines can not detect the smell of victory

I love being a dog. Even up here in Doggie Heaven where inequities between Master and mutt are revealed in perfect clarity, I don't want to be anything other than me. Even now that I understand concepts like humor, drive, passion, envy- my allegiance is pure. It's the genius of God to bestow such complex higher intellect on us and yet, here in Doggie Heaven, we still manage it to our level of simplicity. All this revelation. All this intellect. All this commentary. All put to use to lobby for my rightful earthly legacy- the protection and continued establishment of my domain in time. The purpose is no different then when I was just a "dumb dog" on earth.

I may have complained at times about our Heaven being second rate but really I'm just exercising my new skills. I know humor so I crack a few jokes. Sarcasm just seems to flow naturally as well. I see no reason I shouldn't question things of my environment now that I can. That doesn't mean I want to be with you humans glowing sedentary in an environment that I consider void of humor, drive, passion and envy.

Okay, that's a harsh and ignorant view. I'm sure heavenly peace and tranquility suits you. I'm just glad we don't have the togas. I assume the humans that made it to Heaven were searching for that ultimate contentment and believed it was in the afterlife. They couldn't wait to shed all petty issues of their advanced brains.

You know, when we shed fleas they simply jump to another host. I wonder if that's what is happening between our Heavens. Those corrupting, confusing, petty human emotional issues jump to us. When humans die you often donate your organs. Maybe your earthly consciousness is donated down to the next logical species. This is pure speculation but why not throw it out there now that I can speculate. We seem to have inherited in Doggie Heaven what your Heaven has expelled. But I guess if on earth we could consider a higher afterlife endowment, this would be what we'd want.

What I'm trying to say is that I'm just glad we got this higher consciousness and that it's comprehendable and controllable to us ascended dogs. It all seems perfectly manageable, and might I say, we wear your second-hand consciousness quite comfortably. Even though I've inherited this powerful change to my being, my being hasn't changed because of it. My focus is as singular as it was on earth.

When I returned from the kennel, I was never more singularly focused. No fence, physical or metaphorical, was going to hold me. I wasn't going to put up with any more bone'n....

"Ouch!" (Pause!)

As I was sayin'. I wasn't going to put up with any more bone'n....

"Ouch! Damn it!" (Pause!)

Well, anyway, I'd had it with lookin' over my shoulder. I wasn't sayin' I could defeat General. I could run or I could fight. I just wasn't going to expend my free time peekin' around corners. My first order of business was to try and establish some return of the vibe us dogs had developed. I flaunted myself in front of the other dog's homes. I'd sit out on their sidewalk and chase every damn car that had the slightest muffler issues. I'd bellow every breath in my lungs to try and top the decibel level of my chase. I'd bark so forcefully all afternoon I could barely muster a hoarse gurgle to be let in at home.

Once the dogs were let outside I'd do all sorts of antagonistic stuff. I'd steal items from their yards. I'd eat their food. I'd intimidate little kids that passed along their streets. Over the next few weeks Sugar started to come around. I could tell he was gettin' pissy about me roamin' his turf. He was always pissy about his supposed possessions and having to share. He finally started givin' me a hard time and nippin' and growlin'. That was cool, as I wanted to rile him. I guess being a dog of chaos requires some reorientation and I eventually managed to goad him on to bigger things than just being pissy.

We picked a semi tractor-trailer as our first renewed venture. It was coming into town about 45 MPH and I was pleased to see Sugar take the lead in the chase. He went after the front set of tires on the trailer section. Soon the speed of the monstrous beast got away from him and he laid off. Problem was, he assumed the whole beast was past him and as he cut his chase he veered into the road. Obviously, the back of the trailer was a mere second behind him and the back set of thunderous wheels were about to flatten him into the pavement. As he realized his error he dodged further under the trailer and it passed right over him. The force of its currents had him doing a flip or two right in the middle of the road and a car behind the truck came to a screeching brake, again almost making a doggie pancake. I thought Sugar may be dead and the driver of the car frantically got out of her vehicle but Sugar was on his feet momentarily. He limped off the road and was sore for a few days. With all the years of street smarts that dog had accumulated you'd think he'd know better- and he normally did. It just goes to show how General had us all off our game.

I was just trying to get these dogs to realized what they'd lost because of that bone'n...

"Ouch!" (Pause)

Anyway, because of that bone'n...

"Ouch!" (Pause)

Damn! Something strange is going on here. Let me test something.

I was just trying to get these dogs to realize what they'd lost because of that friggin' dog. That freakin' dog. That piss-head dog. That testicle-brained dog. That ass-wipe dog. That mamma-mountin' dog. That poodle-humpin' dog.... Okay, here we go- That bone'n...

"Ouch!" (Pause).

Ah ha! Seems someone with a little higher power than me has just found out about my "friggin" substitute. Every time I use the substitute word I get a rectal charged jolt of electricity. It makes me concerned that I'll never be able to safely lick my ass again. In that case I guess I'll stop using the substitute word. We dogs have so few pleasures that are uniquely our own. Tongue on rectum is a part of our identity and I'm not willing to sacrifice that.

I guess here in Doggie Heaven a certain reverence and restraint is expected for not only using God's name in vain but also for creating any doggie substitutes whose intent is to mirror the human's seven dirty words. However, notice how long it took before anyone caught on. Do you believe me now that maybe our little paradise isn't being fully prioritized?

"OUCH!!!!"

Let me digress. Doggie Heaven is wonderful place to spend eternity. If you get a chance you should vacation here before floating off to full enlightenment.

(Pause)

(Sigh) I'm so glad sarcasm isn't a rectaly-charged offense. I guess I can continue.

I was just trying to get these dogs to realize what they'd lost because of that "FRIGGIN" dog! Sugar just needed a kick-start. Not that he forgot General could be lurking on any trip uptown but once he got comfortable in his old routine he could at least focus on the freedom lovin' tasks that were presented to him around South Street. Scamp needed a different type of boost. He needed to trust that someone was watching his back now that it was realized he couldn't be the sole force and protector.

Sugar certainly didn't convey that confidence during their Rexford Falls bridge incident. I could rant and rave in front of Scamp's house all day but barks and flaunting weren't going to sell my point. His father, Laddie, was a dog of few barks and impressionable actions. I'm not saying he needed a father figure but I certainly knew how to make an impression. If an action or circumstance was required, I've often noted that the opportunity at some point usually arose. If you recall, it's my little law of necessity. My little impressionable necessity came to play on a warm evening in early summer, 1982.

Tom Mody

Master Tom and Beaner had returned from an ice cream run to the Dairy Isle. As you know, I like ice cream and it's perfectly lickable textures. Particularly soft ice cream. Usually when someone comes home individually from the Dairy Isle they get a cone and I'm often allotted the last bite of the damp wafer. It's acceptable but unsatisfying. When someone makes an ice cream run for the family it usually means sundaes. When Master Father makes a run he generously gets me a small cup to put in my bowl. Master Tom, however, is not so thoughtful with Master Father's money. He knows that the more change left over from the twenty dollar bill means more expendable cash for later that night at the Pizzeria.

So, everyone is scoopin' up their creamy smooth delights and I'm siftin' from Baby to Nat to Grandpa to Master Father and on down. No one is given up anything and I'm pissed. Master Mother heads to the kitchen but I pay her no attention hoping for some handouts from the remaining family. Little did I know she dumped the remainder of her sundae in my bowl. A little "here Dallas" communication between species woulda' been nice. Instead it sat there over night and the next morning I had spoiled vanilla soup mixed in with my morning kibbles.

Sure, dump it all in there. Week old roast beef, stale hot dog rolls, fridge crusted creamed corn, currently expired canned oysters, less than crunchy bran cereal, and of course, fresh Alpo. Yeah, that's right; as long as the Alpo is fresh I won't notice the oysters have expired. Gimme' a break!

I finally did get to lick some fudge off Master Father's spoon and retreated to my balcony. And I do mean retreat. The house had become a "blip" factory and there was no escape. Everything beeps and blips and bludgeons my sensitive ears like a Chinese water drop torture. I've already noted the video games losing their soothing constant flow. At least if I went into the den I knew what to expect. Now Master Tom runs around the house with these hand held "blip boxes". Little lighted red dots and lines are zigzagged against God controlled dots and red lines. They're suppose to simulate your modern day sports games but I never saw

Master Tom out in the park scoring points against oversized glowing LED pylons.

Anyway, him and Beaner were engaged in some annoyance that even got under Master Father's skin and they were asked to take it in another room. Baby and Nat followed like they were hypnotized by the blippin' gadget. I sat upon my balcony, brimming with a new confidence as of late. I was feeling like the king of the kingdom again. But could I prove it?

Scamp had ventured downtown. I saw him go towards the park and as usual I went off barkin' and splashin' spit upon the window. Like a thousand times before Master Father verbally scolded me from his recliner. I paid him no attention. Scamp could hear my muffled outburst from across the street but he caught a glimpse of something and ran into the park. Seconds later, General passed by my window and I went berserk. I didn't think. I didn't ponder. I didn't consider. I just reacted like I was that naive pup from years past. The whole "blippin'" family came bursting into the room as I went on a verbal assault slammin' my face against the large pane. General snarled back in what was about the doggie equivalent of flippin' me the finger and headed on his way.

Not this time he wouldn't. I leaped from my balcony and tore past Master Father who was approaching me with a freshly pressed rolled up Sherburne News edition. It only took me three giant strides and I was out the front door. It wasn't open- I leaped right through the large screen as if it were a mirage. My paws barely hit the slate steps as I flew down the walkway and stood on the sidewalk challenging General to do an about face. He did!

The yellow on my belly had been washed away by the kennel's mud and we collided. I must admit the impact was far greater than I had anticipated. It lacked any hesitation I had noticed in Snyde's conflict. I, however, now had a purpose in my conscience and absorbed what I could before being knocked back. It wouldn't be until later that I let his noticeable strength impress me. I was determined to stand up to General and I came back at him with my own impression of force hoping he'd stand down. He didn't!

By then everyone was out the door behind me and the ranting mob of family scared General off. I doubt the mop Master Mother was waving would be enough to keep General from tearing us limb by limb but he wasn't one to attack humans. Fresh in his mind was a recent beating he endured when he took a nip at one of his Master's guest. He had no quarrel with his Master's race at the moment and went up town a little puzzled at my chest pumping bravado.

I wouldn't go so far to say that General was impressed but someone else was. Scamp had watched the incident from the dark shaded safety of the night. It seemed to him that's how he'd been livin' his life since the Hobie murder. He needed to realize that's how we all had been livin'. As he came forward from deep in the park, the illumination from the streetlights was more than symbolic. A sense of security came over him as he approached the street. I made eye contact with him for a brief moment but Master Father grabbed my collar with his ink-stained hands and dragged me back into the house. Our eyes didn't need to meet for long. Once Scamp walked out of the dark the streetlights allowed him to notice the confidence and purpose in my stare. He didn't need to be afraid to come out of the dark alone anymore. In this new light he once again could trust in the convictions of another.

That night I bore some new holes in the blue blanket. I actually got what you might call carpet burn on my privates and I spent the remainder of the evening laying them on the cool slate near the fireplace. It mighta' been the only time I coulda' benefited from a doggie condom. The discomfort was only temporary but the confidence and virility I regained from my kennel incidents had held firm. Although, I wish my virility carried a bit more humility. I shoulda' stopped humpin' that blanket when Grandpa came through to go in the "little room" but I was in doggie fantasy back on the kennel breeding grounds and it was a good place to be. I never did get to take advantage of that dog humpin' chaos I instigated. Grandpa spewed forth the usual rant- "gosh damn dog actin' like an animal. Get outta' the house". But I was too tightly engaged with the blue blanket for him to mess with me and he went about his business in disgust.

That night was the near final piece of what I'm starting to think may have been pre-destined events. You see, a convergence was about to take place. This requires numerous random incidents affecting multiple parties over an extended period which ultimately comes to its destined conclusion through a final random interaction of all parties by an unforeseen event.

Huh!

Didn't realize I could speak lawyer. All I'm sayin' is that somethin' big was about to happen that needed to happen but couldn't happen because as dogs we couldn't make it happen so only destiny could.

Huh!

Ah Shit! Just figure it out.

Convergences can be measured like earthquakes but you have to feel a certain destiny towards them or it just falls under the "shit happens" category. For instance, it's been recorded that alligators got no "gator heaven". So if they were led up stream by an injured baby hippo swimming for safety and then a suspended bridge carrying gator hunters being chased by cannibals collapsed on top of them, that may incorrectly seem like gator chowin' destiny to you. Not quite, they're just alligators and shit happens. Of course, it may have been a convergence for the gator hunters- a bad one!

For creatures of a higher purpose a convergence can take on many forms. There are numerous random little incidents of time and circumstance that place the participants of a twelve-car pile up to that potentially destined event. Many times shit just happens but some times you gotta' wonder if there was more to it. A hero emerges. A reporter makes a reputation. A policeman gets a promotion. And unfortunately, people (and animals) die.

You can't measure a convergence on its perceived catastrophic outcome. The drama of the event must be weighed with the necessity and consequence to all involved. Afterwards you must be retrospective, marveling or cursing at the little things which set the stage. A broken alarm clock. A Last minute telephone call. Maybe even a loved one begging you to stay home because of an awful premonition. Or the fact that you are a murderous old bastard and the law was coming to haul your ass away. As was that exact situation set at General's home.

He had raided the coop one too many times at the farm west of the Game Farm. The farmer had identified the dog in town and informed the police. Now, they weren't coming to take General away but Master George didn't know that for sure. Scuttlebutt got passed around and he was told the makeshift dog warden had a summons. He was also told who ratted his dog out so he loaded General in the truck to go confront this supposed cow-stroking slanderer.

Steamy and sweaty dog days of August were upon us. The kind that make you edgy. From my doorstep it was a good fifty droolin' pants just to get to Quinn's for a late morning crate piss. Plums were the fruit of the week. Just ripened in the late summer and now extra salty if not washed first. The clammy damp air in the village wreaked of dog food as it hung low and thick in the humidity. It was a busy day at the chow factory. A huge load of unsuitable dog food (if you can believe they actually have standards) was being trucked out of town for some charitable purpose. Maybe the famished dogs of Africa or somethin'. The dry kibbles were shoveled loose in a mound on some open topped rickety wooden cargo bed.

I wouldn't have even ventured towards the factory that morning but a parade of bikes came zoomin' past me at Quinn's door way. Master Tom, Master Mark, Lew and Cappy, all toting an inner tube. A few seconds behind them was a panting and pouting Sugar. If he had been following them the whole way on this hot day then he had to be pooped. Fortunately the intersection's red light held up the boys and we caught up to them. Master Tom ordered me home but it goes in one floppy ear and out the other. He seemed poised to try and escort me home but Cappy told him to just let me be. They were all even nice enough to slow their pace down so we could keep up.

As we past by the Pizzeria, Sugar and I could see the activity in the chow factory lot and ventured over for an inspection. Strangely, the seemingly unsuitable dog chow actually smelled remotely appealing and the workers who had just began loading the truck tossed us some unsuitable treats. Sugar quickly scarfed up all he could find and tried to begrudge me any with an attitude. Same old shit with him and we began gettin' pissy. Our impending spat attracted a supervisor who scolded the workers for charitably attracting dogs and we were chased away.

We ran back to the road and could see the boys in the distance. Sugar took the lead in their direction. He still had his tail up his ass and was kinda' snubbin' me off. You humans have one word male genital slang for this type of attitude- Pud! Wanker! Dick! Yeah, I like dick! Sugar was bein' a dick! Once past the west bridge the boys and us followed a short trail to a pooled area in the Chenango River. You can imagine it, boys, dogs, water, inner tubes on warm August day- pretty wholesome stuff. Sugar was still bein' a dick but I could kick his ass anytime I wanted so I just tried to have doggie fun even if I wasn't overtly welcome by my brethren. To my surprise Master Tom actually warmed up to me being there considering it seemed anyplace I went chaos followed.

After a while we could hear popping up the river. Sugar and I ran off to investigate. Master Jimmer and Beaner were just a short distance south off the railroad tracks. Master Jimmer had brought his rod and was fishing a hole but Beaner kept igniting firecrackers so no fish were being caught. We ran up to them but it wasn't a very welcoming day and Beaner tossed some explosives at us. Out of the brush came Sam who'd been following them from home and was uncomfortable with Beaner's bombs so the three of us ran back towards the bridge.

We could hear the noontime whistle hit and the serenading of dogs in the distance. We all joined in from our location west of the village. Scamp happened to be waiting outside the Pizzeria for his Girl Master when the siren hit and he went howlin' away right to the village intersection.

T o m   M o d y

Cars beeped, people yelled, yadda yadda, ruff ruff, same ole, same ole. Some other mutt he'd never seen before, presumably a stray, came and joined him in the chorus. After the ear bludgeoning had died down the damn mutt took a nip at Scamp but they were forced outta' the intersection by impatient human drivers that gotta' go where they gotta' be. They mighta' got to see a good dog fight for their troubles but humans got more important things to do.

They both dodged the pushy metal beasts and got to the curb corner of the bank. Scamp was going to engage this mutt but its Master came out of the pizzeria because she forgot her money in her car. She was angered to see her dog loose and scolded the mutt for jumping out the window of its parked ride. The poor little pest musta' been a country dog-probably never had been in town.

On this day any creature with heightened aromatic endowments would be overwhelmed. Maybe this mutt normally minds its Master because she put the dog back in the car but still left the window rolled down. We all can appreciate that. A dog could die quickly unvented in these conditions. Aroma from the village was just cryin' out to all who could smell it and once his Master was out of view the crazy mutt's snout got the best of him. He jumped out the window again and ran towards the chow factory. Scamp followed him.

The cargo bed had just been filled and its two chow loaders went to put their shovels away. That crazy mutt musta' been fed dirt or somethin' because that truck full of unsuitable dog chow had him droolin' and insane. He ran up the ramp and dived in the truck. Once he fell in, Scamp couldn't even see him so he just started barkin'. Scamp knew somethin' was wrong. The loaders came back and shooed Scamp away before removing the ramp. I guess that mutt was gorging himself in the back of that cargo bed because he wasn't making a sound. And yes, as any Murphy's Law aficionado could have guessed, the workers got in the truck and headed out the parking lot.

Scamp could see the woman, with pizza box in hand, frantic over her dogs disappearance. He barked with some purpose to the situation but he was just workin' on instinct. It may have seemed normal to her and she paid him no attention. The truck went out the parking lot and headed west outside the village. Scamp followed it. It was Laddie inside of him. Reading the concern and needs of others and acting only for the purpose of being man's best friend. There was no self-importance and no other motive to his actions. Scamp finally was his father's dog.

The speed limit in the village was 30 MPH until the west bridge but the old truck could barely carry its cargo. Traffic followed behind it annoyingly close as Scamp pleaded his case barking at the tires and acting like a pesky village mutt. Right before the truck crossed the bridge Scamp made a final attempt to get noticed practically throwing himself at the driver side door. The startled driver stopped the truck abruptly. The convergence was on.

A pickup truck with an angry tailgating driver slammed into the back of the rickety chow truck. General, the passenger in the bed of that very pickup truck, was thrust forward and violently impacted against the back of the cab. Master George, already seething and on his way to address allegations made against his dog, gathered his rage and attempted to exit the truck but the door was stuck. Pounds and pounds of seemingly unsuitable dog chow was raining down on him, quickly burying the cab.

We heard the crash from below and both boys and dogs from all directions ascended upon the accident. Of course, us dogs were leapin' in the dog chow like it was snow. It really was pretty good stuff considering how much I hate that damn dog food factory. Maybe it was just really hot and we all were really hungry. Maybe it was just the excitement of the moment and leapin' around in piles of dog food was the dog lovin' chaos thing to do.

We were surprised to see Scamp there- actin' just as crazy. It became apparent he was milling about the chow with more purpose than the rest of us. He almost seemed frantic, like he was diggin' up something. Sam noticed this with concern and went to his side. He began sniffin' around Scamp and came to an aromatic realization. There was something other than dog food buried in the mess. When Master Jimmer went to pull Sam away from the situation he heard yelps as well. Beaner assisted them in diggin' out that crazy mutt and set it to safety on the roadside. The previously buried dog was definitely dazed and puked on the side of the road. The dumb thing probably just ate too much unsuitable chow.

Master George finally got himself outta' the truck and was screamin' at all who would listen. Particularly at the chow truck driver. His ranting awoke General from a short period of unconsciousness and the startled beast leaped out of the truck bed on a rant of his own. You might say the mood for us dogs changed quite rapidly. He didn't look too well at first having to halt his verbal abuses in order to get his bearings. I don't even think he knew we were there. I got the impression he didn't want to be around Master George in his abusive state and he stumbled away from the accident to the roadside. With a clearer head and wider view, his two eyes met our eight eyes.

Sugar was the first to crumble. He ran off towards the bridge and when he got there he looked back to wonder why the doggie hell we weren't right behind him. Sam was never too intimidated anyway so it was his policy to stay cool until another reaction was necessary. Scamp just looked at me- at my eyes. Curiously eager for my lead. If he had ESP he probably woulda' been askin' me if we really were going to do this. We really were!

I was going to finish what I started a few weeks back and I was expecting to have some help. It was however, up to me to make the first move. I growled. I heard a second in my ear. Then a third. Clearly I was not alone.

If my head had just slammed at high impact into metal, I might be rethinking my aggressive tendencies as well. For all I know, General was seeing double. That would make six of us in his blurry mind. Could he back down? Would we let him? If he couldn't see straight he was at least thinking clearly. He did the only thing any violently aggressive dog could do that didn't want to dissipate his reputation in an overmatched battle. He took off- but towards Sugar.

It certainly caught us dogs off guard and we weren't quite sure what to do at first. Seconds Later Master Mark caught an eye to the inevitable and the boys ran towards the river. We then realized he wasn't running away, he was attacking Sugar.

Sugar had safely maneuvered down the embankment but General was still a bit disoriented and he stumbled, ultimately rolling down and splashing into the water. The boys and us dogs were right behind them and I must say what we saw next was quite shocking. General was in a shallow water area but he was just flippin' out. I'd say he looked terrified. The water barely was up to the bottom of his torso and he was flailing in circles like he was on fire. Sugar, who had made it to the other side of the river, even halted his escape to stare at the petrified bully.

Something snapped. Some psychosis exploded. The dog was deathly afraid of water. Before Master George's family had purchased the dog his Breeding Master was unhappy to have not sold him along with the rest of the litter. He made General feel as if there was something wrong with him and he was treated as quite the nuisance. Any puppy would act and behave in a difficult manner that didn't feel wanted. At some point a chewing related incident of little mention occurred and the Breeder inexplicably became enraged. He grabbed the tiny pup by the scruff and violently carried him to a fishpond behind the barn. General's head was submerged in the shallow shore and his tiny snout buried in the marshy mud. The dog flailed away on the brink of survival but he managed enough leverage to sink his youthfully sharpened fangs deep into the palm of his punisher.

Momentarily free, he ran back to the barn area, the only place he'd ever known, but the angry punisher snatched him even more violently than before. With bleeding hand now over his snout he was carried to the river which was raging in the rush of spring rains and the past winter's melt. He tossed General in the currents with the intent that he'd drown or simply be swept away and on his own. Problem was, one of the punisher's young sons was nearby collecting fieldstones and he saw the incident. He screamed at his father once he realized what was done and rescued General a short ways down the river. The boy actually ratted his father out to his mother and she was horrified the adult would do such a thing in front of his son. The mother made a greater effort to find this emotionally scarred dog a home and eventually he ended up with Master George and family.

As earthly dogs, and like most humans, we're often not privy to the back-story of those we encounter. Wondering why jealousy, envy, greed or constant narcissistic grooming manifests unhealthy in people is anyone's guess. Maybe we'd be more understanding if we knew about the plight of the former pimply-faced kid who now annoys us with his mirror mugging rituals. But we sure wouldn't absolve him of murder, even though for us dogs it may seem tightly within the borders of ancient animal law. It's a domestic world for us now and we are fightin' for our freedom.

Did your revolutionaries care that the King of England was dispassionately conditioned since birth to protect his birthright? That British Parliament members most undoubtedly had not only the drive of personal greed but the greed for king and country instilled since birth. That's no reason to accept them raising your tea tax now is it? Of course, the colonists already knew of their throne sitter's pious eccentricities. I, however, didn't know until now why the seemingly meanest dog on the planet was actin' like such a spaz in the water that day. I had considered he couldn't afford a good cup of tea to help calm him down.

The boys began throwing rocks but actually at Sugar to entice him further on his way. He was just too mesmerized at the circles of insanity General was spinnin'. General was vulnerable and I led the charge to the water. We were too late to catch him in the water as he had managed to flop and wail his way to the bank but we caught him on the other side and started jumpin' on him.

Maybe if General was in a sound state of mind we could have managed some impressionable beat-down of him. The damn dog was so traumatized that he was just wild beyond our ability to control him. We never gave him a moment to gather himself and he was completely smothered the second he got ashore. In his mind he was still drowning. He wasn't feeling pain nor was he aware that retribution was at hand.

I'm recalling revelations of my generation when humans injected themselves with something called "angel dust". They would become psychotic and their glands would secrete chemicals at extreme abnormal levels giving them super strength at the height of their panic. Groups of people couldn't contain them and their desire to flee would send them off rooftops. That was General's state as he slammed his head into Sam and he gouged Scamp's eye and he slammed his head into mine and ran off. Our take on it was that we had him scared. Score a point for us. We ran after him and Sugar was so impressed he joined chase.

The chase went along the stony shore, up the bordering brush and eventually on to the outer trails of the Game Farm. These trails are a maze of pine needles and dirt that weave through the small marshy state park. It's a quiet environment where Rogers Center visitors can explore and absorb the habitat of a New York forest. However, I don't recall New York State Parks ripe with psychotically panicked German Shepherds and bitterly vindictive gangs of mutts spreading dog lovin' chaos throughout its ecosystem. Nope- only in a place called Sherburne, puppy!

There was no chance of humans spotting an owl or a flying chipmunk or a blue bird or even a damn squirrel on that afternoon. The five of us were runnin' and howlin' through those delicate grounds like a bunch of savages. No predatorily sensitive little thing would dare stick it's head out its hole, nest or leafy underside with us rampaging the place. We probably scared them stiff for at least the rest of the day. Poor timid creatures probably hadn't heard a ruckus like that since the last time hormonally expressive humans discovered they were exploring the birds and bees in a patch of poison ivy.

The trails were sparse with humans and we ran a few off the beaten path when encountered. General had a good pace ahead of us, but for him, the place was full of traps.

Mainly the old wooden bridges that ride low, just above the swampy water. There wasn't the separation of space and fencing that overhung Rexford Falls. As he approached one he stopped on a dime but we quickly came into view. It was the moment he needed though to gather in what was taking place. He never had a second before to just catch a breath. It was muggy and we were quite winded when we reached him. Everything in his body language made it apparent he was going to defend the bridge rather than flee across.

He may have been more dangerous than ever before. Defensive. Backed in a corner. Mentally unstable. And now with a moment's clear headed understanding of the situation. Fatigue was an issue with us four. Over the course of the day's incidents and chase maybe the reality of our situation was now setting in. Maybe adrenaline wasn't as explosive as it was a while ago. We still had numbers but again, we all just looked at each other with our menacing fang exposed grins. Were they just painted on masks? Were those nervous gurgles emanating from our lungs trying to mask the pants of fatigue?

There was quiet in the forest. Not a bird, not a bug, not even a breeze to whistle through the trees. Just ten eyes, none of them blinking. Only the humid air to keep them moist. A moment of truth was at hand for the freedom lovin' Dogs of Sherburne and yet, there we stood. Our enemy was injured, dazed and trapped- yet there we stood. I don't think it was yellow streakin' my belly. I think it was just that moment of contemplation as to what my actions could really mean- both good and bad.

Maybe we had made the point to General that we couldn't be oppressed. Maybe we'd seen him at his most vulnerable and he wasn't feeling so empowered anymore. Of course, we all really weren't thinking- we're dogs. I'm just trying to translate the gut instincts that churn waiting for chemicals in our brains to tell our muscles to do something. The sorting of learned images in our heads of what brings us pain and what gives us pleasure. The effort to make any electromagnetic connection which can gap the bridge from desire to action to contentment. Only God knows how it all works but it's clear that something larger was giving pause to the moment. A little thing called destiny, which I now feel, had manipulated this whole convergence.

It's difficult to be a nervous insignificant bystander at a tense standoff. Any cough, sneeze or unexpected release of gas can set off an explosive situation. It's true for any species and the little tiny frog that was mere inches from the back foot of General was about as tense as any creature could be. One nervous twitch on his rear leg muscle set him off into a leap and his flop in the swamp resonated like an alarm through the silence. General adjusted his stare to that location to see the rippled water radiating its circular waves. A reminder to him that he was mere paw steps away from his most dreaded fear. A reminder that for aggressors like him, the best defense is a potent offense. So, while we were contemplating the moment, General struck.

He lunged right at me sensing I was the heart of this resurgence. It was not like before with his demented enjoyment and ego boasting confidence. It was a cockfight. He was thrown in the ring and there was to be no thoughts of glory or honor in his battle. He was prepared to die but not ready to die- not yet.

Am I awash in melodrama? I don't think our intent was to kill him but I guess it was possible. He surely was capable of killing us. It was a survival based attack on me that just wasn't anything I'd experienced before. I was able to match his aggression and even counter his offenses but he was making an impact. There was too much analyzing the experience on my part where as his head was blank to consequence and pain. Every claw that hit my head, every nip that pinched my hide, every smack of my head against his registered. I couldn't get to his level of disassociation. Still, I had confidence and purpose. This was important because it kept me from running. I never expected to defeat him alone and once he gained the advantage, the others came to my rescue.

Scamp had been there before. Had Master George not injured his father during that fateful confrontation years ago in the park, the two of them may very well have defeated

General that day. Of course, as my scarred back is proof, I also can vouch for Scamp's skills in gang attacks. Scamp rode General as best any cowboy could to an angry bull while Sam and Sugar tried to defray the jaws of death from getting to my neck. General turned to Sam and tried to impress upon him that he could keep me pinned and viscously scar him as well. However, Sugar and Scamp were making headway and Sugar was able to draw first blood sinking a painful jaw strike into Generals lean ribs. I also gouged a nasty rip with my front claws to Generals neck.

The sensations of pain may have finally found a connection and he used all his strength to bore through us and escape our grips. Now that he had us momentarily separated he again chose to single out someone- and that was Sam. He thrust into him knocking Sam into the swamp. Score a point for General. General obviously would not follow in after him but Sam was having a difficult time freeing himself from the grip of the muddy shallow water. Free of one combatant for the moment General made short work of the weakest link and just overwhelmed Sugar in a burst of fang and claw that drew blood in numerous places. Score another point for General.

Scamp and I jumped General again and Sam soon managed himself out of the swamp. The three of us extricated General from Sugar and it all became one blur after that. Fur and spit and blood and skin. Everyone managed to donate something to the cause yet we still couldn't impose our will on him. He broke free again and realized the swamp was keeping him penned. He couldn't fight us so closely grouped with no place to separate us and so he made a bold move. He fled across the bridge conquering a fear of unimaginable proportions.

It may have been a triumph for him but to us it seemed a victory of sorts getting him to retreat. Score another point for us. With that confidence we gave chase again through the trails. Ultimately a clearing came and General fled to a familiar grounds- farmland that bordered the Game Farm. We chased him a ways on the property along the borders of the corn stalks. Once we reached some cut grass grounds he had the open space he was searching for.

Farm animals were cluttered about us. Chickens, goats, even cows had viewing privileges. General turned to take us on and we just pummeled him straight on. It probably looked no worse than an act of sorts to the other animals. We all were so spent it was more like a game of twister than a savage dogfight. All our paws and limbs intertwined and we're just trying to keep balance and not fall over with exhaustion. You might say the fizzle in our purpose was beginning to go flat. We practically were holding each other up and anyone able to get in a nip was more likely to tickle than harm. Our panting barely allowed us to even compress our jaws to a closed position. In fact, if it had gone on any longer General might have drowned by getting drooled on to death.

Sugar was the first to give in and as he fell off the whole pile collapsed like a house of cards. Now free, General managed some distance but he knew his tank was empty as well. We were safe for the moment as we laid out. He tried to mask his injuries from the day with a growl but it was barely a hiss. He couldn't even put up an offensive front. This domestic-murdering, freedom-sucking, life-scarring excuse of a dog coulda' and shoulda' been dealt justice. And yet, there we laid. As dogs of war we left a lot to be desired.

I had to act. I had to ensure that he knows I alone was capable of making him live with pain- or even determining if he lives at all. He was unsteady and unsure when I arose. He looked at the others still sprawled out in the hot sun. Dried blood lined his neck and torso and he licked it for nourishment but when he lifted his head up he became disoriented. I can only assume he had a pounding headache from the concussive impact in the truck. I stood still for a moment to gather my strength. His head was swaying back and forth and he was about to fall over when a chorus of hens just started cacklin'. The calm had made them nervous and they just kept up their chants, scurryin' around the grounds. When General focused back on me I knew that's when I'd make my impression and I ran at him.

This time he tucked tail avoiding a one-on-one fight and fled through a group of chickens with me in chase. I caught up with him after about twenty strides and for once I was on top and I let loose with every jaw chomp and claw swipe I could muster. He wrestled to his feet and I clamped on to his neck with my jaws. From there I froze. I don't know if it was fatigue or a domesticated reservation as to putting the full clamps on him. I could taste blood and it wasn't setting me off into some animalistic savage regression. I wasn't sensing the kill or gaining pleasure from my revenge. It was just satisfying enough to be on top of this bully for once.

My advantage was short lived as he powered away and slammed the side of his head into mine. We both were disoriented and stumbled apart. When the pain cleared I could see General looking over my shoulder with concern. Sugar, Scamp and Sam were now on their feet behind me. Outmatched, General fled a few more strides but in fatigue he had blinders on. He ran on to a wooden dock that protruded over a small fishing pond. It didn't take long to realize he was trapped over water and he began howlin' and shakin'. The four of us approached the dock with obvious intent to pursue him. He didn't even take an aggressively defensive posture as I stepped upon the dock from the grass. He just howled with fear- defeated. I strutted towards him to collect my final point- game over!

All our heads turned at once.

"You're not gonna kill any more of my chickens", rang out from a distance followed by an ear shattering explosive sound. Next thing I knew I was looking up at the sky and I couldn't feel the sun. A shadow came over me as General leaped across my numb body. As he passed the sun hit me again and I started feeling warmth. Problem being it was my insides leaking out warm blood down my torso. I tried to roll over but the pain set in and I began whimperin' from shock. I rolled again in any direction out of instinct and was fortunate I hit grass below me. I could have easily rolled into the pond and drowned. Uncontrollably I continued whimperin'.

When I exhausted the air inside of me and felt my lungs tighten, I thought I may have experienced my last breath. However, the momentary internal stillness was a necessary calming point allowing a force of nature to come into play. We're just animals when something like this happens. We don't think about blood loss or consequences of future actions or even pain of our next movement. We do what our instincts dictate until we can't do it anymore. A fleeing response overcame me as air again filled my lungs. Trauma stiffness had yet to set in and I got to my feet and built up a pace to the cornfields. Numb and in shock I drifted deep into them until I felt safe. At that point I just collapsed, shielded from sun and shotgun among the stalks.

Next thing I remember was the sound of farm equipment in the distance. The sun was in a much lower position and my body temperature was quite cool. Night had come and gone and I had lived to see another day. I tried to get up but I was weak and I needed to adjust to the pain, which now wasn't just exclusive to my wound. That's what us animals do- we adjust to it. Something would have to be physically broke to keep us from our next survival mode. If I could move and I felt that finding water was my only chance of survival, I would adjust to the pain and search for water. My adjustment needed to be made quicker than expected as the farm equipment was getting closer by the second. It sounded big and it sounded mean so I dragged my hind legs a few yards to get the blood circulating and was able to extend them in a standing position. I managed to exit the cornfields before someone's corn on the cob had dog hair embedded in it.

The river fortunately bordered the cornfields and I all but fell into the cool water, cleansing my wound and quenching my thirst. I may have laid there a few minutes- maybe an hour. All's I know is that I started to smell that God forsaken dog food. Interestingly, it smelled like life to me. I guess anything would have smelled good at this point- I was famished. Getting food was next on my survival to do list and I managed the pain and disorientation back to the house. Mind you, a trip of indescribable heart and fortitude. I could hardly call it painful as every step sent a searing jolt through my system blocking any memory of the pervious step. Possibly nature's way of keeping the trauma from compounding itself mentally. Later, when the compounded pain caught up to me, I was mercifully weaving in and out of consciousness.

I didn't even bother barking at the front door. I immediately went to the back hoping my outside dog food dish would be full. It was- full of stench and ants. I licked whatever stained chow I could scrape from the sides of the bowl and was grateful for the flavor of the ants. I again collapsed at the foot of the porch steps.

Maybe minutes, maybe an hour later Master Tom came to the back door in utter relief that I was home. He opened the door and I just was hoping I could learn to float. A second, maybe ten seconds later I realized that wasn't an option and I again managed the pain to get up and enter the house. The dog dish was full- thank you God! I don't even know what I ate but I was thankful it wasn't ants. My final collapse was on the living room floor between the two lounge chairs, and as I stated, I weaved in and out of consciousness all day.

Master Mother and the girls had gotten an early start and weren't home when I arrived nor did anyone come home other than a few runs through the house by Master Tom. Sometime in the late afternoon my unchanged position in the house caught Master Tom's curiosity. He asked if I was all right and knelt down to inspect me. There was dried blood on the carpet and this alarmed him. I was laying on my side and he lifted my front leg up exposing my chest. He gasped.

He could practically see right inside. To him it looked as if someone had taken a knife and attempted to gut me. Knowing my reputation in the village he probably thought it was a distinct possibility. He yelled out to Master Mother who had just come home and arrangements were made to immediately get me to the vets. I was pretty numb by then and I think someone even managed to carry me to the car. It was all gravy to me from that point. A shave, some stitches, pain and antibiotic injections and I was good to go- but not necessarily in that order. I didn't stay over night and I was never even x-rayed to see what happened. It wasn't until a few years later that an x-ray revealed I'd been shot. That slug was in me for the rest of my life. A slug that was meant for General- I think?

I don't know exactly how close I came to dying. These animal mending mechanisms are quite advanced. My tongue alone can all but cauterize the wound licking away harmful organisms with God like efficiency. As long as we can breathe and get sustenance our bodies rarely give in to premature death. I wonder, though, if I was close if I could have seen the light? You know, at the end of the tunnel. I wonder if Hobie and Laddie could have spoken to me and told me I did good? Imagine that, getting a "good doggie" from the afterlife then just fading back into consciousness. Would I have evolved? Would I sense life differently? Would I be at peace for the rest of my years?

My God, I hope not! I just managed to finally defend my independence from a freedom-sucking, life-depleting, over-the-shoulder looking neck pincher of an evil dictator. I didn't want calm or to evolve and mature. I wanted dog lovin' chaos and all the leg-humpin', car-chasin', wet-dog-sprayin', fruit-crate-pissin, rock-barkin', center-of-town-traffic-stopin' howlin' I could squeeze into every day I was alive. And I wanted ice cream- lots of it!

Revelation 15

Dog tags aren't big enough to tell a story

I awoke one morning to repetitive echoing thumps. It wasn't anything new, I was use to that sound. It had just been many months since I last heard it. But I knew why it started again. I could smell it in the air, and more than ever, feel it in my bones. That defining day that separates winter from spring and by 1986, the warm weather was more welcome than ever to this old dog.

The same thumping awoke Master Tom. He was now neither a boy nor a teenager but a freshly minted twenty year old adult. Eastern standard time of 9:00 AM was still much earlier than his internal alarm clock was set but he knew the thumps as well. I was eager in the kitchen when he came down stairs, unshowered and in gym shorts and a sweatshirt. He broke off half a banana and shoved it down his throat. I motioned to the door and waited for him to put on his sneakers. I knew what I would see when that door opened- a brown muck but no snow on the ground for this unseasonably warm March morning. He snagged my collar and held me while he stuck his head out the door to address the thumping perpetrator.

"Mark, what the hell! All right, gimme a minute. I need a drink".

Master Mark, like his gangly old mutt, had a knack for just showing up unannounced. Well, Master Mark's way of announcing was to snag a basketball from the garage and help himself to some hoops shooting. Master Tom got his drink and we exited the door to a burst of spring air.

Master Mark addressed me. "Dallas you old man, that muff keeps getting greyer".

Normally, all I'd hear was, "Dallas, yak, yak, yak", but I actually heard nothing. I was too focused on the squirrel in the neighbor's yard. That first squirrel chase of the year where there was no snow encumbrances. I had every expectation it would be like years past. I'd leap the steps in mid air, burst across the yard, trampoline over the iron fence border and yelp up a tree for ten minutes trying to persuade the squirrel to come down so I can kill it.

I lunged forward to the edge of the stoop but some last nanosecond chemical reaction in my brain halted me before takeoff. Going airborne didn't feel comfortable. The flight off the stoop was aborted and I decided to taxi each step. I didn't think much of it and began my burst across the yard. With some speed behind me I now dedicated my energy to go airborne over the iron fence. My takeoff was sluggish but my front paws cleared the hurdle and landed.

"Son of a... AROOOOOOF"! (translated... "OUUUUUCH").

There was extreme sharp pain and pressure near each side of my testicles- but they were intact. The back end of me never hit the ground and my forward momentum halted to a dead stop. My hind legs were still frozen in the air with pain shooting to each leg. I couldn't move. The back half of me was stuck on the fence. I came down on two dulled iron spikes. Fortunately, I wasn't impaled. This never happened before. I could withstand the pain but I was nervous in my stuck position and yelped like a scared little puppy.

A bird, a crow actually, landed on the far end of the fence and looked down at me with all the knowledge, experience and security of a "wise old bird". It knew I was no longer a player in the... Nah, I'm just kidding. It would be ironic for that to happen- have the story come full circle like that but I'll just stick to the facts.

Master Tom and Master Mark ran over and carefully lifted the backside of me off the fence. I was fine but my body was talkin' again, and for once, I began listening. That past winter I had been ignoring the stiffness walking up stairs and the trepidation at traversing to my balcony. I couldn't consider the cold weather as the cause for this anymore. It finally registered- I was old.

Dogs don't fret over this stuff. If I can't jump then I can't jump. If I don't feel like chasin' anything I don't ask why and sulk over glory days of my youth. If old age makes me feel like I simply don't want to do anything then that's how I feel. I enjoy the rest.

I was managing for a while but by summer's end I couldn't get up to my balcony and I couldn't go up stairs and at times I lost my bark. Many a day some cat lovin' bastard kids would laugh at me in my efforts to force anything out my lungs other than dust. The images of my past were now playing a part in my dreams both day and night- particularly recalling my last few years.

Those were a glorious time for all the free roamin' dogs of Sherburne. After General was confronted on that farm we had a lot of confidence- particularly Scamp and myself. We would have engaged him at any necessary encounter. Maybe it wouldn't have come to that. General may have gotten the message that we could no longer be bullied. We'll never know. Shortly there after, General's family moved out of the village and we never saw him again.

We roamed the streets of Sherburne as legends- and not always in our own minds. Accorded the respect we earned through our years as village icons, we comfortably seized every moment of dog lovin' chaos. Well, maybe it wasn't as exuberant and antagonistic as our younger years but we did what we felt like doing with no encumbrances of animal or human law.

Much of this new appreciation was heaped upon us by the former kids of the village who in the past found us a pain in the royal doggie ass. Perceptions change- usually along the male hairline. Humans hold so dear to their childhood people, places and things. To revisit home and see us old dogs about the village and especially me perched up in the big bay window, it's as if time had stood still. Sadly by the fall of 1986, time was standing still for me.

Days on end would pass and I'd slumber away most of it until that damn "ding" would go off. I'd make the motion to get up but some days my legs just wouldn't respond. By the second or third ding I'd make a mess of the shag carpet and not even have the strength to go hide in a corner. I could still hear much from the outside world as I laid below my balcony, taking in the baseboard register heat for some added warmth. The sounds were different though. Cars were much quieter with their new fuel efficiency. The park which once was a bustle with the smokin' hippies throwing frisbees or causing a commotion was now a relaxing place for the elderly- myself included. Most disturbing was the lack of dogs barkin' in pesky chase or howlin' at the noontime whistle- victims of a leash happy new breed of Master and law.

Come to think of it, almost a year had passed since I saw any of my chaos lovin' brethren. It was right before the winter set in for the '85-'86 season. Of all that damn gang it was Scooter who I encountered last. The meek little tripod was reaping years of safe harbor under our new regression of hostilities. We bumped snouts in front of the Big M supermarket which was a building down from the Inn, and yeah, I growled at him. I gotta' be me, right. He probably was waiting for Master Mark but I intimidated him and he waddled across the parking lot. Almost getting treaded, not once but twice in the process. He did make it safely on his trot back home.

I watched him the whole way until he just about faded down the sidewalk. My mind was churning trying to think- trying to comprehend as best a wise ole' dog could. How did this three legged hobblin' ass kisser of a beagle survive the greatest era in free roamin' dog history?

He'd been run over, dismembered, displaced by an adopted brother, hunted by predators and down right kicked around by beast and metal beast alike. As his round little ass was just about a spec in my vision I saw a human approach him and give him a gentle pat on the head. Then I realized the damn dog survived on being beloved at first sight. I gotta' toss him a bone for that. Yo dog, Scooter, you set the standard because now in this new century that's all a dog's got to mark his place in time.

As this revelation hits me now, I couldn't be more at ease here in Doggie Heaven. You don't need my sheer dogmatic will to influence you about my legend in time. The proof is in every lame-ass, fat-ass, kiss-ass, sorry-ass dog that came after me. The very ones who at the beginning of my rants I accused of causing my legend to fade. Until some apocalyptic destruction of lawyers and lawmakers takes place allowing us to run free again, no dog can touch me. My legend is intact.

A short time after our encounter, Scooter would be rummaging through a pile of leaves on the curb side and get run over by a school bus- dead! I told ya' some time back, those damn beagles get treaded more than any other dog. Maybe that same bus came back to finish the job because Scooter had cheated death so many years ago at his first bus treading encounter. Again, it would be cool to have things work full circle but it was just a case of a beagle not paying attention. It had to catch up with him eventually.

Another dog who met a less than storybook ending was Scamp. He had accompanied one of his Boy Masters on a cross-country skiing hike up Hunt's Mountain. Scamp ran off and returned on a number of instances throughout the day but during one period he was away his Boy Master heard gunshots and Scamp never returned. Tracks couldn't be followed because it was snowing and Scamp's bones still lay upon Hunt's Mountain to this day.

It's usually when a dog is put to sleep that a family gets to say goodbye but Sam was able to die naturally and have closure. He had experienced great peace because the kids of the family had all come home for a wedding and Sam sensed he may never see them again. He was very, very old, a few years shy of 20. A week after the wedding his Master Father left the front door for work as Sam laid lame on the front sidewalk. His Master said, "so long" to him as he went off to work. Sam wasn't there to greet him when he returned home. Later in the evening he walked out to the garage and he saw Sam laying close by. He called to him but Sam didn't respond. His Master, and friend, left him there for the night to rest in peace. The next day he was buried near the canal behind their yard. It wasn't a direct goodbye but it was better than many dogs get.

Sugar and I had similar experiences of Master loneliness during our last months. Master Mark had traveled overseas as an exchange student and Master Tom moved to Los Angeles in the fall of '86. Talk about abrupt life changes. For all we knew they were dead. It was sad to not have those last few months with them but our lives had been lived full. We achieved so much, particularly a stray mutt like Sugar. Maybe a gunshot or a rubber treading would have been the more fitting end to the dog that taught me the art of promotion. Instead, it was a quiet and somber ending with the prick of a needle in the sterility of a vet's office. I guess in some fitting irony it was actually the neighbors who had the job done, not Master Mark's family.

Master Tom returned home for Christmas that year, disturbed at my declining health. As they opened presents Christmas morning I laid away from the gifts below the staircase banister- barely a part of the family gathering. Thankfully, that damn decorated tree blocked my view of the tower I had ruled upon for so many years. My life was now just moments lived by minutes passing. There was no more future ambition. I was content in what ever spot alleviated my aching joints. Content to stay there with nothing else to prove.

You might think I had wished to be window bound one last time but it all had changed out there so drastically. I'd seen it all, done it all. There was nothing for an old dog like me to want from that place. My only real wish occurred to me late Christmas night as Master Tom was the last one to bed. He kissed me on the head and I watched him walk up the stairs from below. I would have loved to have been up there one last time. My days were sadly uneventful but at night I could have much appreciated the docile forum for quiet and rest among my family. Instead, I was separated from them by lame arthritic legs. It was just a strange feeling a dog wouldn't know how to process but any way you look at it, that's how I felt- what I would have wished for.

Master Father is an early riser and not much for taking days off. The day after Christmas he was back to the grind- as you humans say. He grudgingly cleaned my mess from the carpet and looked me strangely in the eye. He asked me to come with him and I was afraid he was going to leash me to the post on that cold winter morning. Instead, he gently guided me down the back stoop and lifted me to the hatch of the station wagon. He talked to me a bit on our short drive to Norwich.

I knew our eventual location well. I had been to the vet a few months earlier, my Master getting the bad news on my failing health and the interesting news that an x-ray revealed a shotgun slug in my gut. Now at the vets again, I looked up at my Master Father. I'd like to say when we arrived there I sensed something different in this visit but at first I didn't- I couldn't. I was too nervous with my own pain and dull senses. That all changed though as I was lifted upon the table by the vet and Master Father. When I got to his eye level my quivering legs became still. I could see tears in his eyes and I felt it in my being. A recollection of sorts.

Years ago the house was empty except for him. I heard sounds in the bedroom and I went upstairs and found him sitting somber upon his bed- tie loosened around his neck and his hand over his eyes. I noticed things had felt strange those past few days and I knew something was wrong. He had just returned from burying his father and was holding in a dam of emotions. Finally he was alone and it was all flooding out. I stood in the doorway and whimpered. He looked up at me and motioned me over. I just sat next to him and let that raw emotion pour over me. What a joy of feeling something- anything. Connecting with your Master one on one. It didn't matter whether the emotion was happiness or sadness, fear or calm. To become a conduit for human emotion is a powerful experience for any dog. It may be the most useful feeling we could ever attain. We are dogs of man, remember.

On that table at the vets I then knew that emotion was about to be revisited. Finally, something would come full circle in my life. As I sensed back then that some type of great loss had occurred, so I was positive of it occurring again. I knew it was concerning me, that we were to be separated. I wasn't all flipped out like I was being left at the kennel. A sense of completion had overcame my being. As I was with him and absorbed his grief over his father's passing, so he was with me now to calm me in my last breaths as the fluid ran warm into my vein.

As I passed beyond I could hear Master Tom calling me throughout that old house, confused and concerned at my absence. Master Mother broke the news to him and regretfully, we never said goodbye. He often talked to me like I was a real person, occasionally expressing his feelings to me in words. Now that I can recall and understand him, I'm left to wonder what he woulda' said.

If I coulda' said anything to him it would have been very simple, from my heart and of my deepest most desire. "Go hump someone in honor of me for I, Dallas, cannot be replaced!"

Born February 3rd 1966, Tom Mody spent his entire childhood living in the small Upstate New York village of Sherburne.. He has two younger sisters, Lisa & Natalie. He was a high school basketball player and took up the guitar at the age of 14, joining his first band at age 16.

After Graduating High School in 1984, he spent a few years (and earthquakes) living in Los Angeles and San Francisco returning to Sherburne in 1990. Out west he attended Sound Master Recording Engineering School in North Hollywood and began his entrepreneurial business, The Mody Company, while in the bay area. In 1987 he wrote a movie script which he never submitted. his first and only long form literary piece until The Dogs of Sherburne novel completion 20 years later.

Throughout the 90's he continued playing in bands and recording music while growing his business endeavours. During the summer he could be found daily on the tennis court and during the fall organizing the Sherburne holiday nerf football games, He met his wife Lisa on New Year's eve 1990 and they were married a short time later... March 20th 1999. He currently lives in the rival city of Norwich, New York where The Mody Company developed into a successful home based internet marketing entity. Their daughter, Antonia, was born in 2002, and son, Julian, in 2006. Tom also has a home recording studio where he makes music with his long time friend and bandmate, Jeffrey Harris and other areamusicians.

The Modys are currently dogless.

CPSIA information can be obtained at www.ICGtesting.com
Printed in the USA
BVOW070235081111

275555BV00005B/2/P

9 780983 450306